Truth

Rod Stewart, Ron Wood and the Jeff Beck Group

First published in Great Britain in 2006 by Cherry Red Books
(a division of Cherry Red Records Ltd.), 3a Long Island House,
Warple Way, London W3 ORG.

Copyright Dave Thompson © 2006

ISBN: 1 901447 60X

Design: Dave Johnson
Printing: Biddles

Truth

Rod Stewart, Ron Wood and the
Jeff Beck Group

Dave Thompson

ACKNOWLEDGEMENTS

For encouragement, enthusiasm, knowledge and more, grateful thanks to Amy Hanson, Mark Johnson, Mike Griffiths, Anton Karis, Jo-Ann Greene, John Donovan, Mark Strand and everyone at Cherry Red Books.

To the musicians and associates who took the time to speak with me over the years, in and out of the interview room, the most special thanks, of course, go to Jeff Beck, who so graciously detoured from promoting his (then-) latest albums to recollect a couple of far older ones. I am grateful, too, to: Brian Auger, Jack Bruce, Donovan, Mick Fleetwood, Graham Gouldman, Peter Green, John Hewlett, John Paul Jones, Ivan Kral, Lulu, Phil May, John Mayall, Alan Merrill, Simon Napier-Bell, Davy O'List, Andrew Loog Oldham, Suzi Quatro, Bernie Tormé and Twink.

Too many of the other players who contributed to my researches are no longer with us: Long John Baldry, Pete Bardens, Kim Gardner, Nicky Hopkins and Noel Redding all gave generously of their time and memories. Thanks, too, to Peter Grant, whom I interviewed during the mid-1980s for a proposed book on independent record labels. The book never happened, but Grant's openness more than compensated for that disappointment.

A tug of the forelock to everybody else who helped bring the beast to life: Anchorite Man; Bateerz and family; Blind Pew; Mrs B. East; Ella; Gaye and Tim, Gef the Talking Mongoose; the Gremlins who live in the furnace; K-Mart and Snarleyyowl; Geoff Monmouth; Nutkin; sundry possums and raccoons; Sonny; a lot of Thompsons and Neville Viking.

And finally – this is for Sprocket, square chops and all.

Contents

CHAPTER ONE

In 1985, with a new single, "People Get Ready", reuniting him with vocalist Rod Stewart for only the second time on vinyl since 1969, Jeff Beck was lined up to be interviewed by one of the British music weeklies of the time.

A writer was assigned, a date was set, and then the guitarist's office started moving the goalposts. He wanted the cover of the magazine. He wanted lots of pictures taken of his collection of vintage cars. And finally, that was all he wanted to talk about – the vintage car collection which he'd been painstakingly assembling his whole career long.

The interview never happened.

Reminded of all this, close to 15 years later, Beck laughed, sighed and apologised all in the same movement. And then he explained.

"What happened was, I got on the cover of *Auto Week* magazine, and I was the first rock'n'roller ever to do that. It was a bizarre thing, it was one of those magazines which had drag racing stars on, and all the Formula Whatever drivers, and all of a sudden, because I have this collection, and people know about it, I was put the cover of that. And I got more bizarre questions and coverage with that than you would imagine, which was great, because I was going through this very anti period, when I didn't want to talk about music or guitars. In a way, they're pretty boring things anyway, so unless you've got some hilarious new angle on it let's not talk about it. I didn't want to be asked about string gauges or flame maple necks and how many fingers I use and stuff. Cars were just more interesting to me at the time. But it was not intended to be in any way flash, I can assure you."

Although Flash was the name of your album at the time, wasn't it?

"Yeah... oh, Christ. Freudian slip."

That story is told to illustrate one point. That Jeff Beck has always been a contrary devil.

In the late 1960s, while he and Rod Stewart led the first, greatest, incarnation of the Jeff Beck Group to proto-metal bluesbreaking glory, Beck alone doubled as a teenybop pop idol, taking the likes of "Hi Ho Silver Lining" and "Love Is Blue" to the toppermost of the British chart.

Through the 1970s, when the world was crying out for the raw rock electrics that he, alone, was capable of wringing out of a guitar, he meandered off into jazz fusion territory.

And today, when peers as venerable as Paul McCartney and Eric Clapton have come proper croppers with their toothless attempts to embrace modern electronica, Beck has turned the whole debate on its head by coming up with a clutch of albums that make the Prodigy sound like a powercut. He called the first one Who Else! – and that was contrary as well, because most people hearing it for the very first time would have been more likely to turn round and demand, "who?"

But Beck shrugged away any confusion, and instead compared Who Else! to every other truly great, but absolutely unexpected, record he has ever been involved with, from the Yardbirds' eponymous studio debut, alive with experimentation, madness and flash; through Truth and Blow By Blow, on to Wired, and thence into every other spanner that he's ever thrown into his own iconic works. "What the hell do you do to impress anybody these days? That's what kept (me) going in a way, trying to come up with something fresh and exciting which would make people go 'wow,' but which wouldn't just appeal because it was clever, or because no-one had done it before. It had to be alive."

Who Else! was certainly that. Film-maker Peter Richardson heard it, then told Beck that he thought it was precisely the kind of record which Hendrix would be making, if he were alive today. And an overjoyed Beck admitted, "I thought that was the ultimate compliment, because when Hendrix came along..."

When Hendrix came along, Beck knew that he – and the rest of the Swinging London glitterati – had better stop messing about with their celebrity and pull something truly remarkable out of the hat. And one by one, they did so. Within six months of the American touching down in the city, the Beatles had unveiled "Strawberry Fields" and were now planning Sgt Pepper, Eric Clapton and Cream were scheming Disraeli Gears, the Who were working towards The Who Sell Out.

But, of all the albums that were released as the late 1960s rushed into the post-Hendrix history books, any number can claim to have hastened that already precipitous end; to have served up a taste of the decade to come in the very last years of the decade in hand. Just one raises itself above the parapet of the Critical Favourites, to survey the wasteland that was still to come, and admit – proudly or otherwise – "I did that." That album is Truth, the first and, in many ways, the only album by the Jeff Beck Group.

It is not necessarily the most obvious pioneer, and certainly not the most heralded. There was no deluxe remastering for the album's 30th anniversary in 1998 (just a somewhat desultory repackaging for its 37th); and the Group itself has never reformed to pursue the multitude of options their original demise prevented them from taking in the first place. There was no vast reservoir of out-takes and rarities for collectors to spend their daydreams salivating over and, though the album was massive in America, it didn't even chart in the Jeff Beck Group's British homeland.

But adherents of the band will argue that the first Led Zeppelin album was a virtual carbon copy of Truth, and most of what has been perpetrated in the name of rock (hard, blues, heavy, metallic, whatever) in the years since its release can be traced back in some form to the standards set by the Jeff Beck Group.

Not only its standards, either. Its very personnel have dominated the music scene for 40 years now. Vocalist Rod Stewart and bassist Ron

Wood emerged as legends before their lunch break was even over, first in tandem with the Faces, then via careers which shot off as solo star and Rolling Stone respectively.

Jeff Beck himself remains one of the Gods of rock guitar, and the roll call of other musicians who passed through the band as it burned up and out across two-and-a-bit years includes some of the most ubiquitous players in British rock: drummers Mickey Waller and Aynsley Dunbar, pianist Nicky Hopkins, guest musicians Keith Moon and John Paul Jones.

Yet Truth still hangs over all of these players, and all their achievements, because it was the album that introduced the world to the manner of achievements the individual band members were capable of: Beck, the string-bending, neck-snapping, axe-wielding architect of the post-blues rock explosion that everyone had been waiting for but nobody knew how to shape; Stewart, the white boy who sang the blues as black as any cat; and Wood, the best little bass player who had never played a bass before.

This was the combination which created Truth; this, with Waller a powerhouse behind his band mates, was the quartet which helped shape the hardest rock of the looming 1970s – and beyond. Honed to razor-sharpness by over a year on the road, squeezed to switchblade shapeliness by the deadlines of the day and then left to their own devices for a few days in the studio, the Jeff Beck Group went in to make a record, and came out with the Holy Grail.

"Truth was only ever a blueprint", Beck declared. "It was never really developed, and I've had to sit back here for the past (nearly 40) years, watching people perfect it. But that's fine, because I would never have stayed playing that same stuff over anyway. I get vibes from people like Joe Perry and Slash, the really great rockers, the people I like to believe when they tell me things. I know they must have been impressed by that album because I can hear it in their performances. It seems to me that record played a very large part in what's going on today.

"What surprises me is, the whole thing was so incredibly dangerous and rickety that it was a wonder we made any records at all! There was no organisation at all. One day there was no Truth album, the next day a Truth album existed. That's how things were, and that was kind of the appeal of the whole thing. It was the equivalent to a decade earlier, when Little Richard used to record in the back of a bakery in Macon, Georgia, somewhere, that's how it was.

"We were practising in pubs for ten quid, then going out on the road, or in to record. It was pretty rough going, but we just got on with it, because that's what you had to do. It wasn't until things started picking up for other bands that we were able to function properly, where proper gigs were being put on the slate with proper money. Otherwise we were just playing for petrol money." And he laughed when it was suggested that Truth itself came together more by accident than design, because that's how the Jeff Beck Group got together in the first place. "When I was first talking about leaving the Yardbirds and going off on my own,

I didn't have a clue what I was going to come up with."

"Going off on my own." Musicians do that all the time these days, rising up the ladder in cahoots with whichever band they started out in, then departing to follow their own dream someplace else. It wasn't so common in the mid-1960s, though, when rock'n'roll was still a pre-adolescent brat and bands themselves were mythical musketeers, all for one and one for all.

True, the occasional frontman would break away from his buddies. Hogging the headlines in October 1965, Wayne Fontana chose a solo career over life with the Mindbenders and swung the axe in the middle of a live show, turning to guitarist Eric Stewart as he walked off the stage and saying, "It's all yours." A few months later, Paul Jones walked out on Manfred Mann, and how he must have envied Fontana; loyal soul that he was, he not only forewarned his band mates of his decision, he agreed to remain on board until they found a replacement. Six months later...

Frontmen were different, though. People knew their faces, knew their names, recognised their voices. When Fontana left the Mindbenders or Jones quit the Manfreds, it was the musicians that worried whether they could go on without their mike-wielding talisman. The singers thought they had it made.

You had to track back a long time to discover the last time a 'mere' musician had quit for a life of his own and emerged without any commercial regrets. Back in 1962, Jet Harris and Tony Meehan walked out on Cliff Richard and the Shadows, announced they were forming their own eponymous group, then grabbed a chart-topping single straight out of the box.

But Cliff and co were massive back then, and each of the stars had his own superstar following. Of course Harris and Meehan did well – it would have been more surprising if they hadn't. The Yardbirds, on the other hand, were just one more pop group in a sea of such things, and Jeff Beck was just one more guitar slinger.

Of course he had his acolytes, but so did his predecessor in that band's august ranks, and where was Eric Clapton now? Still blazing the same old blues he'd always bundled up in a new band, name of Cream. But did anyone outside of the music press especially care? Not to judge by the sales of Cream's debut single – "Wrapping Paper" was released in November 1966, just a couple of weeks before Beck left the Yardbirds, and, though it would ultimately make a minor dent on the charts, reviews were lousy and the disappointment loud. Jack Bruce, another former member of Manfred Mann, remembers Cream sharing the *Ready Steady Go!* stage with his old bandmates, and the looks on their faces told him all he needed to know. "You could just see it in their eyes. As far as they were concerned, we'd blown it."

Of course, Cream would make out all right in the end... more than all right, in fact. But as Jeff Beck sat in his Kansas City hotel room, determined to walk away from the Yardbirds, he was more frightened than anything else. After all, if Clapton couldn't make a go of it on his own, the man whose name was a by-word for God on the walls of the

London club circuit, the man whose fans still hadn't forgiven Beck for presuming to walk in his footsteps, what chance did Beck have?

But he couldn't just stay where he was. Seismic cracks had been spider-webbing across the Yardbirds for six months now, ever since they replaced their original manager, mercurial Russian Giorgio Gomelsky, with the whizkid efficiency of Simon Napier-Bell. Paul Samwell-Smith, the bass-playing heart of the original band, had already quit, and Beck talked of departing at the same time.

At that point, he was dissuaded, partly by his own uncertainty but also by the band's choice for Samwell-Smith's replacement, Beck's own best friend, Jimmy Page. But still he was miserable, and he was growing worse every day. His health was fracturing, his tonsils were torturing him, he was exhausted in every way that was possible – physically, emotionally, mentally, the lot. And how did management respond? By booking the band onto Dick Clark's Caravan Of Stars, a 600-miles-a-day tour that lined the Yardbirds up with Gary Lewis, Brian Hyland, Sam the Sham... and it was a sham, a horribly dispiriting affair that the group had been dreading from the moment their participation was confirmed but which they had no alternative but to complete.

Beck's suffering was palpable. He missed shows, he was frequently ill, he was at odds with his band mates. There were times, the rest of the group muttered behind his back, when his entire being appeared to be devoted to rocking the boat in the hope that it would capsize. Now that it was apparent that it wouldn't, he took the only other available option. He hurled himself overboard. "Jeff walked out on the tour", rhythm guitarist Chris Dreja shrugged. "He did one show and quit."

But what a show it was. The drama kicked off backstage when singer Keith Relf – never Beck's best friend in the band – made some kind of disparaging remark to the guitarist. Beck, who was cradling his instrument in his arms at the time, did not answer. Instead, he wheeled around, raised his guitar over his head... when Jimmy Page walked into the room at that precise moment, his first thought was that Relf was in for the Les Paul-shaped mother of all headaches. But Beck didn't hit him. Instead, he brought the instrument down on the floor, shattering it.

"The neck came away", he said later, "and the pick-ups flew in two different directions. Jimmy Page was horrified, (and) so was I, when I realised what I'd done." Mortified, Beck turned to the still-seated Relf, whose own face was contorted in astonishment, and asked, "Why did you make me do that?"

Beck played the show that evening and stacked up a heap of future anecdotes as the night wore on. According to some people's memories, he smashed another guitar onstage towards the end of the performance; according to others, however, he never hung around even that long, stalking off mid-show without a word.

Either way, the tour bus dropped him off at Corpus Christi International Airport the following morning, and he was in LA by nightfall. The Yardbirds had lost another guitarist. And rock'n'roll was about to gain another legend.

CHAPTER TWO

"I wasn't at all surprised when Jeff left the Yardbirds", Mickie Most once revealed. "In fact, as I got to know him better, I was more surprised he hadn't left them sooner than he did."

It was not the first time, after all, that Beck had threatened to quit and then put that threat into action by walking out of the door. He was miserable almost from the moment he joined the group... maybe not miserable, but certainly frustrated by the nature of the workload, the pop-tinge of the music, the limitations of the budget and by his band mates. They drove him crazy.

"The Yardbirds were a miserable bloody lot. They really were", manager Simon Napier-Bell later reflected. "They didn't give him enough freedom to show off his talent and, consequently, he spent most of his time with the group in a huff."

Whereas other musicians in Beck's position might have sulked or worse, Beck chose to take the opposite approach. He made himself indispensable in the knowledge that, without his mercurial guitar-playing, the Yardbirds would find themselves facing a dilemma that only Oscar Wilde could have found entertaining. To lose one great guitarist is unfortunate. To lose two is carelessness.

The Yardbirds had been around since early 1963 when they were formed by guitarist Tony 'Top' Topham, vocalist Keith Relf, drummer Jim McCarty, bassist Paul Samwell-Smith and rhythm guitarist Chris Dreja, a bunch of R&B-loving west London teens, whose savage cross of purist sensibilities and wild on-stage shenanigans quickly brought them to the attention of Giorgio Gomelsky, the bear-like leviathan who sat at the centre of the regional R&B boom.

The son of a Russian doctor and a French mother, Gomelsky arrived in Britain via stints in Italy (where he organised the country's first ever jazz festival) and Chicago (where he discovered R&B music). He'd started out in London running a jazz club. Now he masterminded the Crawdaddy, one of the hottest nightspots in town, and was promoting blues tours across the UK.

Together with the Marquee Organisation's Harold McNair, Gomelsky was responsible for the British leg of the 1963 American Folk Blues Festival tour, perhaps the single most crucial catalyst in the growth of Britain's own R&B scene. Alone, it was Gomelsky who discovered the Rollin' (as was) Stones, and who was grooming them for some kind of regional breakout when Andrew Loog Oldham happened upon them and catapulted them onto an even vaster stage. And hungrily, seeking out a replacement, Gomelsky happened upon the Yardbirds, installed them in the Stones' old residency at the Crawdaddy Club and watched as they established themselves as firmly as Jagger and co once had.

It was with the arrival of the unknown Eric Clapton to replace Topham in late 1963 that the Yardbirds' stock truly began to rise. Over the next year, the newcomer's deft blues guitar came to shape the 'birds' entire being – but it was also holding them back, as Clapton's puritan devotion to the blues rendered him increasingly resistant to his bandmates' desire to take their fame to the next level. Two singles and a churning live album passed by with a nod of approval from the blues hounds but little commercial activity, and Clapton was happily anticipating their next respected-but-scarcely-saleable single, a faithful cover of Otis Redding's "Your One And Only Love", when the band dropped a bomb on him.

The Otis song was to be scrapped. Instead, they were going ahead with a harpsichord-driven version of untried Manchester songwriter Graham Gouldman's "For Your Love" – a song their record company, Columbia, had already rejected once, when Gouldman's own band offered it to them. But Paul Samwell-Smith had come up with a terrific new arrangement, and even the suits were now tapping their toes, convinced that the Yardbirds were on the edge of the hit single they'd always so-deserved.

But at what price? Clapton was a blues purist at a time when such snobbery was a badge to wear with pride. "For Your Love", on the other hand, was beat commerciality at its most pristine – a wonderful song, an excellent performance, a spellbinding production. But it wasn't the blues, and Clapton knew that the Yardbirds would never return to them once the pop bug had sprinkled their wallets with silver. He played on the record, then quit the group, just seven days before "For Your Love" was released

It was mid-February 1965, and the search was on for a replacement.

The Yardbirds themselves had eyes for just one guitarist. 17 year-old Jimmy Page, the choirboy-faced prodigy who was already cutting a serious swathe through the London session circuit. He'd played on Jet Harris and Tony Meehan's hit single "Diamonds", Lulu's "Shout" and a whole crop of singles by Mickie Most, PJ Proby and Dave Berry. The Yardbirds knew it would take a lot of persuading to prise him away from such a lucrative career, but it had to be worth a go. Didn't it?

Maybe. Page turned the offer down flat, and for precisely the reasons his suitors expected. He was making a more than healthy living in the studio – and, besides, he had no desire whatsoever to sacrifice a civilised working day in order to rattle around the country in the back of a band bus. But he thanked them for asking and told them that, if they were really stuck, that they could do a lot worse than check out a close friend of his, by the name of Geoffrey Arnold Beck.

They did as he suggested and, between February 1965, when Beck played his first ever show with the Yardbirds, and November 1966, when he grimaced through his last, the group proved to the world that lightning can strike twice. In Eric Clapton, they'd boasted one of the two greatest guitar players Britain had ever produced. In Jeff Beck, they discovered the other one.

Growing up in Wallington, a little-known suburb of Croydon, Surrey, Beck's ears had been attuned to music since he first heard Les Paul's "How High The Moon" on the radio one day around 1951. It was not the man's guitar, or even the song that captivated him, but the slapback echo that resounded through the record, a sound that an excited Beck still describes as "a hurricane blowing through. I just thought of sparks flying and metal, which you'd never associate with a guitar."

Not at that time you wouldn't, and Beck certainly didn't. His parents originally saw him as an aspiring pianist, and put him through two years of lessons before the boy finally ripped one of the black keys off the family's grand piano. He wanted to play drums, he declared, and he spent hours snare-and-brushing along to his father's collection of jazz records.

Cello was next, thanks to a classical-loving uncle, but Beck simply couldn't get to grips with the notion that he had to caress the strings with a bow. He wanted to pluck them with his fingers – and, when an attempt to pick up violin went similarly askew, it was clear where his heart really lay. The advent of rock'n'roll confirmed it.

First Bill Haley, then Elvis Presley, and then a million splinters of shattered floodgate... Presley's "Hound Dog", Beck avers, "floored me." But it wasn't Elvis who won his heart, it was the guitar solos, peeled out of thin air by Scotty Moore. "They put me on the floor for several months", Beck continued and, for the first time, he understood "what rock'n'roll was all about. The outrage... hips wriggling, greased-back hair."

It was Beck's sister Annette, four years his senior, who was the greatest aid to his initial musical education, albeit without actually being aware of it. She was buying records regularly, fragile 78s that she would keep wrapped up and hidden away from prying sibling eyes – "and I used to dig them out when she'd gone out." But if any one moment crystallised everything Beck was searching for in a musical instrument... in music itself... it was the day in 1956 that he saw a poster for *The Girl Can't Help It*, the cataclysmic movie that made a superhero out of Little Richard, a sex kitten from Jayne Mansfield and a god out of Gene Vincent.

Of course he had to enter the cinema, of course he sat enraptured through the film. And, when the movie finished, he sat through it again; then returned to see it every day that he could. And each viewing reinforced two things in his mind. Yes, he wanted to be a rock'n'roll guitar player. But the rock'n'roll he wanted to play belonged heart and soul to Gene Vincent.

"When I was learning guitar", Beck enthused, Vincent's guitarist Cliff Gallup "was the biggest influence on my playing – the cut was pretty deep and the scar has never healed! It was just so radical." Like the rest of Britain, the first Vincent record he ever heard was "Be Bop A Lula", and he admits, "it probably doesn't sound metally or threatening now. But if you were back in June '56 and turned the record right up... Boy! The term 'rock'n'roll' had hardly been bandied about and all the other 'rock' records of the time were very polished and audibly nice and round. Then you put on Gene Vincent, and had this guy screaming and these raucous guitar solos – it was unheard of – and no one has done anything like it since."

That did not stop Beck himself from trying, however.

The sight of Vincent, the sound of Gallup, didn't simply ignite young Geoffrey's musical ambitions. They rewired his entire concept of what rock'n'roll music was capable of – and would remain capable of. Thirty-plus years later, Beck would repay Gallup for all his influence by recreating his magnificence across the Crazy Legs album.

Even this young, though, he was already aware of the rebellion the music apparently presaged; had seen the roaming bands of Teddy Boys who marched down England's high streets on their way to tabloid immortality, who razored cinema seats to show their approval of films and kicked in heads to test the strength of their brothel-creepers. But that was all he was, aware of it. It took Gene Vincent to actually spell it out for him, to paint rock'n'roll in terms of a revolution that could sweep away all the old values of 1950s England.

Now Annette was willingly abetting the boy in his voyages of discovery. Nightly, she'd sit with him as they struggled to listen to Radio Luxembourg, a static and hiss-drenched clatter that drifted nightly across the North Sea on 208 metres medium wave, to fill juvenile heads with DJs Keith Fordyce, Barry Alldis and Alan Freeman; the audio adventures of *Eagle* comic mainstay Dan Dare; exclusive live sessions from the big bands and orchestras of the day; and, increasingly as the decade wore on, rock'n'roll. Lots of rock'n'roll.

"Luxembourg... was just fading and cross-fading and flanging. You couldn't hear a bloody note", Beck recalled. "Then one glorious cascade of electric guitar notes would come out and it was tuning into a God somewhere."

Often, it was Annette who pointed that cascade out to him. "She would never say 'oh, I love this guy,' or 'Elvis is great.' She would point out a guitar solo. I was most interested in bands that used the guitar to great effect, people like Scotty Moore, Cliff Gallup, James Burton (alongside Ricky Nelson), all of them in the States, which is where my musical roots are." He still remembers how outraged he felt when he discovered that the people whose names were actually on the record – Elvis Presley was first – didn't actually play the sounds that he most relished.

"In those days, album info was nothing. You find me an early Elvis recording that says Scotty Moore (is) on guitar, and Bill Black (is) on bass. That upset me to the point of learning the guitar style, adopting it. And once I got over the first rung of the ladder, of learning a part of 'Hound Dog', I realised I was better than Elvis because I was doing something he couldn't do."

At first, Beck was content to simply wrestle with an acoustic guitar that one of his schoolfriends had recently got hold of. "It had about one string, but that's all I needed", Beck admitted. "Then that broke, and where were we gonna get another from? I didn't know." Most towns, Croydon included, had at least one music store, but such places were wholly off the radar for a 13, 14-year-old schoolkid with barely enough pocket-money to buy the necessities of the day, let alone the 10 shillings (50p) that a new set of strings would cost. Besides, what was the point of buying a whole packet? He'd only broken one. He replaced the casualty with a length of piano wire and got back to grappling with the complexities of his instrument.

Beck's next guitar was a home-made effort, carved from heavyweight plywood and so hopelessly out of proportion that he remembers the neck as being "about 14 feet long." That's an exaggeration, but still it was easier to look at the guitar than play it, so that's what he'd do, "prop it up in an armchair and look at it."

That guitar perished at the hands of Beck's father, following a heated row. But the boy had already set his sights on creating a new instrument, modelled on the Fender he saw on a Buddy Holly album cover. Well aware that his own carpentry skills could never attain the level of perfection required, Beck called on outside help – a friend who seemed to know his way around so intricate a project. Once again, however, the finished item had very little to do with the musicality one might expect to find in a guitar – bright yellow, and festooned with wires and knobs, "it looked like half a pine tree, had about 400 frets (spaced according to whim and appearance, as opposed to any understanding of their actual purpose), and the neck was still a couple of miles long."

It was, however, playable, particularly after Beck finally plucked up the courage to start frequenting one of the local music stores, and shoplifted a pick-up. "I had so little money", he excused himself to *Guitar Player* magazine, "and (playing guitar) was the thing I wanted to do so much."

. His next project was to build an amplifier – an economical 30 watts, housed within a cabinet that stood 15 feet tall. Of course there was no way to get it home, much less convince his parents that it was a worthwhile adornment to the house, so Beck took the next best route and plugged his guitar into the family radiogram. It sounded horrible, and the volume was negligible. But, if you pressed your ear right up against the speaker, as Beck did as often as he could, the effect was unmistakable. He was on the radio.

Time passed. A friend of his owned a Pye Record Maker, a magnificent appliance that, within the wooden case of a standard radiogram, was capable not only of playing records but recording them as well via a specially adapted cartridge and a coated magnetic disc. The Record Maker was eventually supplanted by the reel-to-reel tape recorder but, while it remained available, it allowed the aspiring young recording star to actually achieve the Holiest of Grails – making a record.

Soon, Beck was as proficient on the instrument as any "snot-rag 14-year-old kid" could hope to be, and had circumnavigated most of the misconceptions that blighted the majority of his contemporaries. He no longer naively believed that you could plug your guitar directly into the wall; was no longer convinced that the colour of a guitar lead dictated its volume (red was the loudest). And he had long since graduated past the need for lessons, as he proved when he dismissed his first and only tutor because he "knew less than I did"; then when he convinced his father to accompany him to a local music store to try out a white Fender Telecaster he'd become enamoured by, the store owner wouldn't allow the boy to touch it without adult supervision. "Finally, one Saturday, I've got it in my hands and, as I'm running over riffs by Scotty Moore, people are stopping to listen."

On another occasion, he was riding a bus up Charing Cross Road when he spotted a bright red Stratocaster in a shop window. Shouting "stop the bus!" he leaped off to stand with his face pressed up against the window, just gazing.

Fenders – indeed, any American guitars – were nigh-on unobtainable at that time. As Britain continued her slow recovery from World War Two, and the mountain of debt left behind by the Lend-Lease agreement with the United States, the economy of the day placed an import ban on most American goods, Fender guitars included. Private individuals could bring them in, so a handful of stores might have one on display (Cliff Richard apparently brought the first one into the country for Hank Marvin), but the cost was prohibitive all the same. So Beck started collecting the next best thing – Fender catalogues. "I used to leave them on the table so people would think I was going to buy a guitar. In fact I couldn't afford them."

Beck's ambitions received another boost when he met Jimmy Page. Again, it was Annette who made the historic introduction; she was attending art school in Epsom and came home one day to tell her brother, "There's a bloke at school with a funny-shaped guitar like yours."

Beck was astonished. "I went 'Where is he? Take me to him!' I couldn't believe there was another human being in Surrey interested in strange-shaped solid guitars." Nor that Annette had actually noticed him. When Beck and his sister were younger, after all, "(Annette) was always the first to say 'Shut that row up! Stop playing that horrible noise.' (But) when she went to art school the whole thing changed. The recognition of somebody else doing the same thing must have changed her mind. She comes home screaming back into the house saying, 'I know a guy that does what you do.' She told me where this guy lived, and said that it was okay to go around and visit. And to see someone else with these strange looking electric guitars was great.

"I went in there, into Jimmy's front room. It seemed to me he was only 15 or 16, and he got his little acoustic guitar out and started playing away. It was great. He sang Buddy Holly songs. From then on we were just really close. His mum bought him a tape recorder and we used to make home recordings together. I think he sold them for a great sum of money to Immediate Records." (Two Page-Beck guitar jams, "Chuckles" and "Steelin'", later became part of Immediate's Blues Anytime series of compilations.)

Most of the money Beck had was now going on records, but occasionally it would stretch to a live show as well; in March 1958, he caught Buddy Holly at Croydon's Davies Theatre and later described it as the best gig he ever attended. Ever. Gene Vincent remained closest to his heart, however and, just a couple of months after the Holly show, Beck made his first ever public appearance, as part of a trio (completed by a forgotten singer and a cello-playing double-bassist) who regaled Carshalton Park's May Day parade with an extraordinarily ramshackle version of "Be Bop A Lula."

"I couldn't find a (proper) bass player, so this art student came along", Beck recalled. "He still had his duffel coat on, and he didn't have a bass. He had a cello, and it looked ridiculous. He was six feet three inches, and he played this cello like an upright bass. I said 'put it on a chair...' – we got through half a number before we folded up and couldn't remember the rest of it."

A string of school 'bands' followed... gatherings of fellow musicians who'd get together and play. If it worked, they might do it again, if it didn't, they'd drift off to seek out new permutations. Nothing was serious, nothing was set in stone – even the band names would change from day to day. But every time he came together with another bunch of like-minded souls, Beck would have another riff mastered, another run together, another solo mapped out in his mind.

And then he heard the news he'd been waiting for, it seemed, his entire life. Gene Vincent was coming to England, to play on TV's *Boy Meets Girl*.

CHAPTER
THREE

For all the menace and malice and bad reputation he'd established in the three years since "Be Bop A Lula", Gene Vincent was not the most visual of performers. True, his stance and his scruffiness made him stand out a little – crippled in a motorcycle accident during his time in the US Navy, Vincent wielded his bad leg like a weapon, outraging the sensibilities of an older generation who still believed that the disabled were best kept well out of sight. The rest of the Vincent aura – the sense of debauched evil he wore like a glove – simply followed.

But when you actually took stock of everything else, the tatty denims, the 5 o'clock shadow, the permanent sneer, he was just another snotty kid with a bad case of attitude and a chip on his shoulder. Or so thought Jack Good, the American-born presenter of television's greatest rock'n'roll show, when Vincent arrived at the television studio.

Good had an eye for image. It was he who first squeezed Cliff Richard into the role of England's Elvis that would sustain him while he built up his own identity; it was Good who reshaped so many of Britain's proto-rockers, granting them an inkling of a chance of giving the Americans a run for their money.

In Vincent, however, Good saw something that went beyond merely projecting an image for a single TV performance. He saw one that would survive the decades... today, the look that Good grafted upon Vincent in a draughty television studio in early 1960 remains the quintessential image of rock'n'roll itself.

Off came the jeans, the shirts and the hats that had hitherto been Vincent's sole uniform; off came any resemblance to an even halfway respectable human being. When Vincent rolled out onto the *Boy Meets Girl* set, he was a demon dipped in tight black leather, twisting his body beneath a single white spotlight, barely moving, never smiling, just sweating and as a pick-up band, the Firing Squad, ground their way through steamy versions of "Rocky Road Blues", "Frankie And Johnny", "Wild Cat" and "Right Here On Earth."

Good couldn't have moulded anything if it wasn't there to begin with. But, by the time Vincent set foot back on stage, touring the UK alongside Eddie Cochran, the mutation was complete. Cochran was every cocky teenager's dream come true; Vincent was every outcast's idol. Together on the same concert bill, they reached out to every rock'n'roll fan in the land.

Jeff Beck was disappointed when he first caught sight of Vincent, initially on the television and then onstage in Croydon. Seeing the singer himself was a thrill, and the new look personified everything that Beck had heard in Vincent's music. But he had also been banking upon seeing the Blue Caps, the group that backed Vincent across all his greatest records. He had no way of knowing that the band had shattered long before, that not one of the faces he'd memorised off Vincent's LP covers was even talking to him any more.

"I was heartbroken when he appeared onstage without the Blue Caps. I was a naive, trusting kid of 12 or so, and he was playing with these guys who looked like they had just walked in from a bar. They were pretty good though... (then), when Vincent appeared it was amazing. He was so menacing that you forgave him that he didn't have his own band."

The tour was a phenomenal success. Back home in the States, Vincent's personal renown had been fading for months. Europe, however, adored him – his entire career was undergoing an astonishing rebirth, the old records were still selling, his new ones were moving, his concerts were sell-outs. And then Cochran died, killed in a car crash as he headed back to London for a red-eye flight to LA at the end of the first leg of the tour, on 17 April 1960. Vincent was in the car with him, but while he emerged from the wreck battered but breathing – he broke a few ribs and his collarbone, and further damaged his leg – emotionally he would never recover.

He tried to put a bold face on things. Less than a month after the crash, Vincent was in Abbey Road Studios with Norrie Paramor, recording a new single, "Pistol Packin' Mama", a session that had originally been arranged as a straight-ahead Vincent-Cochran duet. It says a lot for Vincent's fortitude that he could even go ahead with the project, let alone turn in so tremendous a performance, and a Britain mourning Cochran's loss was swift to show its gratitude. "Pistol Packin' Mama" climbed to Number 15, and might have gone even higher had Vincent not peremptorily returned to the US in June, turning his back on a sold-out string of concerts in the process. He claimed he'd received a telegram telling him his 18-month-old daughter, Melody, had died from pneumonia; later however, he admitted that nothing of the sort had occurred. He just didn't want to play the shows.

And so somebody else played them for him. Among the very bedrocks of the infant British rock'n'roll scene was the concept of the domestic soundalike. The biggest stars of the day rarely appeared in person on British shores – some, like Elvis, never would. But audiences still wanted to hear their music, so wily promoters would hunt out performers who could imitate them; not quite note for note, because even the hungriest audience would scarcely tolerate that, but close enough that the village hall would go home happy when the show was over.

Every British player worth his salt (and a few that weren't) was initially launched beneath the banner of the UK's answer to someone or other... usually Elvis, until Cliff Richard came along and made that tag his very own; but Jerry Lee Lewis, Little Richard, Eddie Cochran, every one of them had his own Anglo shadow. And barely had Gene Vincent announced he was pulling out of his projected tour than promoter Bob Potter was looking to fill the void.

Shadowing the cancelled Vincent tour dates, Potter put together a package of performers who, across the course of an evening, could replicate the greatest Vincent gig you could ever imagine. Even he however could never have imagined, just how close to perfection the venture would come. Bill-topper Cal Danger was Vincent in everything but bad leg and alcoholism, while further down the bill Kerry Rapid was a walking encyclopaedia of Vincent's catalogue.

Potter had also forged a band, the Bandits, to back each of the frontmen in turn. Most of the Bandits already knew one another from playing together around their native Hampshire. One new player was drawn in from the auditions, however – and, though Jeff Beck may have been unknown, experienced only in a few school pick-up bands, Potter was convinced of one thing. You could have cloned Cliff Gallup himself and never created such a note-perfect duplication.

Renaming himself Jeff Mason for the occasion, Beck himself cut a dazzling figure from his bleached pompadour on down. But it was his playing that blew everybody away – after all those years spent thrashing away at his home-made instruments, graduating to the real thing, a £25 Guyatone, felt like coming home as sounds and effects he'd sweated blood to replicate now peeled out of his amplifier without a pause for breath.

This was Beck's first ever experience of touring and, no matter how excited he was to be playing in front of an audience, his glee was always offset by his sheer dislike for the touring life. "I hate the idea that one has to go away and live unnaturally and all that", he condemned. But he also knew that he had no choice. Live work was where you learned your trade, live work was where you built your name.

Coming off the road at the end of the Vincent tour, he determined to find himself a regular band. The Deltones had long since caught Beck's eye, speeding around Croydon and the environs in their pink jacket uniforms and a Dormobile van with their name painted across it. When he heard they were in need of a guitarist, to replace the outgoing Ian Duncan, Beck was first in line for the auditions – and sailed through so easily that he was onstage with the band at the Putney Ballroom that same evening.

Like the Bandits, the Deltones neither possessed nor needed any 'original' material. Audiences danced to songs they knew, so it was in a band's interest to stick to the classics and stick to the charts, and build a reputation for doing both very well. The arrival of the machine-gunning out a succession of smash hit guitar instrumentals, was simply added grist to that particular mill. "It was easy stuff," Beck recalls. "Any band with the slightest bit of proficiency on their instruments could learn songs like 'Apache' in a day."

The importance of the Shadows to the eventual development of British rock can never be understated; and the importance of one of them, guitarist Hank Marvin, is even more crucial than that.

Born Brian Rankin, Marvin was not the first rock'n'roll guitar-slinger. He wasn't even the first British one. But he was the first who not only looked good and sounded better, he also made it all seem so easy. The bespectacled Geordie was nobody's idea of a teenage idol – even without the glasses (which at least gave him a hint of the Buddy Hollys), he was tall enough to seem gawky, and gawky enough to look goofy. But put a guitar in his hand and a band at his back, and he was a god, which really wasn't something you expected anybody to say about a British rock'n'roller in the late 1950s.

Rock'n'roll was American; its heroes, naturally, were Americans as well, exotic invaders who filled teenage ears with drawling accents and an erotic twang, a world of lurid neon, fin-backed Chevys and chick-infested soda pops that were a million miles from the drab grey of Anytown, England. Then Cliff and Hank and the Shadows came along, and suddenly rock'n'roll was global, and its possibilities were universal. And in villages, towns and cities the length and breadth of the land, kids were switching on their weekly dose of televised *Oh Boy!* and realising: "If they can do it, so can I!"

They could, as well. Pink Fairies guitarist Larry Wallis speaks for an entire generation when he recalls; "When I heard Hank B. Marvin on the (first) Cliff Richard album, and saw the pic of him with a Vox solid-body guitar, all was truly lost." Whitesnake's Micky Moody affectionately remembers the second-hand guitar his father bought him, on which he learned to play the Shadows' "Apache" on one string; BJ Cole picked up the steel guitar because "I wanted to sound like Hank, only more so." And so on.

Whether clowning behind Cliff, or stepping out in their own right, the Shadows – with Marvin's guitar fully to the fore – dominated British rock in the years before the Beatles. Between the debut "Move It" in late 1958, and the Fabs first chart-topper in early 1963, the team racked up more than 30 UK hits, and no less than 10 of them topped the chart. Which meant that even if an aspiring young musician didn't especially care for the band, still there was no escape from them.

Jeff Beck was ambivalent. He admired the band's success, he loved their look, he enjoyed their music. And he admitted that, had they come from America, he'd probably have been even more impressed. He learned their repertoire – "Apache", "Man Of Mystery", "The Stranger" *et al* – and could play it well. But he still ached to play something else.

"I was only a little sprout, you know, but I had still learned a lot of Cliff (Gallup)'s solos, pretty much aped them off so that it sounded a lot like him. And I was trying to beg the singer to learn the songs but they were already out of date, you see... 1956 to (1960) – hey, it's like a million miles! We used to do 'Be-Bop-a-Lula' – he didn't like singing that, but... And the kids were going, 'Can you play some more modern stuff?'"

And so they did, ploughing their course across the same circuit of youth clubs, church halls and gymnasiums as countless other bands. Some shows would subsequently prove memorable – towards the end of their lifespan, the Deltones opened for the Rolling Stones at Battersea Park, and Beck later marvelled at his first ever encounter with the ruffians, thugs and all-round hooligans that seemed to be cavorting across the temporary stage. "The way they looked, I was wondering why they weren't getting ice cream thrown at them."

He enjoyed their set, but wasn't sure if he could see a future in it. "I was still trying to find out what the hell I should be doing. All the girls were wanting the chart thing – they always wanted the latest things in the charts, as they still do. And so it just went on from there."

On 19 September 1960, Beck enrolled at Wimbledon School of Art to begin a two-year course in fine arts. Just eight months later, on 22 May 1961, he quit, disillusioned not by the teachers' disdain for his extra-curricular activities (the fate of every would-be musician in the educational system of the time), but by the realisation that very few of the people who actually got through art school ever went on to do anything in art.

"You saw people from previous years who left and they were coming back in rags, still couldn't get a job." If Beck was lucky, he told himself, he might hand a career "designing cornflakes packages." But, more likely, he'd end up doing something for which his education had never prepared him... working in a shoe shop, or a factory. Better to get out while he still had options – and music provided that opportunity, both as a member of the Deltones and in the spare time he spent messing around in what he recalled as "hundreds of other permutations of other bands." And slowly, he began to figure out what he wanted to do.

The Deltones were essentially a chart-orientated covers band, and Beck valued the apprenticeship with which they provided him – indeed, when the band finally broke up and singer Del Burchill moved on to a new band, the Crescents, Beck followed him for at least a few shows. He was hankering for a change, however, and his next band, the Nightshift, certainly offered him that.

The Nightshift were rooted firmly in the blues, a music Beck himself was just beginning to become fascinated by. Beginning in mid-1961, west London was suddenly awash with the stuff, as Alexis Korner and Cyril Davies took their own private obsession out of the shadows of their current gig with the Chris Barber jazz band and into the aptly-named bowels of the Moist Hoist, their own R&B club in Ealing. There, they inculcated first a circle of curious onlookers; then a widening sphere of musically curious; and, finally, an entire generation with a deep and abiding love of all things black and American.

"My interest in blues started when the Chicago blues albums first began to reach England", Beck recalled. "I grabbed them. Muddy Waters, Buddy Guy... they're just great. There's a special way the guitars sound, sort of tinny and rough. The Chicago sound (is) like nothing else. I was listening to Big Bill Broonzy trying to accompany himself, and loved that thumping crudeness and the stomping foot."

He quickly discovered, however, that the music only sounded crude "until you tried to play it." That was when the personal variables – feel, mood, emotion – came into play and, as his ears absorbed every new record he could lay his hands on, Beck set himself the target of capturing not the particular feel of the masters, for any human jukebox could do that, but a style and feel that was all his own.

That was always the one factor that set Beck aside from other guitar players of the age, and made him such a great catch for the Nightshift. "The blues shuffle stuff was a prerequisite in those days", he remembers. "Everybody was doing it, nobody wanted their music fucked around with... There were people like John Mayall around, playing completely authentic Chicago blues and, unless you really had a handle on things, you were going to get a bit of a rough time of things." That, however, was the aspect that he relished the most, facing an audience that was fractious and impatient and winning them over by the sheer weight of his determination. Anybody, he'd tell them, can play this... and he'd execute a pristine blues lick. But can they do *this*? And he'd blaze out a variation that could take the tops of their heads off.

The wellspring from which Beck drew his inspiration and education was the man who history best recalls as the catalyst around which the nascent Rolling Stones came together – without ever considering how he was able to do that in the first place.

Stocky, square-jawed, and almost frighteningly devoted to the music, Ian Stewart was the owner of one of the vastest blues record collections Beck had ever seen – as large, some people have said, as that with which Mayall educated the young Eric Clapton, and just as influential. Certainly Mick Jagger, Keith Richards and Brian Jones had never seen anything like it and, even before they started playing together in earnest, the three were regular visitors to Stewart's home to sit and listen through the mountains of vinyl.

Stewart was living in Epsom now, sharing a bungalow with Glyn Jones (the future record producer), and, Beck recalls, "was definitely the cornerstone of the whole of that (scene). He was Mr Blues. Religiously, he actually made you feel guilty about thinking about liking any other kind of music. I was heading in that direction, and he just put a massive boot up my arse."

The first time they met, when a mutual friend invited Beck over to the bungalow, "Stu... played me Otis Rush records and I was just blown away. Knowing Stu was like having a world music correspondent: 2120 Michigan Avenue (home of Chess records in Chicago), that address became etched in there. He told me what mikes they used, and he used to explain about 'hairy' guitar sounds. You knew that every time you saw him, enough time would have elapsed that you were going to get another classic Stu discovery from Flash Records or somewhere like that."

The Nightshift were never to find themselves in a position to take full advantage of Beck's education. But still the group made a few inroads on a club scene that was now bursting with new groups. They made regular appearances at Eel Pie Island, the blues-centric club that was, indeed, planted on an island in the middle of the River Thames, and ventured regularly into Soho to play clubs thereabouts.

One early show saw them headlining over the Stones; others matched them with the Yardbirds, as they took their own first steps out of the rehearsal room, with original guitarist Tony 'Top' Topham still holding down the role reserved for so many later legends. The Nightshift would never make it out of the era's footnotes, however. Though they were picked up for a few hours in the studio by the Pye label's Piccadilly subsidiary, the four songs they recorded in one hectic afternoon – "Stormy Monday", "Corinna Corinna", "Lavender Tree" and "That's My Story" were promptly shelved. They would not see the light of day for another two years and are, in any case, better remembered for the involvement of songwriter Tim Rice (of Rice and Lloyd Webber fame) than for the presence of Beck.

Indeed, Beck spent the first years of the 1960s pursuing a career that appears almost doggedly devoted to frustrating future historians. In early 1963, he was offered a gig with the Roosters, a tight little blues band led by guitarist Tom McGuinness and pianist Ben Palmer, but turned it down... Eric Clapton took the job instead. A few months later, hanging around a guitar shop on the Charing Cross Road, somebody suggested Beck get in touch with John Mayall, who had just moved down to London from his hometown of Manchester, and was still struggling to make even a tiny name for himself. Certainly Beck had never heard of him and, though the salesman did remark "he's the guv'nor, you'd better see him", he never got around to it.

Much of this apparent intransigence was down to Beck's own domestic situation. In July 1963, he married Patricia Brown, a dressmaker he'd been dating for several years, and the months on either side of the wedding saw him very much torn between pursuing his musical ambitions and settling down as a responsible husband. The compromise he eventually settled upon would not, in the event, be sufficient – the marriage was over within two years. For a while, however, he preferred to simply drift through, round and past the opportunities thrown at him by his burgeoning reputation as a guitar player, not truly settling into any band until he joined the Tridents, a Chiswick-based outfit led by the brothers John and Paul Lucas, plus drummer Ray Cook.

Beck himself was already a fan of the group – according to legend, when they asked him to replace outgoing guitarist Mike Jopp in the late summer of 1963, Beck's immediate response was "I wondered how long it would take you to ask me."

"(The Tridents) really were my scene", Beck later raved, "because they were playing flat-out R&B, like Jimmy Reed stuff... supercharged up and... all rocky. I got off on that, even though it was only 12-bar blues."

So did other people. By early 1964, the Tridents were being represented by Rik Gunnell, one of the premier bookers on the London circuit and had landed a weekly residency at the 100 Club. Like the Nightshift, they were also regulars at Eel Pie Island and were the backing band the night that American bluesman Jesse Fuller lured 1,500 people across the rickety bridge to the Thames islet club.

The Tridents' own shows, meanwhile, were regularly attracting audiences of up to a thousand people, while they were also travelling far beyond the blues circuit. Future Pink Floyd drummer Nick Mason recalls one of that band's earliest incarnations, the Tea Set, opening for the Tridents at the Regent Street Poly, while the BBC was so enthused by the group's reputation for wild excitement that they recorded an entire Eel Pie show for possible broadcast. Unfortunately the concert remained in the vault – according to Beck biographer Annette Carson, "the sound engineer was so destroyed by the noises coming from Beck's guitar that he came rushing down, headphones still dangling around his neck, to find out what the heck was going on."

One track from that recording would eventually see release on Beck's 1990s Beckology box set, joined there by the only other Tridents recordings ever to see the light of day: "Wandering Man Blues" and "Trouble In Mind" were recorded under the band's own steam, to be pressed as demonstration discs to send around to potential promoters (two other tracks, versions of the blues classic "Keep Your Hands Off My Woman", and the band's own self-composed "That Noise!" remain unheard).

There was no serious record-company interest, however. No matter how vast the Tridents' live following was growing, every label rep who ventured down to see the group reported one serious problem – the same guitar noises that had so bedevilled that hapless BBC engineer.

Beck was not simply playing his guitar at this time. He was ruthlessly pushing it way beyond any limits that had hitherto been seen as acceptable. He relished feedback; not just the polite squeaks that emanated from the Kinks' chart-topping "You Really Got Me", but full-on screams, squeals and wails, sounds that could reduce a sensitive ear – let alone super-sensitive recording equipment – to mush. "The amplifiers would feed back anyway" Beck explained. "But to use it was a good way of getting out of it. It would start whistling and singing, then you found that you could probably handle it and make quite an interesting noise with it – with an echo, all sorts of mysteries started to happen and it would sound really bizarre."

CHAPTER
FOUR

One of the Tridents' regular gigs, again at Eel Pie Island, saw them booked in as the regular 'interval band' (playing during the interval between the scheduled groups) for Long John Baldry's Hoochie Coochie Men. Baldry's lead guitarist, the mercurial Jeff Bradford, caught his attention – according to Baldry, Bradford was "one of the finest guitarists to ever come out of English blues, (and) one of the few who played finger-style on the electric guitar. I am convinced that all of the guitarists who followed, Jeff Beck, Eric Clapton, Jimmy Page, were all watching Jeff and leaning from him."

Equally eye- and ear-catching, however, was a young man whom Baldry proudly described as his protégé, a flash, lanky so-and-so named Roddy Stewart. He was raw, untutored and seldom sang for more than two or three songs a night, harmonising roughly with Baldry's more cultured tones. The rest of the time he blew a rudimentary harp and posed for the girls on the dance floor. But Baldry adored him, the Hoochie Coochie Men were entertained by him and Beck was at least intrigued, not only by Stewart's performance, but by his very behaviour.

In the terminology of a later age, Stewart was an incorrigible ligger, an intensely cocksure young man who walked, talked and dressed as though he were the King of all he surveyed. 'Rod the Mod', people called him, and whether they were laughing or loving him made no difference. The name stuck so firmly that, a decade later, it still clung affectionately to his shoulders.

"He was the most dreadful poseur", says Mark Woodstrong, a now-retired London cab driver who, in his mid-20s, ran around the same clubs as Stewart. "And he told the most phenomenal stories about himself, none of which were exactly believable but there was always the possibility that they might be. Or close enough, anyway."

Baldry agreed with that summation, and happily recollected the highlights of Stewart's autobiography, as Roddy would reveal it during long nights on the road.

There was the one about how the newborn Roderick David Stewart came within 30 minutes of becoming one of wartime Britain's youngest casualties – just half an hour before he was born, in Highgate, London, on 10 January 1945, a German V-1 flying bomb flattened the local police station just minutes away from the Stewart family home.

Then there were his tales about his days as an Aldermaston Marcher in 1960, adding his presence to the protesting thousands that bore down upon the British Atomic Weapons Research Establishment in Berkshire to protest the ease with which the world could be annihilated by the simple push of a button.

He was not, Stewart admitted, the most committed marcher on the jaunt. "I believed in it of course, but I couldn't really get that involved. I mean, you'd never own up at the time that you were just going along for a giggle, but probably thousands of kids went along to get screwed. There used to be terrible orgies." His own participation in the protests was vindicated when he lost his virginity to a fellow marcher from Bristol – however would he have met her if he'd simply stayed at home in Highbury?

The pair remained together for a few months that summer, finally breaking up – according to a well-buttered legend – the night that she grabbed his acoustic guitar out of his hands and smashed it to pieces on some rocks on Brighton Beach. Admittedly, she had good reason – she'd just informed her beau that she was pregnant, and was asking what he thought she should do. The unrepentant strumming with which he replied provided the answer she had been dreading.

Not that Stewart was in any fit state to become a doting, responsible father at that time. Eight years younger than his nearest sibling, brother Bob, and consequently spoiled rotten by his parents, the teenaged Stewart was one of those youths who believed the entire world was spread out for his own personal enjoyment. Shortly before his Aldermaston adventure, he was hitch-hiking to Paris to sleep rough on the Left Bank for a few nights; shortly after the March, he left home to dwell aboard a derelict houseboat-full of beatniks on the coast at Shoreham.

That particular sojourn ended when the local constabulary descended upon the commune in response to complaints from the neighbours. Under the command of the fiercely bearded John the Road, the self-appointed captain of the ship, the beatniks fought back with any weapon that came to hand – including, unfortunately, an ancient musket that John The Road discharged in the general direction of the assault force. That did it. Scampering back to headquarters, the police collected their water cannon and proceeded to blast the beatniks off the boat. They towed the dilapidated vessel out to sea and sank it.

Abandoning the beatnik life along with the shards of his acoustic guitar, Stewart returned to London to pursue another of his most cherished daydreams, playing football for Brentford FC. Always a promising player at school, he sparkled in the close-season trials and signed professional forms during the summer of 1961. But, after three weeks of cleaning boots, mopping floors and, if he was really lucky, watching the first XI train, he quit. He had not kicked a ball in anger once.

Had he persevered and made the grade, there is every possibility that modern authors would regard Rod Stewart in the same manner as they treat the likes of George Best and Rodney Marsh – not necessarily as a player, but certainly as a playboy. Every penny he had, including the few pounds a week he earned during his time at Griffin Park, was spent on clothing; every spare hour was devoted to haunting the fashionable boutiques and menswear shops that were beginning to pepper Carnaby

Street, that once obscure dog's leg that clips off London's Oxford Circus.

Stewart was already tall, but he chose clothes that made him taller; he was already striking, but now he was positively dandified, especially when compared to the beards, jeans and donkey jackets that traditionally peopled the folk and blues clubs where he was now not only spectating but performing.

Indeed, though he liked to pretend that his only ambition was to get laid as often as possible, there was more to him than that. When he first picked up a guitar, and for some time thereafter, his party piece was an old Eddie Cochran song, "C'mon Everybody", refined by repetition and practised into something approaching perfection, "and then I'd fall down in the gutter outside the pub." But his tastes were blazing new trails now, across the songbooks of Woody Guthrie and Ramblin' Jack Elliott, into the mysterious realms of 'Trad Arr', and then out the other side into the populist musings of Bob Dylan and Joan Baez. He discovered banjo virtuoso Derroll Adams, and promptly picked up that instrument himself.

He went through his own Bob Dylan phase – "who didn't?" he asked. "After Dylan brought that first album out (in 1962), we had thousands of Bob Dylans running about in their Bob Dylan caps. Everybody was doing a Dylan, it was a big scene." Two years later, Stewart was one of the cheerleaders behind Hamilton Camp's first album, itself dominated by Dylan compositions, and that framed his approach even more stringently. "I was doing the whole bit with banjo and harmonica and hat, washed-out denims...."

Other times, he'd be numbered among the army of unknown hopefuls who would leap unbidden onstage with whoever else might be playing, and join in – shouting lyrics, strumming guitars or, in Stewart's case, honking on the harmonica that he'd bought in emulation of Dylan but which could pull off a passable imitation of Cyril Davies as well.

Never one to waste time rehearsing when he could be doing something more profitable, Stewart hit on the notion of busking, setting out every morning with his banjo and a cap, then strumming his way through whichever songs came to mind, to see if they worked – success, of course, being gauged by the number of coins that were tossed into the cap. Then, when it got too dark to continue (or the police had forced him to move along), he'd retire to the Porcupine, a home-from-home for most of central London's most committed buskers, to worship from afar the club's own superstar proprietor, guitarist Wizz Jones.

Jones himself was never especially impressed by the young Stewart – "his voice was pretty nondescript, though he wouldn't sing that much in public, and I didn't even know he played guitar." Stewart, however, saw in Jones all that he wanted to achieve for himself and, in later years, credit him as the guru who first gave the encouragement he needed to make a go of his musical aspirations.

If that was the case, Jones was certainly in the minority. The London police had already proven themselves to be less than appreciative of Stewart's musical abilities, but the law in San Tropez was even less forgiving. Stewart hiked over to Europe in summer 1962, immediately after that year's Aldermaston March, and initially gravitated to Spain and Italy, "wandering around, trying to get myself together."

Finally he washed up on the south of France, just one more in the apparent army of rootless English kids who saw those sunbaked beaches as a nirvana of sorts. Busking with his banjo, he enjoyed but a few days of blissful repose before he was busted for common vagrancy and deposited, penniless, at the British Consul. There he was issued with a third class ticket and sent on his way. When he got home his mother promptly burned the Levi's he'd been wearing all summer long. Even a good laundering could not combat their stench.

Stewart fell back into the club scene, blasting away with every band that would allow him to join them onstage, and sometimes hanging on so long that he all but became an extra member. The Soul Agents, a punchy little outfit from Southampton, would later be able to boast his brief membership, while Brummie beatsters the Dimensions picked him up one night at Ken Colyer's Studio 51 club on Oxford Street, and kept him on board for several months – at least until the band's regular vocalist, Jimmy Powell, finally began tiring of the interloper's constant attempts to grasp the mike.

That was in September 1963; Stewart later reflected his own reasons for departing were financial. "I never used to get any money. I think they thought 'Oh, he's a silly bastard, just likes being on stage, don't give him any bread. I never got a decent deal out of that group." Neither did he truly merit the degree of Dimensions-related fame that was to come his way in later years, when legend declared that he was the harmonica player on Millie's "My Boy Lollipop" hit single. The Dimensions themselves were her backing band at the session, but Powell is adamant that Stewart was long gone by then, and that producer Chris Blackwell remembered otherwise "only because he went on to become the known name."

In fact, Stewart's one experience of the recording studio during this period was doomed to ignominious failure. In 1963, another band with which he was occasionally involved, the Raiders, were invited into producer Joe Meek's Holloway Road lair for a recording test. Stewart went along with them to throw in some backing vocals, but 10 minutes into the session, Meek fixed him with a steely glare and let rip with an ear-bending raspberry. Stewart let himself out of the building.

Not everybody who encountered Stewart, however, was quite so disparaging. One bitterly cold night in January 1964, Long John Baldry was waiting for the late train at Twickenham railway station as he made his way home from Eel Pie Island when he heard another fellow traveller howling away at the other end of the platform, pacing up and down, honking away on his harmonica, riffing on "Smokestack Lightning."

Baldry recalled, "I tapped him on the shoulder and said, 'Young man, it sounds like you've got a good voice there for singing R&B.' Then I asked him if he would care to come down and have a play the following Tuesday at the Marquee."

Baldry was fronting harmonica legend Cyril Davies' R&B All Stars at the time, but Davies was deathly ill – in fact, he would not live beyond the following Wednesday and the band was employing a string of guests to fill in for him. Stewart, having assured himself that the towering stranger was not having him on, agreed – and he made an absolute hash of it. Although he was called upon to perform just one song, "Night Time Is The Right Time", his nerve completely collapsed as his moment approached and, if bassist Cliff Barton had not handed him a tab of speed, he might never have even made it on stage. Instead, "I didn't half sing that number. I was up for three days after, of course."

The R&B All Stars metamorphosed into the Hoochie Coochie Men upon Davies' death, with Stewart hired on as second vocalist and harmonica player. And, at first, he was lousy at both. Baldry laughed, "In the beginning, people were saying 'Ooh, good God, he's awful!' They couldn't believe his shyness. He stood with his back to the audience, he just couldn't handle looking at the audience at all."

Stewart learned fast, though. Soon, the Hoochie Coochie Men's own playbills were highlighting Stewart's involvement, as a clotheshorse if not as a musical attraction. Stewart himself confessed, "I used to be more worried about what I looked like than the music", while Baldry continued, "the promoters loved him. They would call up and ask if Rod would be playing with us that night; I'd say yes, and ask them why, and then get to the gig and find posters for the Hoochie Coochie Men, in little letters, and 'featuring Rod The Mod' in larger ones. Or they'd call him 'The Mod's Delight'."

By the time the Hoochie Coochie Men came to cut their first single, in early 1964, Stewart was confident enough to be given a duet on the B-side, the gospelly "Up Above My Head." He'd also attracted the attentions of his own management team, Steve Rowlands and Geoff Wright, and landed a solo deal with Decca – with astonishingly atrocious timing, he chose to debut with a version of "Good Morning Little Schoolgirl", recorded with, among others, session bassist John Paul Jones, precisely seven days after the Yardbirds (with Eric Clapton still on board) cut the same song for their own second single effort. Stewart's version sunk and Decca dropped him on the spot. He didn't seem to care, though. He was having a blast regardless.

So was Jeff Beck. Though he admits he was "crying out for attention" at that time, he also knew that his personal reputation was already rising far above the circuit on which he plyed his trade. When his old band, the Nightshift, were invited to appear at the National Jazz & Blues festival during the summer of 1964, they instantly called Beck to ask whether he would play the show with them, knowing the mere sound of his maverick guitar would raise them above the run of the mill.

On another occasion, he was offered a few weeks touring with the latest incarnation of the Tornados, the all-instrumental band that hit the top of the charts in 1961 with the Joe Meek-produced "Telstar", and had been tumbling down ever since. They were still a considerable live draw, however, and the tour paid well enough to persuade Beck to take a leave of absence from the Tridents.

Another member of the mercurial Meek's stable, too, had his eye on Beck. David 'Screaming Lord' Sutch would subsequently become better known as the leader of alternative British political party the Monster Raving Loony Party. Through the early 1960s, however, he was a delightfully outrageous, but utterly English, answer to Screamin' Jay Hawkins. Indeed, Sutch admitted that when he first began considering a career in showbiz, Hawkins was the only role model his conscience would allow him to ape – everybody else, it seemed, wanted to be Elvis or Buddy Holly, and where was the fun in that?

Sutch's records never really set the world afire. But his live show was massively successful, and the ever-changing line-up of his backing band, the Savages, proved an academy for a wealth of future British rock legends, including – said Sutch – the young Beck. Indeed, according to Sutch, Beck was responsible for the chunky lead guitar that cuts Hammer Horror ribbons through both sides of his "Dracula's Daughter" single, recorded and released in early 1964. "That was his first time in a studio," the Lord proudly declared.

But Sutch may have been mistaken. "Dracula's Daughter" was produced by Joe Meek, and Beck is adamant that he never met the man. So, unless he sneaked in to overdub while Meek was occupied elsewhere, communing with the spirits or whatever, his involvement with Sutch's noble Savages was probably no more significant than the time he spent with the Tornados, a few weeks of live shows in and around the Tridents' obligations.

Beck himself has never claimed to have played on the Sutch single, nevertheless, he was no stranger to the recording studio. He certainly contributed a tricky lead guitar to the Manchester band Fitz'n'Startz "I'm Not Running Away", a mums-and-dads flavoured pop ballad that was issued on Parlophone in late 1964, while his friendship with Jimmy Page saw him at least present at a number of other sessions, keeping his old friend company. "The session scene was still one generation before, so I was like the New Pick on the Block," Page reflected. So, when Clapton left the Yardbirds, and they offered the vacancy to him, they surely never really expected him to accept. But they did listen when he suggested an alternative option.

Yardbirds manager Giorgio Gomelsky promised to check this Jeff Beck out; and Page promptly invited his friend round to his house, for an evening sitting around listening to records. Suddenly, Page pulled out his copy of Five Live Yardbirds, the band's one and only album, recorded at the Marquee the previous autumn, with Eric Clapton in full flight. "Listen to this and let me know what you think."

Beck listened. Yeah, it was all right.

CHAPTER
FIVE

A s Jeff Beck was making his way onto the British concert circuit of the day, the network of A and B roads that Keith Richard once complained all ran in the same north-south direction, Mickie Most was just coming off it.

Born Michael Peter Hayes in Aldershot, England, in June 1938, Most's own singing career commenced amid the same Big Bang of talent that ignited British rock'n'roll in general in 1957, and his recollections, within Andrew Loog Oldham's *Stoned* autobiography, capture all the youthful excitement that was present at that Creation. A close friend of Terry Dene as he set about jousting at the windmills that were Britain's earliest attempts to produce a credible rock'n'roll star, Most was working at the 2 Is coffee bar in Soho, pouring hot beverages for performers and punters alike, when he formed his first group, the Most Brothers, with Alex Murray.

"I carried my recording contract with me in my pocket for at least a year, because it was really something", Most remembered. "There were only about 12 people in England who had a recording contract." He never even knew what the royalty rate was, he laughed. "I didn't care. I made records."

In fact he made three, "Joke records for Decca, which were funny and that was it. We had no control over them." In 1958, however, he left Britain for South Africa, to be with his girlfriend (and future wife) Chris, and it was there that Most's singing career went into overdrive. A string of hits between 1959-63 included two, "Think It Over" in 1959, and "D In Love" in 1961, which ranked among their year's top 10 best-sellers. He then returned to Britain in 1963, reconnecting with a few of his friends from the 2 Is and, through the auspices of one of them, finding his way to the foot of the bill of the upcoming Bo Diddley/Everly Brothers package tour.

The last time Most had seen Peter Grant, he too was working at the 2 Is, selling tickets at the door, and bouncing any miscreants who might have managed to find their way inside. Since then, he'd enjoyed a stint on the professional wrestling circuit, before moving briefly into acting – Grant doubled for Robert Morley on a few occasions, and stood in for Anthony Quinn during the filming of *The Guns Of Navarone*; other credits included minor roles in *Cleopatra* and *A Night To Remember*, but though he desperately wanted to be an actor, he admitted "I was never quite good enough."

Still intent on remaining in show business, Grant took to roadie-ing at a time when even the best-heeled bands were lucky to have a friend who'd drive them around. Renting a couple of mini-buses, he set himself up as a chauffeur on the then-lucrative circuit of American air force bases that peppered the country, a stroke of entrepreneurial genius that saw him swiftly graduate to more lucrative roles.

Employed by concert promoter Don Arden, Grant next found himself tour manager for many of the American bands that Arden was then importing – Little Richard, Brian Hyland, Chuck Berry and, just as Mickie Most got back in contact, Bo Diddley and the Everlys. And it was during that tour, as it breezed into Newcastle, that he first sighted the group that would alter the course of both his and Mickie Most's careers forever.

Following the evening's show, Grant, together with Diddley's maracas player, Jerome, stopped by a local R&B club to see what passed for entertainment on the Tyne. They arrived in time to catch the Alan Price Rhythm & Blues Combo, an extraordinarily hard-hitting local band whose fans, enamoured by the group's wild appearance and even wilder sound, had already nicknamed them 'Animals'. The name would stick.

According to Grant, he signed on as the group's booking agent before the end of the evening, luring the suspicious Geordies by promising to land them an opening slot on the upcoming Chuck Berry tour. Weeks later, he had also won them a record deal with EMI's Columbia subsidiary, labelmates to the Yardbirds. Mickie Most would produce.

"I was telling Peter that the reason I came back from South Africa was that I wanted to go into the studio and produce artists", Most later explained. "I could play and sing a bit, but I wasn't that wonderful." He could, however, talk a good game. Though he acknowledged that the newly renamed Animals "didn't know me from a bar of soap", he persuaded both the band and their record company that he should handle their maiden recording session and, by summer 1964, the partnership was top of the UK charts with a revolutionary version of the traditional "The House Of The Rising Sun."

"The first thing (Columbia) said about 'The House Of The Rising Sun' was that it was too long" – more than four minutes, at a time when most 45s were still struggling to reach three. So I said 'Why is it too long? What difference does it make how long it is? If it's boring, then it's too long, and if it's not boring, then it's got to be right'." And he was right. Number 1 at home, "The House Of The Rising Sun" soon ruled the roost in America as well, establishing the Animals as one of the top bands of the day and Most as the latest in the sudden tidal wave of young *auteurs* slashing into the music business.

The Beatles had George Martin and, for as long as their relationship flourished, he was untouchable at the top of the pile. But nipping at his heels, the likes of the Stones' Andrew Loog Oldham, the Yardbirds' Giorgio Gomelsky and the Who's Kit Lambert and Chris Stamp partnership were all intent on proving that the old ways of making records were exactly that – old. Most himself later confessed, "I don't think I knew anything about producing records. There are certain producers who spend their whole time painting in sound, and that's great if you've got a good backcloth. What I tried to do is remember that the most important ingredient on a record is the song."

Soon, Most was helming a small empire of hit-making talent. He oversaw America singer Brenda Lee's Stateside comeback, "Is It True"; he cut great 45s with the Cherokees, the Symbols and the Moquettes. Another of Peter Grant's bands, the Nashville Teens, scored with Most's productions of a pair of JD Loudermilk songs, "Tobacco Road" and "Google Eye" – sessions, incidentally, that introduced the producer to the prodigious Jimmy Page. Soon, Most once boasted, Page was playing "on all the records I was making", often in cahoots with multi-instrumentalist arranger John Paul Jones. But Most's most significant triumph, at least at this point in his career, was the discovery and dissemination of Manchester teenagers Herman's Hermits across the world – exactly, says Herman himself, as he promised to do.

Describing Most as "the dashing prince of the record biz", Peter 'Herman' Noone remembers, "the first time I saw him was on a bill with the Everly Brothers. After the show my friends and I were trying to be cool when Mickie came out chatting to Phil Everly. Phil got on a tour bus and Mickie got in a 1963 Porsche. I was pretty impressed!" Indeed, when Herman's Hermits began their search for a producer, "one of the reasons we approached him was because he played the guitar, he had a Porsche, he didn't get on the tour bus and he didn't play golf. All the other producers in England played golf."

Utilising a winning combination of Most's eagle eye for a hit song and frontman Noone's ever-enduring boy next door charm, the Hermits racked up half a dozen million-selling singles during 1965 alone. Their American profile was on a par with the Beatles; their success, in the eyes of the 'serious' pop fan, was baffling. But Most was unapologetic. He was in the business of making hit records. That, therefore, was what he did, even making twice-monthly trips across the Atlantic in search of suitable material.

He would haunt the publishing houses of New York and Los Angeles, determined to get a jump on any great new songs that might be going the rounds, knowing that they might otherwise have taken months to filter over the ocean. Sometimes he'd even record over there as well; Peter Noone recalls many of Herman's Hermits' records were cut in New York while the Hermits themselves were back home. "Mickie and I would fly over to record the next single, then we'd take it back to Manchester and play it to the band."

Neither could anybody argue with the success of these exercises. By the end of 1965, Most was arguably the most successful producer in the country, bar none. "We all know Mickie had a gift for making great records", Andrew Oldham later reflected. "But his greatest gift was that, before he became a producer, he had been an artist, which meant he understood artists and was never taken in by their guile. Whereas part of my job, and other peoples' jobs, was to be taken in by our artists' temperament, Mickie wouldn't take shit from any of them."

For Giorgio Gomelsky, on the other hand, taking shit from the Yardbirds seemed at times to be his life's sole mission, and his own admiration for the newly installed Jeff Beck only added to his troubles.

True to his promise to Page, Gomelsky and his assistant, Hamish Grimes, cornered Beck at the next Tridents gig, at the 100 Club on 23 February 1965, to invite him down to the Yardbirds' next rehearsal, at the Marquee the following afternoon. "(They) dragged me off after the set", Beck recalled. "I was all sweaty, had hair down to my ankles. They said 'You're coming with us.' I said 'Can I swear?' He said 'You're gonna be in a top fucking band. Be at this address tomorrow.'"

Initially, Beck wasn't sure. The Tridents were finally beginning to pick up their own head of steam, there were a couple of record companies looking at them and they were friends. The Yardbirds, on the other hand, seemed a little stand-offish from the start, as though they knew Eric Clapton would be a hard act for anyone to follow and were intent on making the job even harder. "I didn't like them when I first met them," Beck later confessed. "They didn't say 'hi' or anything."

But Beck and Keith Relf had an entertaining conversation about blues guitarist Matt 'Guitar' Murphy, and the group's actual set-up was sound. "They appeared to have good management", Beck mused, "and seemed to be going places." Besides, although there were other guitar players auditioning that day, "I think they knew I was gonna be the one." A week later, with Clapton set to make his final appearance as a Yardbird in Bristol on 3 March, Beck bade farewell to the Tridents. He was replaced by guitarist Mike Jopp – later to form Affinity with bassist Mo Foster, who himself would become a regular in Beck's band during the 1980s.

Beck's hair was chopped back to just over the shoulder, a bit like Mick Jagger. His old jeans and shirt were cast aside for a not-so-new stage suit Eric Clapton had left behind when he departed. Then, a few rehearsals with his new band mates and, two days after Clapton's final show with the Yardbirds, Beck was playing his first, a short, four-song appearance at the Sounds of '65, a benefit for the pirate Radio Caroline.

"For Your Love" was released that same day, swiftly climbing to Number 3 in the UK and launching the band onto a succession of radio and TV appearances, all of which featured Beck blithely replicating Clapton's guitar lines. In concert, however, he could have been forgiven for appearing somewhat less assured. His predecessor had developed an enormous following, the armies of devotees who thought nothing of proclaiming their hero 'God' in spraypainted letters across the country's walls.

As the Yardbirds prepared to play their home ground Crawdaddy for the first time since Beck's arrival, on 14 March 1965, the new boy knew that he stood a fair chance of being slaughtered by the audience. "But I was cocky. It was like 'Alright, you bastards, get a load of this.'"

From the outset, Beck was determined not to try and replicate Clapton, despite his bandmates' constant insistence that he do precisely that. "They were pissed off that Eric had left, they thought that the whole Yardbirds sound was gone. They said, 'Can you play the blues?' I said, 'Slow blues, Chicago blues?' They said, 'Anything.' So I honked around. They said to get rid of that echo... you don't use an echo in

Chicago blues. Yeah. That's just what they said. All I kept hearing in the wagon on the way to gigs was 'Eric this' and 'Eric that.' And eventually I just went 'For fuck's sake, I'm in the band now, so shut up.'"

Beck's years on the club circuit had seen him develop a fine line in blues riffs, but he knew that Clapton had long since made that style his own. Instead, he turned up his amp, turned up the heat and simply savaged the sound, peeling off lines that left the blues far behind to chase Chuck Berry and Eddie Cochran through a burning building, all angles and flash and sudden explosions. A few voices might have cried out for God to return, but they were inaudible beneath the sheer savagery.

Gomelsky was awestruck. "His playing (was) full of passion and intensity. His sense of rhythmic accents, big 'tearing' chords and long sustained single notes added a whole new dimension to the band's sound." Now the search was on for material that would showcase it.

The day after the Crawdaddy show, the band went into the studio for the first time with Beck, to cut three songs for a projected EP. "His baptism of fire", as Gomelsky put it, was a more productive session than anyone expected. Versions of the Clapton-era live favourites "I'm Not Talking", "I Ain't Done Wrong" and "My Girl Sloopy" were on the schedule, but the band was so hot that even the bluesy instrumental with which they warmed up for the recording, "Steeled Blues" (titled for Beck's steel guitar lead), would be deemed suitable for release, earmarked for the B-side of the group's next single.

That would be recorded soon after, as the band returned to "For Your Love" songwriter Graham Gouldman and were rewarded with "Heart Full Of Soul", a song that was just as distinctive as "For Your Love" and, no less than that earlier record, set Gomelsky's imagination racing.

Recording that first hit, he and Samwell-Smith hit upon the idea of augmenting the band's sound with a harpsichord. This time around, Gomelsky heard space for a sitar and a tabla, traditional Indian instruments that had never entered a Western rock band's thinking before.

Gomelsky explained, "With (an) Indian friend's help, we found a sitar and a tabla player, not exactly in plentiful supply at that time in London. On the appointed time, these two characters showed up at Advision Studios with their weird-looking instruments wrapped up in some exotic cloth. I'll never forget the look on the engineers' faces. Recording guitars was hard enough, but these strange-looking acoustic things?"

Still they got on with it. With engineer Eddy Offord taking the helm, the guest musicians were set up in the centre of the studio "and off we went. The sound was incredible," averred Gomelsky, "and we looked at each other awestruck. After a while, however, we came upon what finally proved to be an insurmountable obstacle: timing. Indian musicians have a different way of counting time and bars, and we just couldn't communicate to them that they were supposed to stop after four bars."

For a moment, it looked as though the entire session was about to collapse, that Gomelsky's great idea was simply a time (and money) consuming experiment in failure. And then Beck, who had left the room some time earlier, walked back in. "Hey listen. I think I figured out a way of getting pretty close to that sound with the guitar." And he had. Jimmy Page was in the studio while the band was working (by the end of the session, he had persuaded the sitar player to part with his instrument for a princely £25), and Beck remembered, "I borrowed his Mayer fuzz box to work out the idea. Then when I went to record my part, I used a Sola Sound tone bender, which was one of the first fuzz boxes commercially available."

The result was one of the most remarkable sounding records of what was already shaping up to be a vintage year in British pop – "Heart Full Of Soul" entered the British chart on 19 June 1965, to rub shoulders with the Beatles' "Ticket To Ride", the Who's echo-laden "Anyway Anyhow Anywhere", the Kinks' "Set Me Free" and so many more.

"Heart Full Of Soul" performed as well as any of them – only the electrified Dylan of the Byrds' "Mr Tambourine Man" kept it from topping the chart. But while those other records had their day and then departed, the spirit of "Heart Full Of Soul" would remain in earshot for the rest of the year – the rest of the decade, even. Ears that might never have glanced in the direction of sub-continental drones and ragas were suddenly wrapping themselves around the Yardbirds' sound, and wondering how in heaven the band achieved it.

By the end of the summer, the Kinks' Dave Davies and the Beatles' George Harrison were both experimenting with the sitar; by the end of the year, even the Rolling Stones were on the chart with its sound, each and every one of them opening British pop to even greater experimentation, laying the groundwork for the psychedelic summer to come... and placing an almost intolerable burden on the Yardbirds.

After two singles in such distinctive styles, Keith Relf complained, "people now expect each of our records to be different", an ambition the group itself shared. Yet even they knew they were taking a chance when they decided to co-opt a Gregorian-style chant for the next release.

"Still I'm Sad" was built around an idea that Samwell-Smith conjured up during the last days of the Clapton era, multi-tracked vocals pouring out a mournful chant, over which Relf's vocal positively ached. "We're not really following any one vein of music", he explained. "Our musical policies are like a tree with branches going in different directions from the main trunk. We're using different forms of music and getting more and more experimental..."

Too experimental, Beck sometimes shuddered. "We are overflowing with ideas, perhaps too many", he cautioned *Melody Maker* as "Still I'm Sad" awaited release in October. They worried that the single itself might prove too "way-out", and made sure that the B-side – which, in a brilliant marketing move, was elevated to twin A-side status – was a more conventional rocker, "Evil Hearted You." In concert, too, caution frequently took precedence over cavalier madness. "Even we play to an audience, we are sometimes afraid that, by doing our experimental numbers, people will laugh and think we're playing a joke.

"That's why we include the sort of technical numbers, like a guitar boogie piece, to show people that we can play all the ordinary stuff, like the ravers, but are trying to take them a step further experimentally. We try hard to achieve this and when we feel we're getting over to the audience, we go wild ourselves, hoping and sometimes succeeding in taking the audiences with us."

And sometimes they didn't. As the Yardbirds' penchant for studio trickery grew more and more pronounced, so their ability to replicate it on stage fell further and further behind. Even in the comparatively civilised surroundings of a radio or TV studio, the band was at the mercy of engineers who neither knew nor cared how to recreate the effects and efforts that Gomelsky and Samwell-Smith so lovingly crafted on record.

The group's workload, too, took its toll on their efforts. Like every other band of the age, the Yardbirds made their living from the road; for the most part, a successful record simply meant that more people would want to see them when they played. Attempts to break the United States increased the strain even further, as the band launched onto the first of the country-wide tours that would, eventually, spell their downfall.

Their first visit came in September 1965, shortly after "Heart Full Of Soul" gave the band their first US hit, but before the American Immigration officials actually got round to issuing the musicians with work permits. They played a mere handful of shows and made an appearance on *American Bandstand*, and greater disappointments were to come, as Beck's dreams of a land full of blues fans were shattered on the immovable rock of Beatlemania.

"Where was the rock'n'roll?" he asked. "Where were the greased-back sideburns? Where was Elvis and Chuck Berry?" Like those other British blues aficionados who hit America in search of the blues they'd grown up with, only to discover that they knew more about the music than the people they were meeting, Beck was astonished by the sheer depths to which local ignorance could sink. "I couldn't even get sense out of people", he bemoaned. "It was totally weird. I wanted to see the real thing – Jerry Lee. I wanted to see Little Richard sing 'Lucille'. I wanted to be in the front row, I wanted to see my face in his boot." Instead, it was the British Invaders who carried the musical weight in America, and names like Muddy Waters and Howlin' Wolf were the unknown aliens. It was a disappointment that Beck would carry with him for years to come.

A second American tour at the end of the year brought more rewards, musically if not culturally. "Evil Hearted You" had followed "Heart Full Of Soul" into the charts and six weeks of live shows were solidly excellent. In New York City, the Yardbirds were feted by none less than Andy Warhol, while a trip to Chicago introduced them to the one area in which the American scene *did* excel over its British counterpart, the world of groupies and, most memorably of all, the Plaster Casters – "two young ladies", as Dreja and McCarty recounted in their Yardbirds memoirs, "whose mission in life was to preserve in plaster their favourite part of a musician's anatomy."

Los Angeles, too, overflowed with fleshly memories, although for Beck, one woman in particular would rise above them all. Mary Hughes, "was the epitome of Hollywood semi-stardom (and) Jeff, to say the least, was bowled over," Chris Dreja explained. "It was Jeff's first introduction to a beautiful available woman, like he'd never seen before."

When Beck joined the band, Dreja continued, "he was living in the throes of ending this dull and morbid marriage", in the hinterland of south London's Balham, in "a bizarre flat where the rooms were petitioned off by hardboard. For him (LA) was a total explosion, and he had no qualms about climbing in there and soaking himself in it."

Jeff Beck's affection for Mary Hughes would play its own part in dissolving his links with the Yardbirds, as American tours became more a chance for him to spend time with her than worry about playing with the band. Ms Hughes would even merit a namecheck on "Psycho Daisies", the guitarist's final recording with the Yardbirds.

Other pressures, however, were also being brought to bear on the guitarist, pressures that he initially tried to ignore, but which ultimately became too much to bear. He had long since grown accustomed to his bandmates, deliberately or otherwise, remembering things that Clapton used to do, and wondering whether Beck might want to try them as well – the very nature of Beck's playing style, and the furious assaults he nightly enacted upon the memory of the blessed Eric saw to that. But he was also constantly aware that, in the eyes of Relf, Dreja, McCarty and Samwell-Smith, he remained the new boy, forever excluded from the band's favourite jokes, squeezed out of the decision-making process, barely even tolerated in terms of musical direction.

In the studio, of course, where Gomelsky was always open to fresh ideas, Beck was as equal as any of them – his salvaging of the near-abortive "Heart Full Of Soul" session saw to that. But even that luxury was about to be snatched away from him, as the Yardbirds began to wonder whether Gomelsky was actually capable of taking the group to the next level of fame and fortune, and began to contemplate a coup.

CHAPTER
SIX

The Yardbirds were not Giorgio Gomelsky's only concern during the summer of 1965. Mindful of the manner in which he'd been marooned by the Stones, he was in the slow process of building up an entire roster of acts, all of whom he hoped would come to share the 'birds' burgeoning success. His greatest hopes, however, lay with the Brian Auger Trinity. Indeed, no less than the Yardbirds, the Trinity already boasted its own poll-topping musical prodigy; Auger himself had just been voted *Melody Maker's* Best Pianist of the year, and was the readers' choice for the year's most promising New Star.

A jazz pianist by trade, carving an incandescent path through what was still a tightly-knit, and absurdly elitist scene, Auger was initially very cautious about revealing his R&B leanings, slow to realise that the Ray Charles albums that he was buying when none of his friends were looking, and playing when nobody else was around ("I'd have been run out of town if they found out") were, in fact, his passport into an entire new musical sphere. "I knew it would be a controversial decision (moving into R&B) – there were a few jazz people who never spoke to me again. They felt that I had gone over to the enemy."

Gomelsky, however, didn't simply applaud Auger's decision – he celebrated it by securing him his own deal with Columbia Records, and inviting Auger down to the studio to graft harpsichord onto the Yardbirds' "For Your Love." Auger's own first single followed in June 1965, a seething version of Mose Allison's "Fool Killer." "And nobody wanted to know about it", Auger shuddered. "The jazz people hated it as a matter of course, and the rock'n'roll community all complained that it was too jazzy."

A handful of ears, however, were more accommodating and, accompanied by drummer Mickey Waller and bassist Rick Brown, Auger launched into an endless sequence of nationwide gigging – which is how he happened to find himself at the Twisted Wheel in Manchester on the very same evening in summer 1965 that Long John Baldry was in town, feeling just a little fed-up with the direction in which his Hoochie Coochie Men were headed.

The group was dying on its feet – indeed, before he joined the Trinity, Waller had been the percussive force behind the Hoochie Coochie Men themselves, and Baldry originally dropped into the Twisted Wheel simply to say hello to an old friend. Instead, as Auger recalls, "I came offstage to find that John had sent me a message asking if I would meet with him and his manager, Martin Davis, to discuss working together. I was very keen; John was probably the best blues singer in Europe at that time and working with him would launch me even deeper into the R&B

thing. So I went along to this meeting, and agreed that he would, essentially, be joining the Trinity."

Baldry, however, had even more grandiose plans than that. No sooner had he and Auger agreed to work together, than Baldry was suggesting they bring in a second singer. "John said, 'I have this sort of protégé I'd like to include in the band'", recalls Auger, "and that was Rod Stewart."

Auger was intrigued by the expansion. Stewart was no stranger to him: "I'd seen him with the Soul Agents a few times... he even sat in with the early Trinity a couple of times at the Marquee. We jammed together and things like that, so I said I didn't see any problem. But then I got to thinking, 'well, we've got two male vocalists, but it's not exactly Sam and Dave, is it? Why not extend it even further?'"

Julie Driscoll worked as a secretary in Gomelsky's office where she answered the Yardbirds' fan mail, among other duties. But she both looked and sounded like a star, an astonishingly beautiful and heartstoppingly photogenic 17-year-old whose first single, Charles and Inez Foxx's "Don't Do It No More", had just been released – Auger played on it, Gomelsky produced. "I suggested we include her in this new band as well", Auger continued. "The idea was that I would come on and play a couple of instrumentals, then Julie could do her numbers, then Rod and then John. It would give a unique look to the band and, of course, it would be completely different to anything else that was happening."

The group would be called Steampacket. "It was a package thing", Auger explained. "There was me playing more or less jazz stuff, Julie doing rhythm and blues things from Wilson Pickett through Aretha Franklin to Nina Simone and Oscar Brown, which was quite a variety of material; there was Rod, who was singing Tamla things and straight Chicago blues, and then there was John. It was quite good, really."

Stewart agreed. "It was a very good visual band", Stewart reflected. "Everybody (was) trying to outdo each other with their clothes." Photographs of the band concur, but equally impressive was their live act. Tony Secunda, manager of the Moody Blues (and, soon, the Move), caught Steampacket live on a number of occasions, and recalled, "it was a very powerhouse band. They could go into a club and do the entire evening, each member performing their own speciality piece. It was very exciting."

Driscoll was especially thrilled by the ease with which she and Stewart gelled. "Our voices went well together. We duetted on things like (Mary Wells') 'My Guy'." The only downside to their partnership was the fact "we used to like the same kind of songs, and he always got the first pickings." Still the group stormed their first national tour, opening for the Rolling Stones and the Walker Brothers in July 1965, and were among the dominant turns at the National Jazz & Blues Festival in Richmond. "For what was happening at the time in England", Baldry mused, "I think we were pretty good. Looking back on it now (though), it seems fairly daft." He refers not only to the ambition of the stage show, but also the absolute chaos that was constantly churning behind the scenes. Steampacket was a logistical nightmare, the mutant merging of three sets of managers – Gomelsky handling Auger and Driscoll, Martin Davis overseeing Baldry, and the Rowlands/Wright team looking out for Stewart; three different record companies (Baldry was signed to UA, Driscoll to Parlophone, Auger and, just recently, Stewart to Columbia); and who knew how many different musical agendas.

There was rarely any agreement, there was no common consensus, no-one was willing to give an inch of ground. Essentially, Steampacket would spend their entire career waiting for everyone to sort their differences out.

Even the group's one official recording session ended in disaster. "They did the most terrible things to us," Auger recalled. "We were playing in Newcastle when we got a call from Giorgio saying the only available studio time was at nine o'clock the following morning in London. So we drove 300 miles back, getting in around seven in the morning, and actually made it into Advision Studios." But the musicians had been so intent on breaking the land-speed record to make the date that nobody had given any thought as to what they were going to record. Neither had anyone figured out who would sing first, and not one of the vocalists was willing to give way. The session was abandoned almost before it began.

The group's only outlet lay in the members' own solo careers, and the clutch of 45s that appeared during the Steampacket adventure, each of which featured Auger and the Trinity as the backing band: Driscoll's "I Didn't Want To Have To Do It", Baldry's "I'm Onto You Baby" and the aptly titled "How Long Will It Last"; Stewart's covers of "The Day Will Come" and Sam Cooke's "Shake"; and Auger's still-stunning R&B shakedown through Booker T's greatest hit, subtly retitled "65 Green Onions."

Tapes of Steampacket as a whole do exist, almost all of them masterminded by Gomelsky: a handful of film clips (the band made several appearances on *Ready Steady Go!*), and nine songs, "rough old things", as Baldry puts it, that Gomelsky taped during a band rehearsal at the Marquee. But, once the Yardbirds' American career kicked off that same summer, Gomelsky was rarely around.

"I didn't see him for months", Auger complained. "We spent five or six days a week on the road, and the rest of my time on the telephone, trying to keep things together, picking people up, paying the band's wages, dealing with all the problems that came up, going with John to talk to his manager and having nobody there who could take this load off me." Auger's frustration continued to mount when Steampacket were offered the chance to visit the US in their own right, as special guests of the Animals. "John turned it down, the silly bastard", Stewart swore.

By early 1966, "the whole thing was (falling) on its arse", as Auger puts it. "The band was so popular that we were working an average of five nights a week over a period of nearly two years, driving all those distances and hauling gear up and down. And yet I was getting calls at nine o'clock every Monday morning: 'Would you please come to the office, there's a problem with whoever it was we've just done a gig for.' I was pretty tired, and I was getting to the point where something had to give. It was obvious we weren't going to record; there were all these arguments between the managers, I could see the writing on the wall."

That script turned fluorescent when Steampacket were invited to play a three-week residency at the Voom Voom Club in St Tropez in May 1966. Auger wanted to do it – although the money was appallingly low, the group could at least treat it like a working holiday. There was just one drawback. They wouldn't be able to afford to take the whole band; one of the singers would have to stay at home.

A meeting was arranged between the band's managers, their agent George Webb, Auger and Baldry, a summit whose final outcome was decided the moment it became apparent that neither of Stewart's representatives were turning up. "(They) knew about the meeting", Auger insisted, "and so did Rod. But nobody showed up, and the one person who I thought would vote for Rod's (inclusion on the tour) was John, who didn't say a word. So that was it. If somebody had to be left behind, it was him."

Years later, Stewart complained that Auger had sacked him from Steampacket. "When he became very big in England, I couldn't pick up the papers without reading this", Auger concluded. "But that's bullshit. The truth of the matter is, everybody fired him."

CHAPTER
SEVEN

As far as the Yardbirds were concerned, everybody fired Gomelsky as well. But the end of the road arrived miles away from the group's familiar stamping grounds of west London and even further from their newfound pastures in America. It hove into view in Italy, after Giorgio booked them into the San Remo Song festival, an Italian day out that, in terms of cultural significance, was only a few rungs up from Eurovision. Except Gomelsky seemed to have decided that it *was* Eurovision – or so it appeared, from the songs he presented the group.

In fact, San Remo was by no means a bad move for the band to make. They had already sewn up northern Europe, America was on their side, the records were selling in Australia. The one market the band had yet to penetrate was southern Europe, and San Remo, an annual beanfeast set up by the Italian music industry in 1951 to spotlight local talent, had become the launch-pad for all manner of international talent. The only restriction was that these 'invited guests' had to perform songs entered for the festival by Italian artists.

The Yardbirds were not stepping into unknown territory, then – the previous year's festival had featured both the Hollies and Sonny and Cher, while the event's commercial importance was illustrated by the success of the Bachelors, another of the 1965 entrants. One of the songs they performed became an Italian chart-topper.

The Yardbirds' material, too, had success written all over it, at least on paper. Sharing their label in Italy was Bobby Solo, the 'Italian Elvis Presley', as his PR insisted. What better boost to Solo's career could there be than to have a British band treat one of his songs to their own wild electricity? And what better introduction could the Yardbirds hope for than to perform a song especially composed by the great man?

Unfortunately, "Questa Volta" really wasn't one of Solo's better efforts (the group's other selection, Lucio Dalla's "Pafff...Bum", was marginally more tolerable), and the Yardbirds failed to make it even through the first round of voting. To make matters worse, a stage set up for solo singers with 50-piece orchestras simply couldn't cope with a bunch of electrified hairies, which meant half the audience couldn't even hear their performance and the other half was frazzled by noise. And, as if to confirm the ill-advised nature of the entire exercise, when the band arrived in the studio to record the songs, Beck remained so disgusted by "Questa Volta" that he refused to even pick up his guitar.

Returning home, March 1966 saw Gomelsky accompany the band into Advision Studios to begin work, at last, on their first studio album. Even by the standards of the time, it was astonishing that the Yardbirds had never recorded an LP before – Five Live Yardbirds, almost two years earlier, was (of course) live; and, while an album had appeared in the States the previous year, it was nothing more than a hodge-podge of singles and out-takes spread across the reigns of both Clapton and Beck.

A Yardbirds' Eye View Of Beat, as Gomelsky had already christened the set, would more than remedy the delay. Three past singles and the now imminent explosion of "Shapes Of Things" had already proven the band's studio pedigree, while America had confirmed to Gomelsky himself that "the recording studio was a legitimate place of creation, and not just a singles factory." Visits to a handful of Stateside studios, including the legendary Sun set-up, had filled the musicians' heads with new ideas; now Gomelsky was stepping further into the unknown by arranging a virtually open-ended studio residency for the band, taking over Advision Studios every night for as long as it took to record the album.

Unfortunately, as Gomelsky gently puts it, "fate would not permit me to take this musical journey to its final destination. Some of the fellow travellers got scared, some got petty and some got confused. Success and media attention can seduce you into distorted views of reality." He himself confessed that the earliest recordings for the projected album were "hesitant, awkward if not gawky, somewhat meandering and even a bit inept," and the eight songs that have emerged from these sessions on a wealth of posthumous Yardbirds compilations offer little more than a very raw impression of how the finished record might have sounded.

But there is an unpolished majesty there nonetheless – one which, had the sessions only been pursued to their conclusion, might have resulted in a record at least as revolutionary as that which the group would eventually complete, several months and one shattering change later in the year. Although it was famously inspired by the distinctly unseismic sounds of jazzman Dave Brubeck's "Pick Up Sticks", "Shapes Of Things", the band's latest genre-defying (but, ultimately defining... Heavy Metal begins here) single, proved that, as Bernie Tormé, rock guitarist of a later generation, now explains.

"The thing for me is that Jeff Beck was the first. In 1965, I had never heard of Clapton. Hendrix was two years in the future, and really Jeff Beck on his own totally created THE default lead guitar sound. I had never heard anything like the way the guitar sounded on "Heart Full Of Soul"; that riff, it was just *awesome*. When "Shapes of Things" came out, I scraped all my pennies together and found a shop in Dublin that had it... believe me it wasn't easy! I still think that the solo on it is totally unbeaten. Its a timeless gem; and, as for the B-side, "You're A Better Man Than I", what an incredible solo, sound, construction, playing, all just perfect. Humbling stuff."

Beck's own reflections on the era agree. "As far as the Yardbirds go, my musical utopia was back in early '66, before all the hang-ups. We were all on the threshold of this new thing. The Yardbirds were the very first psychedelic band really, just an experimental psychedelic crazy bunch of loonies from England. That's the strongest thing we had, this underground thing. You couldn't buy it in the shops, you couldn't go and see it on TV. You had to be there."

But you had to be quick to catch it. The Yardbirds relieved Gomelsky of his managership in late April 1966. It was Samwell-Smith, now firmly ensconced as the band's internal leader, who engineered the revolution as he surveyed the band's finances and wondered why, with three (four, including "Shapes Of Things") major singles behind them, the musicians were scarcely better off than they had been a year before. There was no suggestion that Gomelsky had been anything less than honest with the group's finances, but the possibility that a shrewder mind might have brought a lot more cash into the group was inescapable.

Finally, Vicki Wickham, the producer of television's *Ready Steady Go!*, stepped forward with an introduction to Simon Napier-Bell, an almost obsessively ambitious young man who, having already tasted pop glory as co-writer of Dusty Springfield's "You Don't Have To Say You Love Me", was now looking to make a more significant investment in the music industry.

Napier-Bell admitted that, at that time, "I knew nothing about managing a group, and almost nothing about pop or rock music." What he did know (or, at least, had been convinced of) was that "There were four rock groups in the world that really counted for anything, and the Yardbirds was one of them." Besides, "it seemed like quite an easy job." The band already had a booking agent, Marquee Artistes, who were in charge of organising shows. There was a road manager who made sure they got to them; "there wasn't much left for the manager to do but sign the contracts", a task Napier-Bell immediately got to grips with, as he set about renegotiating the band's contract with Columbia, as the band themselves got on with writing Gomelsky out of the picture.

It was not an easy move to make. Gomelsky was more than a manager to the band, he was practically a father figure, and he was intensely hurt by the group's decision. His sentimentality, however, was matched by a shrewdness the Yardbirds themselves did not even begin to comprehend until it was too late. "We somehow gave Giorgio total rights to everything we'd recorded up to that time," Dreja later reflected, "all of which has been coming out regularly ever since, from all over the world, usually in the most dreadful packaging. It's ironic that, in order to obtain a more stable business, we ended up selling one of our most stable assets."

Napier-Bell, too, quickly discovered that he'd bitten off more than he wanted to chew. Everything the Yardbirds asked him for – more money so they could buy houses was their first demand – he had given them. "But still they grumbled and groaned. They didn't like touring, they didn't like doing TV."

On one occasion, Napier-Bell gathered them together and announced, "I'm going to make you a fortune. We're going to tour the world and clean up." "But that's not what we really want," they moaned in unison. 'We want to concentrate on recording; have more time to write our songs and fulfil ourselves artistically. We want to get satisfaction out of our music."

The other thing they wanted to do was argue with Jeff Beck. No less than Gomelsky, Napier-Bell quickly came to believe that "he was the stand-out talent in the group." But whereas Gomelsky knew his way around the studio sufficiently well to negotiate Beck into a stronger position, and knew the band members well enough to make sure they stood back when he did so, Napier-Bell did not possess either attribute and could only stand and watch as Beck's bandmates crowded him out of the picture.

Beck's chief weapon of retaliation was his health. Just days before Gomelsky's departure was officially announced, Beck collapsed midway through a Yardbirds show in Marseilles and was rushed to hospital, where the initial diagnosis was possible meningitis. In fact it was merely a severe bout of food poisoning, but there was no way Beck could continue with the tour – all the more so after the discovery that he was also suffering from tonsillitis.

It was a fortnight before Beck was fit to resume his duties, just as the Yardbirds returned to the studio – this time under Napier-Bell's aegis – to make a fresh start on their album; Gomelsky, of course, owned the rights to the original Yardbirds' Eye View tapes. A new single, the wild Cossack frenzy of "Over Under Sideways Down", was the first order of business, while Beck's mounting frustrations were allayed by the decision to hand him the B-side, the instrumental "Jeff's Boogie"; a week later, that number would be a highlight of the band's next appearance on *Ready Steady Go!*, alongside an airing for Keith Relf's newly-released solo single, "Mr Zero".

Indeed, Napier-Bell was now talking of alleviating all the pressures within the band by arranging for every member of the Yardbirds to step out in some solo capacity or another, a mood that paid immediate dividends for Beck when, on top of "Jeff's Boogie", a BBC session at the beginning of May saw him granted control of Elmore James' "The Sun Is Shining", both as guitarist and as vocalist,

It was not a double duty that he necessarily relished, but he was not going to turn down any opportunity to step outside of the strictures that the band imposed upon him. Indeed, the moment Napier-Bell announced that the band should take a week off to recharge their batteries before launching into the promotion of "Over Under Sideways Down", Beck was booking time at IBC Studios to record a *bona fide* solo single.

He already knew who he wanted to play alongside him – Jimmy Page was hauled out of whichever studio engagement was currently occupying his attention; he was accompanied by fellow session veterans John Paul Jones on bass and Nicky Hopkins on piano; and, on drums, Keith Moon – Beck's all-time favourite drummer, moonlighting from his all-time favourite band, the Who. The pair were already a familiar sight around the London clubs, where they spent their time discussing hot rods and surf music; Beck was not, however, so open about their plans to work together. According to legend, Beck asked Moon to attend the studio in disguise; Moon obliged by donning a pair of sunglasses.

Moon's recruitment was not wholly coincidental. The drummer was going through another of his regular spells of disillusionment – "having a bit of trouble" with his bandmates, as Beck put it – and the guitarist makes no secret of the fact that he was "trying to get Keith out of the Who." Neither were his instincts about the possibilities of this *ad hoc* aggregation at all misplaced.

"That was a momentous session," Beck recalled. He and Page had sketched out an electrifying revision of Ravel's Bolero, retitled for the occasion "Beck's Bolero", and though it was little more, Beck insisted, than "a half-baked song", still it had an energy and effervescence that the most crafted pop nugget could only aspire towards. "We didn't have to play it more than twice before the others were onto it," Beck continued. "There was not an ounce of work in it. We didn't deliberate, we just played it through. Everyone in the control room was aghast: 'these guys don't even need to rehearse.'"

Simon Napier-Bell co-produced the session with Beck, although history would not remember that particular incidental. As Napier-Bell told *Trouser Press* magazine in 1981, "(When Mickie Most) took over producing the Yardbirds, Jeff wanted that track as a B-side for "Hi Ho Silver Lining". I let him have it and (Mickie) put his name on it. Talk about naive, I just said, 'What the hell, I don't need it.' I didn't really – but that track became a rock milestone. Take your name off Mickie, and give it back to me!" (The song's writing credits, too, would become something of a contentious issue, as Jimmy Page grasped them for himself and didn't even allow Beck a co-write. Page told *Creem*: "(Jeff would) claim (it) was his own, which is just not right. Certain parts of it, like the steel part, that was his work over ten chords which I worked out in the studio. He put the other parts on afterwards.")

The session itself, however, was dynamite. "Beck's Bolero" was complete in little more time than it takes to play it, continuing to blaze even after Moon, having already unleashed an unscheduled blood-curdling scream, demolished his drum mike with a cymbal. Then, without discussion, the group slipped into another number, then another... "We did four or five cuts", Beck recalled, "and it just sounded and felt like we shouldn't go anywhere else." So far as Beck was concerned, the only thing the group needed was a singer (he was adamant that "it wasn't going to be me".) But even that was no obstacle. He was determined, "we should just get rehearsing and carry this band."

Moon agreed. According to Jimmy Page, "That's when Keith said 'this is fantastic. We should start a supergroup.'"

The session was still on Moon's mind a few days later, when the Who played the Newbury Ricky Tick. The drummer was now hanging out with the Beach Boys' Bruce Johnston, in London to help promote his band's newly-released Pet Sounds album; with John Entwistle also along for the ride, the pair spent the early evening at a party being staged for *Ready Steady Go!*. By the time the pair remembered the gig, and made their way out to Newbury, Pete Townshend and Roger Daltrey had already started the show, with the rhythm section from the opening Jimmie Brown Sound standing in for the errant party-goers.

Tempers began fraying from the moment Moon and Entwistle took their places on the stage, but it was not until late in the show, during the traditionally explosive "My Generation", that things finally erupted. Townshend recalled, "I got angry and threw a guitar at (Moon); he threw a drum at me." Offstage, the battle continued in the dressing room, and though Moon came off worst, lacerating his leg, he still had the energy to tell a watching journalist that the Who was at an end. He and Entwistle were quitting, to form a new band with Jeff Beck and Jimmy Page. It would be called Lead Zeppelin, because, Moon (or maybe Entwistle – nobody remembers any more) joked that the whole thing would probably go down like one.

"The Lead Zeppelin", John Entwistle chuckled thirty years later. "That could have been good. We even told Kit (Who manager Kit Lambert) and Stiggy (agent Robert Stigwood) about it. Right after that show, we jumped into Keith's car, drove back to London, hunted them down wherever they were that night and told them 'That's it. We're not going back.'"

For a moment, they appeared to be serious as well. Although Entwistle returned to play the Who's next show, Moon remained absent, nursing the lacerated leg he'd picked up in Newbury, while his bandmates battled on with a string of guest drummers hauled out of the audience on the night of each show ("Chaos!" Entwistle shuddered).

Beck, meanwhile, began putting out feelers in search of a vocalist to complete the band. Steve Winwood, the dynamic frontman with the Spencer Davis Group, was considered for a time; so was Steve Marriott, the cocky little devil who led the Small Faces. But Winwood was never approached, and Marriott fell off the radar after Don Arden, the Small Faces' manager, made it plain that dire consequences would accompany any attempt to snaffle his star property. According to Page, Moon ran into Arden at a club one night, and was told "that if he even approached Marriott, he'd never be able to play drums again."

Still the Lead Zeppelin might have taken off. Unfortunately, Beck sighed, "Moonie needed the Who. He wasn't about to leave on the pretence that we were going to form a band overnight, and become huge and successful. He just had a terrible five minutes with them, then made amends and went back. Once he found security in the knowledge that he could do this, he probably went back and said 'Right, I know I'm safe with (us) if all else fails', but it didn't." And that "took the sails out of the whole thing." The greatest supergroup of the 1960s, a band that would have put even Cream in the shade, had survived less than a week.

Beck remained enthused about "Beck's Bolero", nevertheless. "It's... very pulsating and exciting", he told *Disc* in early June 1966. "I'm not going to swear on it, but I think it should go, it's so strong. You've never heard such a thrashing sound." But while the paper reported that "Jeff's disc... will be released in about seven weeks' time", it never did, and

Beck was beginning to wonder if there had ever been any intention of it doing so.

Officially, the release foundered when it became apparent that there was no sign of a B-side. Or, at least, nothing that was practical. "I thought it would be great if we just had a two-and-a-half minute silence, with a bit at the end saying 'well, that's it – goodnight,' Beck laughed. "(But) that sort of idea sounds good at the time, but if you did it, it would sound corny."

Unofficially, however, Beck was beginning to suspect that the entire affair was a set-up. "Simon Napier-Bell was doing all these little things to keep my mind away from straying again, like letting me sing a song ("The Sun Is Shining") on the new album. He was trying to avert my attention from other things by letting me have this arena, and I should have said, 'Look, I don't want to sing, I want Keith Moon. I want to fuck off and do this other thing with him.' But I didn't."

The Who was not the only band that "Beck's Bolero", and all this talk of Lead Zeppelin, was intended to scare, of course. The Yardbirds, too, heard whispers of Beck's latest enterprise and realised that they, too, needed to tread carefully if they weren't to shed another guitar hero – for, no matter how hard the band members tried to hold Beck back, still he shone in the eyes of the public.

Yet barely had the Yardbirds returned to action in late May than the group were up to their old tricks again. At the end of the month, the Yardbirds went into Advision Studios to continue working on that long-delayed album – or, at least, most of them did. Beck, however, was told to sit tight until he got the call from his bandmates, by which time all the rhythm tracks, most of the vocals and every arrangement would already be nailed into place. All he needed to do was overdub his guitar in the places he was told to.

Napier-Bell, who was co-producing the session with Samwell-Smith, was mortified by the announcement, but he was powerless to intervene. He could not, however, help but take a certain satisfaction from Beck's own way of dealing with his band mates' pettiness. They were working on "The Nazz Are Blue" at the time, and the moment had come for Beck to lay down his solo.

"The others talked about it like it was a gift on their part, a generous offer, granting him the right to be heard for a few seconds", Napier-Bell recalled. "It was a blues number, and Jeff's petulant reaction to their indulgent attitude was to stand there and play one long note through the solo." The funny thing was, once the sessions were complete, "his subtle one-note solo turned out to be one of the highlights of the album."

The album that the group would title The Yardbirds, but which history prefers to call Roger The Engineer (from Dreja's cartoon drawing of engineer Roger Cameron, that appears on the album cover), would be released in late July, and proved as revolutionary as the band could ever have hoped. Bernie Tormé, still a teen in Dublin, recalls, "The greatest thing was that it was not just blues rock. It was London, eastern, melodic, cello-like in places, definitely psychedelic, really groundbreaking. I really started to learn to play from that album, and I still think the control in Jeff's playing is just incomparable – nothing is wasted, every note counts."

By the time the album appeared, however, the shape of the group would have changed immeasurably, although not in the direction that many observers were expecting. While Beck continued glowering in the corner, it was Samwell-Smith who departed in mid-June, to launch a new career in record production.

The Yardbirds were playing Queen's College, Oxford's May Ball at the time; the booze had been flowing all evening, and Keith Relf was certainly somewhat the worse for wear when he decided to enliven the proceedings by changing the words to some of the band's songs.

"The students were really funny in those days", Chris Dreja explained. "They were really stiff and jerky... upper-class academic types... and Keith had great difficulty relating to (them). Our first set was okay but there was no response, not a thing, which made Keith uptight – and so he drank more." By the time of the group's second set, Relf decided "if he couldn't get a good reaction, he'd get a bad one. For one complete song, he raspberried into the mike, insulted the audience and rolled around on the stage. We eventually got him off and did 20 minutes of instrumentals." By the time the band came offstage, utterly horrified by what they'd witnessed, Samwell-Smith had made his decision. He'd been thinking about quitting for a while, to pursue his growing interest in production. There was no time like the present.

Among the audience that tumultuous evening was Jimmy Page, escorting the American singer Mama Cass Elliot to the show. As soon as he heard about Samwell-Smith's departure, he astonished everybody – including, possibly, himself – by volunteering to fill the gap until the band could seek out a full-time replacement. The fact that he had never really played bass in the past didn't bother him, and the band weren't going to say no. Page made his Yardbirds debut the following Tuesday at the Marquee, gearing up for a flood of shows on both sides of the Atlantic.

Still awaiting release at the time of Samwell-Smith's departure, Roger The Engineer was to become the second momentous record in the Yardbirds' history ("For Your Love" was of course the first), to be issued in the wake of a key member's departure. Few audiences, however, truly noticed the substitution and, of those that did, most were probably thrilled to see just who had stepped into the breach. As New Musical Express journalist Keith Altham pointed out when he reported on the split, "with Jeff and Jimmy in the same group, the Yardbirds have, with the exception of Eric Clapton, two of the most creative guitarists around the group scene today." And the emphasis on "guitarist" was no misprint. Rhythm guitarist Chris Dreja was already learning bass; as soon as he had mastered the instrument's rudiments, he and Page would be switching instruments and the Yardbirds would head out with the most savage twin-guitar attack imaginable.

The question was, would they survive long enough to take advantage of it?

CHAPTER EIGHT

At the end of July, the Yardbirds were back in the studio to cut their next single, the manic psychedelia of "Happenings Ten Years Time Ago". Page played rhythm guitar, John Paul Jones played bass and Beck let rip all over the disc.

But his tonsillitis flared up again the following day, pushing a handful of British dates into the dumper and delaying the launch of the next American tour; and, once that tour did get underway in August, it was only a matter of time before he took ill again. Against his own doctor's advice, Beck had decided to postpone the much-needed tonsillectomy until some hopefully distant future date. And no sooner had the tour arrived in San Francisco on 23 August, than his senses were shattered by a violent recurrence of the ailment.

Or so he said. Jimmy Page, however, had a sneaking feeling that maybe the guitarist's tonsils weren't quite as afflicted as he liked to let on. "Beck showed me his tonsils, said he wasn't feeling well and was going to see a doctor. He left for LA, where we were headed in two or three days time anyway. When we got there, though, we realised that whatever doctor he was claiming to see must have had his office in the Whiskey. He was actually seeing his girlfriend, and had just used the doctor bit as an excuse to cut out on us."

The Yardbirds played San Francisco as a four-piece, Dreja getting an altogether unexpected induction into the life of a bass player, while Page took over Beck's lead. Neither player was happy by the precipitous nature of the proceedings, but they got through the gig – and just as well. It was a line-up with which they were going to become wearyingly familiar over the next few months.

Beck remained out of action for the remainder of the American tour; he finally reunited with the rest of the band in New York on 12 September, in time to catch the next flight home. There was another quick visit to the studio, to record the projected B-side to the next single ("Psycho Daisies"), and a couple of days spent filming a cameo role in Michelangelo Antonioni's latest movie, *Blow Up*, crashing through a blistering "Stroll On" before Beck threw himself into the demolition of one of the hollow-bodied guitar shapes that the director had thoughtfully lined up for the auto-destructive finale to the sequence. The problem was, Napier-Bell quickly discovered, "Jeff so enjoyed Antonioni's directions to smash up all his equipment that he became addicted to it, and after that he wrecked guitars and amps night after night."

He got his first chance to demonstrate this new gift on 23 September, at the Royal Albert Hall. The Yardbirds had been taken on as support for the Rolling Stones' latest outing, a thankless task given the sheer hysteria the Stones were capable of whipping up, but one that they seized with both hands regardless. Even the mysterious decision to place them first on the bill, with Ike and Tina Turner dividing them from the headliners, could not dull the Yardbirds' appetite and, from the moment they took the Albert Hall stage, with Beck and Page now fully embroiled in their twin lead guitar incarnation, they kicked up such a racket that *NME* reviewer Norrie Drummond complained that the "outrageous cacophony... completely drowned out Keith Relf's voice." If Beck, he snarled, "cut out the gymnastics with his guitar, the group might find some semblance of music."

But the band loved it and, as the Yardbirds set out for their fourth American tour on 21 October, it was armed with a confidence, even a contentment, that had rarely been glimpsed in the past. Or it would have been, if it wasn't for Beck.

Almost from the outset, he was at odds with everything and everyone. The first night of the tour, at the Comic Strip in Worcester, Mass, all but imploded as Beck demolished one of his amps. Other shows would invariably end in anger as Beck found fresh fault with his equipment, his instrument, the venue. Few of the theatres that the band was playing boasted more than the most rudimentary amplification, and the sound quality, even on stage, was often horrendous. In the past, Beck had accepted that was just the way things were. Now, however, he'd had enough. Bad enough that the band was trapped into a day-in day-out routine of too many shows and not enough money. If he couldn't get the sound he wanted either, what the hell was he doing any of it for?

He finally reached breaking point as the band came away from their own set of dates to join up with Dick Clarke's Caravan Of Stars, the night he only narrowly avoided demolishing his own band's singer. They dropped him at the airport the following day, and Jeff Beck was a Yardbird no longer.

Beck would remain in California for the rest of November and December 1966, recuperating from the battery of ailments that had been bothering him and relaxing on the club circuit. Work, when it crossed his mind to do anything, revolved around writing one, maybe two, of the monthly columns he was then authoring for *Beat Instrumental* magazine, and the only steadfast commitment he seemed to have made was in refusing to comment on his relationship with the Yardbirds.

Rumours were flying around the events of his last evening with the band; everywhere, whispers insisted that he'd left the band. But Beck's magazine column let nothing slip. Indeed, though he did acknowledge, and mourn, the destruction of his treasured Les Paul (admitting "it wasn't an accident"), he was also celebrating the success of his partnership with Page. "I'm just hoping that we can stay on form." As Page later agreed, the pair had already formulated "some great plans for what we could do with the two lead guitars, (which) was really unique for its time, because nobody was doing that."

Now nobody would – but for now, nobody was admitting that.

Management refused to be drawn upon the possibility that, for the second time in two years, the Yardbirds had let one of the greatest guitar players in the world walk out on them. Nobody was denying that Beck was no longer on the road with the band; that they were now playing as a four-piece, but Napier-Bell was adamant in the pages of *Melody Maker*, "we haven't been told (he) is leaving, and he hasn't told us he is leaving. I've not heard anything."

Keith Relf, likewise, seemed to feel that nothing was amiss. "We've been hearing rumours too, but I can assure you they are not true." Rather, he pointed people towards the statement carried in the most recent *New Musical Express*, blaming "mental exhaustion" for Beck's departure, and assuring the world he'd be returning soon.

Just two days later, however, Napier-Bell was back on the phone with the papers, catching them just as they sent the 3 December issues to press, to deliver the news that they'd suspected all along. Beck was leaving the Yardbirds. Ill-health had finally got the better of him.

The worst-kept secret of the season was out, and Beck immediately swung onto the defensive. "I can't say I'm sorry", he mused in his next *Beat Instrumental* column. "In fact, now I can't think why I didn't do it sooner." Even so, he confided, "there's a great deal of information that I (can't) really pass on. It concerns all sorts of things, like money, ungratefulness, sheer stupidity and thoughtlessness. I was never really fully accepted into the group and, when things got a little rough, as they did on the last American tour, most of the moans were directed at me."

For the first few weeks after he returned from California, Beck was all but homeless, trying to figure out what he wanted to do while sharing a Sussex Mews flat with Rick Brown, the singer with the Misunderstood – a Riverside, California, band who'd relocated to London six months earlier, and whose entire *raison d'être* was built around precisely the same sense of experimental loudness that was Beck's fondest memory of the Yardbirds.

It was to be a short-lived sojourn. Despite there being an ocean between Brown and his homeland, the 19-year-old had just been drafted into the United States army; he would be flying back to the States on 5 January to fight the call-up. (He failed.) Much of Beck's time, then, was spent talking with Brown about the upcoming battle – it took his mind off his own predicament, and also diverted it from both the ringing telephone and his waiting instrument. For weeks, Beck never even touched his guitar, "and when I came to play again, I was hopeless."

The occasional visitor would drop by – Jimmy Page was one of the first, as the Yardbirds finally came off the road and prepared to consider life without Beck. It was not, Page told his friend, going to be easy; on 22 December, the newly-shorn band entered the studio with Paul Samwell-Smith producing, to try out some new material, their own "LSD" and a new Graham Gouldman song, "You Stole My Love." It was a disaster. Samwell-Smith had already produced a version of the Gouldman song for its composer's own band, the Mockingbirds, and was unhappy about being asked to make another one.

Keith Relf didn't turn up for the session, so the recording couldn't be completed whatever happened, while Page himself was constantly at odds with Samwell-Smith over the direction the recording was taking. By the time the group's attention turned to "LSD", Page too had left the studio.

If Beck took any pleasure from his former bandmates' obvious discomfort, however, he did not let it show. Some of the other voices around him were suggesting that the seemingly imminent demise of the Yardbirds might open up a void into which he could step. But that was not a possibility he wanted to contemplate. He was out of the band, out of the music industry, and out of patience with any suggestion that he get back on the merry-go-round.

Still he was also painfully aware that he couldn't remain inactive forever. Despite Napier-Bell's best efforts on the band's behalf, Beck was scarcely any better off now, financially-speaking, than he had been under Giorgio Gomelsky's reign. He was also aware that Napier-Bell himself continued to hold high hopes for him.

Six months ago, Eric Clapton had finally stepped out of the shadows of his tenure with John Mayall's Bluesbreakers, to launch a new band with Ginger Baker and Jack Bruce, the audaciously-christened Cream. So far, however, the group had done little more than bask in the accumulated hype that surrounded their creation, whereas Beck's achievements over the past twelve months had seen him soar so far ahead of old Slowhand that, when *Beat Instrumental* published its 1966 Gold Star Awards poll, Clapton finished in a lowly third place. Beck, on the other hand, displaced the previous year's winner, Hank Marvin, to be proclaimed the greatest guitarist in the country. That kind of support, Napier-Bell reasoned, had to be worth something.

He was not alone in thinking so. Mickie Most was also eyeing Beck's renown with thoughtful eyes.

Around the same time as Beck was getting out of the Yardbirds, Most and Peter Grant were getting into business together, finally cementing their long-standing partnership by opening RAK Artists Management.

It was a shrewd move for both men, all the more so since Grant had spent much of the last couple of years trying desperately to stand on his own two managerial feet, and failing quite abysmally. Overseeing the likes of the Flintstones and the She Trinity, he had enjoyed just one moment of fleeting success when 1920s revivalists the New Vaudeville Band rode the same brand of Anglophiliac madness that had already made an American star out of Ian Whitcomb and topped the US chart with the novelty "Winchester Cathedral" in October 1966. But there was no follow-up there, no long-term career prospects, and Grant knew he could not spend his entire life flitting from one one-off project to another. So, when Most suggested that they pool their resources in RAK, he had no hesitation in agreeing.

Most himself had wrapped up 1966 by somehow making even his accomplishments of the previous year look insignificant. Herman's

Hermits continued to sell in vast quantities, while a couple of other acts he'd recently picked up were likewise repaying his faith with the first links in a chain of hits – and, most satisfying of all, nobody had given either of them a hope in hell before he picked them up.

Lulu, for example, was already two years past her sell-by date when she first went into the studio with Most. A 19 year-old with a big voice, but a persona that was thoroughly locked within the belting R&B novelty bracket that gave her a monster hit the first time out ("Shout" went to Number 7 in 1964), she'd "gone cold" as Most put it, had not sniffed a hit in over a year, and looked like staying that way. In late 1966, however, Most signed her up, placed her with Columbia and, though their first hit together, "The Boat That I Row", would not materialise until the new year, he was already looking forward to putting the knockers in their place. "We (just) had to find the songs, and that has always been my job."

He had high hopes, too, for Donovan, a Scots-born St Albans folkie with a serious Dylan fixation who had likewise been hitless since a trio of hits in 1965. The pair were originally brought together at the end of that year – the union was arranged by Allen Klein, already representing Most in the US, and now doing the same for Donovan, and the singer acknowledges that it worked better than anybody expected.

"I wanted my ideas to go into pop culture, and so I made my songs more accessible by welcoming the relationship with the hottest pop producer in the business. The songs would appear frivolous, but when you listen to the lyrics they would make you think differently about the world."

His first single with Most, "Sunshine Superman", was recorded that December, and scheduled for a January 1966 release, only for Donovan's UK label, Pye, to suddenly realise that Most's contract with EMI prohibited any other label from employing him. The single was canned, at least in the UK (in America, where Donovan was newly signed to Epic, it was released in July and became an immediate chart-topper); it would be December 1966, a full year after the song was recorded, before Most, Pye and EMI finally worked out their differences and the record could be issued in Britain. It entered the chart on 10 December, just a few weeks before Most pulled off one of the most surprising deals of his career so far, by buying up Napier-Bell's stake in the Yardbirds career.

It was no secret that, having entered into his relationship with the band in such high spirits, Napier-Bell was now despairing of ever enjoying himself again. The band wore him out, sucked him dry and then came back for more. Constantly whining, constantly complaining, constantly threatening to shatter, the Yardbirds were every manager's worst nightmare come true.

Most's name initially entered his thoughts as a possible producer for the band; Page cornered Napier-Bell just hours after that abortive pre-Christmas session with Paul Samwell-Smith and almost begged him to make the call.

Napier-Bell, however, spotted other possibilities entirely – namely, the escape route he'd almost despaired of ever finding. And it did not prove a difficult sell at all. Most had known Jimmy Page for more than three years now, and had worked with him on dozens of recording sessions from the Nashville Teens to Brenda Lee, Donovan to the Hermits, Page had played on them all. Most knew exactly what Page was capable of in the studio; knew that, whatever else was happening in a session, he could rely on Page to get the job done. No matter how many horror stories he heard about the Yardbirds' famous recalcitrance in the studio, Most knew that Page would guide the session through. And besides, it was not as if he was making a long-term commitment to the group. "They were on the point of breaking up... but, before they could do that, they had a commitment to finish another album." All Most had to do was make it with them. "It was", Napier-Bell reasoned, "a relationship that suited everyone very well."

The negotiations were swift. Most would produce the Yardbirds; he would also (through RAK) manage them. The deal was done and dusted in a matter of hours. As they wrapped up the Yardbirds, therefore, Most brought up the subject of Napier-Bell's other headline attraction. "I told Simon that if he ever thought Jeff might want to do something, he should give me a call."

Why wait? On Boxing Day 1966 – that is, just four days after the Samwell-Smith sessions told Page that the Yardbirds needed to make an entirely new start – Napier-Bell's Nomis organisation issued a press release announcing that Jeff Beck's management would now be split jointly between Napier-Bell and Peter Grant, and that, too, thrilled Napier-Bell. "I (thought) that simple talent won out." he told writer Chris Welch. "(Beck) was and is the greatest blues guitarist ever, I think. Eric Clapton almost wrecked himself trying to play the blues. Jeff Beck drank a cup of tea and played better anyway."

CHAPTER NINE

S hortly after Christmas 1966, with his new management firmly in place, Beck finally found somewhere to live, an 11th floor penthouse near Banstead, Surrey. It was an eye-catching set-up, dominated by a Union Jack tablecloth, a Yardbirds poster and his collection of toy cars, all ruled over by an Afghan hound named Pudding – his real name, Kehm Karahn, was too much of a mouthful. Pudding worked a lot better.

Guests continued dropping by to visit. Page was back in the United States with the Yardbirds, undertaking their first full tour as a Beck-less quartet; now it was Ron Wood and Kim Gardner who'd taken it upon themselves to drag Beck out of the doldrums.

Two years before, the pair were members of the Birds, a west London-based R&B band whom Beck had been on at least nodding terms for a couple of years, ever since the Tridents opened a show for them at the 100 Club in August 1964. Wood and Gardner themselves went back even further, to 1963, when they first linked up as the Thunderbirds, rehearsing in a record shop and jamming on the same mix of Chuck Berry, Bo Diddley and Motown standards as every other band on the circuit.

Sharp, enthusiastic and Moddishly eye-catching, the Thunderbirds in general, and Wood in particular, quickly became familiar faces around the clubs, both as onlookers and, occasionally, as substitutes – when Keith Relf's asthma forced him to miss a Yardbirds show one night in early 1964, Wood was among the audience members who leaped onstage to make sure the show could go on, blowing a breathless harmonica through the band's set.

"Everyone knew Woody", Kim Gardner laughed in 1995. "There was just something about him, the way he looked, the way he was always grinning, and so fucking cheerful – you could be having the shittiest day on earth, and then Woody would stride up, slap you on the back, "'ello mate, what ya doing?' and you couldn't even bring yourself to tell him – ah, me budgie died, me girlfriend left me, the rent's due and my amp's packed up. You'd be, 'yeah, everything's great,' and the next thing you'd know, you'd be having the time of your life." As the Birds stepped slowly but confidently onto the circuit, it was Wood's chirpy effervescence that pulled them along.

Taking over a weekend residency at their local, West Drayton, community centre, the band's newly abbreviated name was unveiled when they launched their own Nest Club, and became a regular sight on the streets, transporting their gear (two amps and instruments) in a massive home-made wheelbarrow.

By early 1964, the Birds had graduated from a clutch of gigs around west London to a tour of the Midlands, and turned semi-professional following an apparently phenomenal performance at the Uxbridge Blues festival in April. Gardner recalled, "We built a following, and soon our manager had us working the length and breadth of England, seven nights a week, packing and unpacking our equipment and all piling into the back of a van."

In August 1964, Beck could only look up to the Birds, as his Tridents filled the opening spot at their month-long, once-a-week residency at the 100 Club. But, while he moved onto the Yardbirds, the Birds established themselves as little more than a hard-working R&B combo. The big break that so many predicted for them never arrived. They did well at *Ready Steady Go!'s* talent-spotting Ready Steady Win competition in late 1964, but while the ensuing record deal with Decca saw them fling out a crop of great singles, only one of them, a cover of Holland-Dozier-Holland's "Leaving Here", even threatened to bother the chart – it reached Number 45 in early 1965.

The following year, the band landed a cameo in director Freddie Francis' low-budget horror film, *The Deadly Bees*, being shot down the road in Twickenham, but their performance was barely more memorable than the movie itself. And, when finally a bright hope did present itself, as the group left Decca for Robert Stigwood's newly-launched Reaction label, any excitement the band may have felt at sharing a label with the Who and the newly-formed Cream dissipated the moment it became apparent that those were the only bands on the label Stigwood was bothered with.

It was clear, as 1966 wrapped up, that the Birds were on their way out, but Wood and Gardner refused to give up on their partnership, if not the band itself – Wood himself even turned down an invitation to audition for the Yardbirds, to play rhythm behind Jimmy Page's lead, preferring instead to stick with Gardner and launch into another project entirely, Santa Barbara Machine Head.

Part loose collaboration, part exploratory jam session, Santa Barbara Machine Head linked the pair with Tomorrow drummer Twink, organist Jon Lord (from Ron's brother Art's dead-on-their-feet Artwoods) and producer Gus Dudgeon. The band was Lord's idea, one of several he had as he awaited the inevitable demise of the Artwoods (they'd just been dropped by Decca) before Deep Purple kicked in. Twink recalled, "I was sharing a flat with Jon Lord, and Ron and Kim used to come over all the time. Jon took us into Decca studios one Sunday afternoon. And we had this structured jam on three titles."

Soon to become staples of the Immediate label's apparently endless sequence of blues compilations, Santa Barbara Machine Head was never likely to go far, if only because Twink's Tomorrow finally looked to be going places. Lord, too, would discover fresh diversions, as the Artwoods transformed into the St Valentine's Day Massacre and scored a Number 1 hit in Denmark. Only Wood and Gardner were at a loose end of sorts, and that looked to be over the night Wood and girlfriend

Krissie walked into Blaises night club in Queen's Gate, a few nights before Christmas and were immediately sought out by a passing Jeff Beck.

The club was packed that night, jammed with ears curious to finally witness this hot new American guitarist that had just stormed into town, name of Jimi Hendrix. Newly imported to British shores by Animals bassist Chas Chandler, as he commenced his own new career in artist management, he was already widely feted as the future of rock guitar – in October, just days after arriving in London, Hendrix guested on a couple of songs at a Cream show, and so shattered Eric Clapton's self-belief that the Englishman went straight back into the rehearsal studio, and piled pyrotechnic feedback over every song the band had. "I've got a tape of it", Cream bassist Jack Bruce recalled decades later. "Eric was trying to play (like) Jimi and failing miserably."

Word travelled fast after that. Soon, people who'd never even heard the man play were repeating the belief that he was God's gift to rock guitar, while anyone who did catch him in action, sitting in with whoever might be onstage at whichever London niterie that Hendrix was gracing, was usually rendered so speechless that all they could do was gasp. "Jimi Hendrix? Wow."

Even before he arrived at Blaises, Beck was determined to be less impressed by the new kid in town – and he succeeded as well, walking out of the club while the performance was still in full swing and bumping into Pete Townshend, who was just walking in. "He's banging his guitar against the amp", Beck growled. "You'll just have to tell him that's your thing."

Ever the masterful self-publicist, Jimi ensured that the mere presence of a fellow performer at one of his shows was twisted to imply admiration – when the Experience played a private showcase at the Scotch of St James, to an audience of wall-to-wall superstars, Hendrix smiled, "Chas brought all his friends along to see me. Mick Jagger, the Beatles, Eric Clapton, Jeff Beck. Mick told me that I was the sexiest performer in the world, after himself… whatever that means."

Beck, however, was adamant that he was simply checking out the competition, bemoaning the fact that, from the moment word of Hendrix started to spread, "suddenly, you couldn't do anything remotely flash or clever because people would just say you were ripping Hendrix off." But still he wasn't simply going to lie down and let Hendrix, Green, Cream or anybody else take all the glory.

"For someone like me, Hendrix was a bloody disaster, for no other reason than he took over the guitar, lock, stock and barrel, and 'you lot can all piss off, I'm doing this gig now.' And for me, it was my gig he took away! I couldn't do any fancy stuff on guitar, for fear of being called a rip-off of him, and that had to be considered big time. I thought I might as well become a bus conductor." He certainly didn't want to be a guitarist any longer.

No matter that different guitarists had been doing different things, developing the visual trademarks that complemented their playing, for years. By the sheer force of character, style and, it had to be said, exotic novelty, Hendrix created an amalgam of all of them, and was now making them his own. Yeah, the boy could play guitar. But he didn't have a single original visual idea in his head. He just did "everything we all wanted to do."

Wood, on the other hand, was totally bowled over by Hendrix's performance, but even as he and Krissie headed home, their conversation was less about the American than something Beck had said while they were waiting for the show to begin – that he was thinking of forming a new band; that he was looking for mates, rather than musicians, to play with; and that maybe he and Wood should get together sometime, to have a play and see what happened. When Wood suggested bringing Kim Gardner along as well, Beck was all for it.

Beck's moods changed like the seasons, though. The next time Wood spoke to him, he had withdrawn back inside his shell, sick of the music industry, sick of musicians, sick of the sight of his guitar. And so it went on, Beck vacillating between optimism for the musical future and despair with the whole rock'n'roll lifestyle. What Wood originally thought was the promise of a new band had instead become transformed into a rescue mission, with Wood and Gardner as the sisters of mercy who had to nurse the guitarist back to life.

"We knew Jeff was feeling down", Gardner remembered, "so Ronnie and I used to schlep our guitars over to his place. 'Oh hi mate, we were just passing...', then sit around and do whatever. We'd play together, just jamming around, or we'd go out for a meal and a drink, whatever he wanted to do."

Occasionally, they would steer conversation towards the future. "A lot of people were telling Jeff to get back out there and do something, his friends as well as his managers, and we talked a few times about – nothing concrete, but the Birds were on their way out at that point and we used to say 'Wouldn't it be great if...'; talk about singers and drummers we'd like to work with, that sort of thing." Proof that the duo's jam therapy was working arrived when Napier-Bell called Beck in early January to ask if he'd fancy a spot of session work.

Around the same time as the Yardbirds began to disintegrate, Napier-Bell found his attention being drawn to a new band, the Leatherhead-based John's Children. Unrepentantly anarchic, utterly chaotic and (though it took some time for Napier-Bell to realise the fact) more or less incompetent as musicians, John's Children were nevertheless an exciting live band, with the looks, charm and character to go a long way.

Their partnership with Napier-Bell started well – drummer Chris Townson even found himself earning some extra pocket money when he was employed as a babysitter for Beck's dog, Pudding, while the guitarist was touring with the Yardbirds. "Smashed Blocked", John Children's debut 45, meanwhile, nudged regional Top Tens as far apart as California and Florida (albeit under the less provocative title "The Love I Thought I'd Found" and, though legend exaggerates any further US chart action (the record decidedly didn't make the national Top 100), still it was sufficient to send the band back into the studio, to cut a follow-up single.

In fact, "Just What You Want, Just What You Get" would be the work of sundry sessionmen, hired by Napier-Bell because he knew John's Children themselves could never have cut it. Impressed by the band's enthusiasm, however, Napier-Bell did agree to let them play on the B-side, "But She's Mine" – then, once they'd finished work, he called Beck into the studio to overdub a guitar solo. "It was at IBC studios in London", bassist John Hewlett recalled. "Simon asked Jeff if he would put a solo on. We went out, and it was there when we returned – although I also have a memory of watching Jeff in the middle of the huge IBC main studio."

It was a painless experience, a gentle reintroduction into the life of a working musician, and Beck admitted that it sparked a new enthusiasm in his breast. But session work was one thing, a career was something else entirely, as he discovered when he arrived for the first time at the RAK offices – a vast 40-foot long space, six floors above 155 Oxford Street, in a building owned by the camping goods chain Millets.

Mickie Most sat at one end of the room, Peter Grant sat at the other, while the tiniest staff they could manage – an accountant, a shared secretary and a receptionist named Irene – busied themselves in-between. Beck walked in and headed straight for Most's end of the domain; years later, Most took no prisoners as he recalled the guitarist's exact words. "He came to me and said he wanted to be a pop star."

In fact, he really didn't. Indeed, he was still utterly undecided over what he wanted to do, but he also knew that he needed to decide. And, when he woke up one morning, put on the radio, and heard hit after hit after hit by performers who didn't sound like they'd even broken sweat in the studio – just turn up, do your bit and leave – a new idea began to germinate in his mind.

Groups were great, but they involved too much work, too much compromise, creatively and financially. His time with the Yardbirds had proved that, forever driving from one gig to another, never seeing the same bed for weeks on end, neither tasting real food nor meeting real people. It was a nightmare, and he'd finally woken up. Beck wanted a nine-to-five career. Pop star just seemed the most obvious and, besides, the remark certainly broke the impasse that his conversation with Most had hitherto been butting against.

Before coming out with the pop-star remark, after all, Beck had been musing on the possibility of forming a blues band, an idea that Most was almost desperate to quash. "All that wangy-yangy Hendrix stuff is history", Beck remembers him saying – even though, in January 1967, Hendrix himself was still a brand new arrival (his debut single, "Hey Joe", had barely left the factory at the time).

Beck personally dismissed Most's comment. "History? No it ain't, pal, not as far as I'm concerned." But he was also smart enough to realise, from the direction that Most's mind was already moving, that he had two simple choices: "The prospect of unlimited exposure via Mickie Most, or get thrown out of the office to pursue my blues band."

He chose the former. "We all wanted to be Billy Big Bananas back then." And who was a bigger banana than the deep breath's worth of names that inhabited the upper reaches of the charts in January 1967: Tom Jones, Paul Jones, Wayne Fontana, Engelbert Humperdinck? He was speaking Mickie Most's language at last. So Most asked him the most obvious question of all. Could Beck sing?

"Not very well."

Most shrugged. So what? He'd heard the last Yardbirds album, and their latest B-side come to that. Neither "The Sun Is Shining" nor "Psycho Daisies", Beck vocals both, were likely to give the average big balladeer too many sleepless nights. But the guitarist could hold a tune, he didn't lack for expression, and did it really matter anyway? You could do anything in the studio these days if you knew the sounds you were looking for, and Most had never been lacking in that department. A good chorus to carry the song, a good band to handle the melody and a good-looking frontman to make it all seem convincing. Kid's stuff.

Beck continues, "So Mickie said, 'Well, if you want to be a star, if you want to be on TV, you have to sing.' And, according to the letter of the contract I signed with him, I had to do what I was told."

In later years, Beck revealed, Peter Grant actually pinned that contract to his office wall…"That's (how) lopsided it was… he had it framed as a joke. And it's probably still lurking around somewhere, as a warning to other aspiring young musicians. But back then, I had to do it."

What he had to do was "Hi Ho Silver Lining", a song that Most had unearthed during his most recent trip abroad, a few days in New York that saw him drop by the offices of Helios Music. Written by Scott English and Larry Weiss, "Hi Ho Silver Lining" was a stupendous singalong, a bouncing rubber ball of an anthem that Most knew would prove irresistible to the record-buying public. The only problem was, they'd have to move quickly. Across town, Don Arden, too, had his eyes on the song – in fact, he'd actually beaten Most to the punch, picking up an acetate a full week before Most got to New York and securing the sub-publishing rights for it as well.

Now Arden was preparing to go into the studio and record it with a band he'd just picked up from his latest business deal, buying up promoter Ron King's Galaxy Entertainment agency. It was a great purchase – Arden was still seething at the time over losing the Small Faces to Andrew Loog Oldham's Immediate label. The arrival of the Amen Corner, the Move and the Attack (among others) certainly put the smile back on his face, and the thought of what the latter might achieve with "Hi Ho Silver Lining" thrilled him to the core.

Most was determined to wipe at least some of the smile off Arden's face. Financially, the self-styled Godfather of Pop would not suffer… his publishing income would be the same, no matter whose version did the best. But in the eyes of the public, only one of the records could be the hit, and Most was determined that it would be his – especially once he put his ear to the grapevine, and discovered that the Attack's greatest attribute was their guitarist, a Leicester lad named David O'List who, though he was barely 16 at the time, was already being compared to some of the giants of the instrument... Eric Clapton, Peter Green and, of course, Jeff Beck.

Telling Beck to make sure he took good care of his voice, Most went into organisational overdrive. A session was booked at De Lane Lea Studios on 19 January. Clem Cattini was called in to play drums, John Paul Jones was booked for bass, and handed a copy of the acetate so he could work out the song's string arrangements ("so you can punch him out for that one", Beck joked later). All Beck had to do, Most told him, was turn up.

One night, around a week before the session, Beck was wasting time at the Cromwellian, one of the principle watering holes on the Swinging London circuit, when he noticed "this guy ploughing into some food and getting drunk on his own. He didn't even look at me, so I went over to see what was happening."

It was Rod Stewart, although neither he nor Beck seemed to recognise one another at first. Recalling the meeting when he and Beck were interviewed for MTV in 1984, Stewart declared, "I came up to you and said 'Are you a taxi driver?' and you said 'No, I play the guitar'. You said 'Are you a bouncer?' and I said 'No, I'm a singer'." In fact, the only thing that either was at all cognisant of was, it was 3 o'clock in the morning, and they were the last two people in the club.

Recognition dawned on Beck first. "He was really drunk, so I asked him whether he was still playing with Steampacket. I'd seen him with them and he was outrageous. He said no, so I said, 'If you ever want to put a band together...'"

Stewart had been out of Steampacket for some six months at that time, since he was voted off the San Tropez trip. This particular evening, he was mourning his departure from yet another band, Shotgun Express.

Like Steampacket, Shotgun Express was designed as a self-contained revue – and, like Steampacket, was built upon the foundations of a driving organ-led combo, Pete B's Looners – "more or less an instrumental band playing Booker T type material", leader Peter Bardens explained. "But the Looners just weren't diverse or remunerative enough to remain a viable proposition, so we decided to restructure."

Noting how the demise of Steampacket had opened up a very real hole in the club circuit, out went the solid instrumental set and in came Liverpudlian vocalist Beryl Marsden, a Tony Stratton-Smith discovery with a stream of excellent, but unsold 45s behind her. Rod Stewart followed her in, agreeing to join at a time, he later confessed, when his self-confidence was at an all-time low. "For the first time, I was really worried about what I was going to do. I was really into my music by then, and I felt I'd given a lot to (Steampacket)."

Bardens' call might even have stopped him from jacking it in altogether – but, rather than learn from the mistakes that had helped undo his tenure with Steampacket, Stewart doggedly stuck by the management team of John Rowlands and Geoff Wright who had guided him thus far. The rest of the band, on the other hand, was firmly contracted to the all-powerful Rik Gunnell agency, while guitarist Peter Green seemed to be wanted by every talent scout and entrepreneur in the country. Indeed, barely had Shotgun Express coalesced around the demands of the members' respective managers than Green was out, heading to John Mayall's Bluesbreakers, to replace the recently errant Eric Clapton.

For the moment, it didn't matter. John Moreshead came in to replace Green, and drummer Mick Fleetwood recalled, "(We) were quite successful for a few months; we had a lot of work, playing mostly Northern clubs, and we went down well because Rod, who liked to sing Sam Cooke songs, and Beryl put on a good show." The band even stepped where Steampacket never had, and cut a single, "I Could Feel The Whole World Turn Around", in October 1966.

But slowly their momentum began to slide. "Beryl was perpetually at the hairdresser, Rod was always in bed, and the administration got to be too great a problem", Bardens mourned. "It didn't matter where we were playing, we never left for a gig before four o'clock, so we were always late."

Finally, the band collapsed as Brian Auger explained, watching from afar. "They just couldn't get to the gigs, they were so disorganised. In the end, John Gunnell invited them up for a meeting and, once they had all arrived, he took a piece of paper out of his desk and said, 'Now you're all here, I have something to show you. This is your contract.' He then tore it into shreds, threw it on the ground and screamed, 'Now get the fuck out of here.' And that was the end of the Shotgun Express." The group played their final show on Friday, 13 January 1967. Twenty-four hours later, Stewart met Jeff Beck.

Agreeing that they were unlikely to decide (or, at least, remember) anything in the state that they were in, Stewart and Beck arranged to meet up again the following afternoon in the somewhat more sober surroundings of the Imperial War Museum. There, they ambled around the exhibits, but barely glanced at anything. Instead, Stewart listened as Beck outlined his own immediate plans.

He was recording a single with Mickie Most, and he thought it would probably do well. His dreams of becoming a pop star, however, had been dented somewhat by the realisation that 'true' pop stars spend their entire careers bouncing between groups of session men, not one of whom would even laugh at a joke unless they received Union scale for doing so. Unable to face that particular hell, Beck had decided to put together his own band – but, just as he told Ron Wood, he didn't want musicians. He wanted friends, people whose company he could enjoy as much as he enjoyed their playing.

Stewart, who'd spent most of his life being the life and soul of the party, was becoming more excited by the moment. Who else, he asked, did Beck have in mind? The guitarist's response left him speechless, and it was only later that Beck came to share Stewart's incredulity. "Jet Harris and Viv Prince. What was I thinking? I don't know, I just don't have a bloody clue what that was about."

CHAPTER TEN

n that distant world before the Beatles blew up everything, Hank Marvin wasn't the only icon in the Shadows. Drummers looked to Tony Meehan, singers to Cliff Richard (who was an integral part of the band back then, even if he did receive star billing), and bassists looked to Terry 'Jet' Harris... in fact, everybody looked at Jet Harris, even when they knew they ought to be concentrating on Marvin's winged fingertips or Meehan's flailing drumsticks

"He wanted to be James Dean", recalls Shadows rhythm guitarist Bruce Welch. "He dyed his hair blonde and used Vitapointe to make it shine." He was also "one of the best musicians I had ever come across, one of the innovators of the electric bass guitar." In fact, the Framus Star bass that Harris was introduced to in 1956, during his time with Tony Crombie's Rockets, was one of the first – if not positively the first – electric bass guitars to be seen on a British stage.

That kickstarted a whole bunch of imitators, but so did everything else about Harris. "I knew I'd finish up playing bass when I saw Jet Harris' sweater on the first Shadows LP", Fairport Convention's Dave Pegg admitted. His looks, his presence, his attitude, the salmon-pink Fender Precision with which he replaced the Framus... everything carved Harris out as a role model, and continued to carve him long after the Shadows' brand of twanging guitar rock had been pushed aside by the blues and the Beatles; long after their every record was a certified chart-topper before it was even recorded; long after Harris himself left the band, to form a new duo with Tony Meehan, and then disappear from the public eye.

"We all wanted to look like Jet Harris", confessed John Paul Jones – who, at 17, had already left behind his Shirley Douglas bass tutor (*The Easy Way To Rhythm & Blues For Bass Guitar*) to serve as a session musician alongside Harris and Meehan. But Harris himself shrugs the imagery away. "I was a rebel without realising I was being one. I didn't think 'Right, I'm gonna have a rebel image.' I just acted as myself." It didn't help that he had a stomach full of ulcers, either. "(People) thought I was a moody-looking bloke, but I was just suffering on stage. I was in pain, and people didn't realise that."

What they did realise, years before the Beatles bought their first leather jackets, the Stones grew their first defiant hairstyles and the Who cut up their first Union Jacks, was that Jet Harris embodied the face of British rock'n'roll as thoroughly as Hank Marvin wrapped up its sound.

"Jet was an idol of mine, I used to idolise him when he was in the Shadows", Beck recalled. Cool beyond words, even when the band relaxed into one of their slow numbers, which they did an awful lot of, or started joking around with a novelty song, Harris would still be standing just off to one side, part of the band but apart from it too. It was as though the Shadows were simply the vehicle he'd chosen to drive him towards his main objective – which was to smoulder in front of as many people as he could.

It wasn't a pose. He was an excellent bassist; aside from the Rockets, he played with Wally Whyton's skiffle-shaped Vipers, gigged with Terry Deane and Wee Willy Harris, and even toured behind the very young Mickie Most and the Most Brothers, before he was ever drawn into the Shadows – none of which were gigs you could readily drift through.

But still, when you looked at Jet Harris, you weren't looking at a member of one of the most successful bands in rock history. You were looking at the embodiment of rock'n'roll as something that was out of control; that had stepped so far beyond the rules and regulations of regular society that even the spotless Cliff and the boy-next-door Hank were somehow tainted by its presence – just how goody-goody could either of them be, after all, if they were hanging out with someone who looked like Jet?

Joe Meek was chasing the Jet Harris look when he designed the singing heart-throb Heinz. So was Bill Wyman when he started coming on moody as the Stones began gaining popularity. The Beatles' Stuart Sutcliffe had a hint of the Harrises about him and, after he departed, George Harrison adopted the same mantle for himself. Once upon a time, people in pop groups were all smiles and dance steps for the cameras. Jet Harris proved that they didn't need to – one of them could pout until the cows came home. Within the ranks of the Deltones, the Tridents and the Yardbirds, Beck grasped that role as though he might never smile again.

Harris' final appearance with the Shadows was at the *New Musical Express* Poll Winners' Concert in April, 1962. A fortnight later, with TV producer Jack Good acting as both his manager and producer (there was no need, this time, for Good to tweak the image), he signed to Decca and, over the following 12 months, Harris and Meehan spat out a stream of singles, each as memorable as anything they'd accomplished with the Shadows – indeed, there was one period, in early 1963, when the only acts that had a chance of topping the UK charts were Cliff, the Shadows or Harris and Meehan. But then came tragedy.

In September 1963, as Harris and his girlfriend, the singer Billie Davis, were travelling home from a Davis gig in Evesham, their chauffeur-driven limo was involved in a collision with a Midland Red bus. The bus was a write-off, and Harris wasn't much better. Davis, herself in agony from the broken jaw that would essentially end her own career, pulled his unconscious form from the tangled wreckage, convinced that, were he not already dead, he would be soon. The head injuries he sustained would require no less than 34 stitches and demanded months of convalescence.

But there was no time to rest. "Applejack", Harris' latest single, would have to fend for itself. But early 1964 would see the music press trumpeting 'The Return of Jet Harris' as he joined one of the most eagerly awaited, and over-subscribed tours of the age. The Rolling Stones, John Leyton, Mike Sarne and Mike Berry joined Harris among the headliners of All Stars 64. Harris' performances, however, were tentative at best – it was clear that he was still in pain, and it was apparent that the much-vaunted return had been scheduled far too soon. When his contract with Decca lapsed in February, following the release of the scarcely noticed "Big Bad Bass" single, Harris did not even attempt to find a new deal.

He would remain out of action for the next 18 months. In July 1966, he made a tentative stab at a comeback, signing with Fontana for the one-off single "My Lady", written for him by the Troggs' Reg Presley, and produced by Tony Meehan. It didn't sell, however, and again Harris slipped into obscurity, surfacing only briefly in December when the law courts finally got round to considering the accident. There he was awarded £11,150 in damages, with the judge, Mr Justice Donaldson, explaining the high (by the standards of the day) fee by reminding the court that, though Harris "was no Beatle and possibly no Cliff Richard, he was nevertheless at the top of his profession". He was, and perhaps he could be again. Beck got in touch with Harris early in the New Year. "I thought, 'Let's get a face on the bass,' and I immediately thought of Jet. Then I found he was a boozer, and he'd had an accident, so I thought 'Well, he sounds just right – a tragic character with blonde hair, that sounds perfect.'"

Viv Prince, on the other hand, was pushed into Beck's consciousness by Jimmy Page. "I remember Viv being revered by Jimmy Page for being a hooligan, and I couldn't get that expression out of my head. I thought that's what I want, a drummer who's a hooligan. And I couldn't get Moony. I wanted Moon, and I got so close when we did those sessions for "Beck's Bolero", it was so tantalisingly close. But he wasn't budging, and I thought, 'Well, who the bloody hell do you get on drums, when you've seen a guy like him? We don't want any pussies around the place, any namby-pamby drummers.' I still wanted a thug on the drums, that was my driving force. And while there were no other Moons, there was nobody like Viv Prince either at the time, so I got him."

Like Jet Harris, Viv Prince had more or less drifted into legend by early 1967. The son of band leader Harry Prince, he had already cut a distinctive swathe through the trad jazz world when he fell into rock'n'roll as a member of Carter Lewis and the Southerners.

A fabulous drummer, he was also a fabulous showman, as wild as any drummer could be. If a show was going well, he would reward the audience by demolishing his kit. If it was going badly, he would punish his bandmates by demolishing it again. Onstage and off, Prince lived a life that, in years to come, would be described as archetypal rock'n'roll. For now, most people simply concurred with Jimmy Page. He was a hooligan.

Prince was introduced to the Pretty Things in early 1964, shortly after they signed with Fontana. In the studio for the first time, producer Jimmy Duncan was growing increasingly frustrated by the band's then incumbent drummer, Viv Andrews, and insisted they use sessionman Bobby Graham instead. Graham, however, would not be available to gig with the band, and with Andrews having now departed the scene, the search was on for a full time replacement. Duncan suggested they contact Prince.

Prince was reluctant. Like the young Jimmy Page (with whom he'd already played several sessions), he was in no mood to join a band; he had, in fact, already turned down an offer from the Kinks. That band's inducements, however, had amounted to nothing more than the promise of a bright future. The Pretty Things, on the other hand, promised £40 a week and a brand new Ludwig drum kit. Prince agreed and seven days later, received his first pay packet. It contained eight pound notes.

Pretty Things vocalist Phil May recalled the advent of Prince. "We were sort of novice lunatics (at the time), then suddenly they hand us the high priest of lunacy. And we all caught on very fast. In fact, we had to sack him in the end, because he was so bad. We couldn't finish a concert."

Yet Prince had his admirers among fans who adored his unpredictability, musicians who envied his unconventionality – and the young Keith Moon, who actively trailed the Pretty Things round the clubs, and watched every move that Prince made. Watched and remembered. "Before Viv, playing drums was quite sedentary", Phil May explained. "Boring. And through Viv, you'd suddenly realise you could be a drummer, but also an extrovert. You could be a star, and play your drums too. I think Keith realised he could be Keith, and he didn't have to switch instruments. He could still play drums and let out all his lunacy through the drum kit. 'Cause Viv was amazing. He'd hit anything – mic stands, anything near him, fire buckets, just anything he'd play. Drummed on the floor, on the mike stands, on the guitars themselves."

Books can (and no doubt will) be written documenting the madness that Prince wreaked upon the world – the copious amount of alcohol he'd consume in the studio, while his bandmates were soberly attempting to complete a recording; the concerts where he turned up drunk, then proceeded to get drunker; the fires he lit, the officials he outraged, the bans he collected... and his seemingly infallible ability to promptly forget what he'd done within moments of actually doing it.

The night before he was sacked by the Pretty Things in late November 1965, Prince and some friends ran amok in the pub across the road from the Stockport theatre where the band was playing that evening. Breaking furniture and raising hell, Prince earned a lifelong ban from the establishment. But the following evening, with the Pretties still in town, he was back at the same pub, absolutely unable to understand why the staff refused to serve him. So, realising that most of the people in the pub would be crossing the road to attend that evening's show, he determined that he'd repay them by refusing to perform. "They could drink and he couldn't", recalled Phil May. "So he wasn't going to play for them."

From the Pretties, Prince returned to session work. When "Have I The Right" hitmakers the Honeycombs played the London Palladium, Prince was brought in as drummer so that the group's regular percussionist, Honey Lantree, could move to the front and sing. A few days later, when Keith Moon was taken ill, the Who themselves agreed that, if you couldn't have the Master of Mayhem, you should take the person who'd taught him everything he knew – Prince sat in for Moon on some half a dozen shows around the English south and west that December, and audience members who did not spot the swap were left only to marvel at the sight they saw. 'Moonie' was really on form tonight!

Prince faded from view through most of 1966 – Rod Stewart certainly couldn't remember the last time he'd heard the man's name mentioned in anything approaching a contemporary context. But, as he walked into the Goodge Street pub whose upper storeys housed Beck's rehearsal studio, the thunder that echoed off the walls informed him that something truly tumultuous was occurring up the stairs. It was only once he'd actually joined the rehearsal that he realised that, sometimes, tumultuous does not necessarily translate to music.

The band looked great. Even as Beck stood and watched the entire afternoon collapsing into cacophony, he remained convinced, "with Viv and Jet there, and Rod with his cockerel haircut, I thought 'This is going to be worth looking at, even if it sounds like a pile of shit'." Unfortunately, he also had to admit, that was precisely what it did sound like.

Harris had scarcely touched his instrument over the past couple of years, while Prince seemed long ago to have decided that playing his was the least of his required duties. There was also the problem of alcohol. Nobody remembers precisely how many rehearsals this quartet actually completed – it may just have been the one Stewart recalls ("it was a stupid band"), there might have been a couple more. But for Harris, it was one too many. He'd been up most of the night with Beck and Stewart, knocking the drinks back without a care. "And then I woke up in my car in the car park, and it was six o'clock... But the problem was, I didn't know if it was six o'clock in the morning... because it was winter you know. I thought: 'Now is this morning or night?'"

Friends had already cautioned him about his drinking – "(They) all said 'Hey, you're knocking it a bit aren't you?' 'No, I'm not, you know. I'm alright.' But I wasn't. Very sad." That early morning (or was it evening? He still isn't certain) awakening, however, finally convinced him that maybe those other people had a point. He quit the Beck Group, quit drinking, and quit the music industry. Beck later admitted that, from a purely musical point of view, he was not sorry to see him leave.

CHAPTER
ELEVEN

The nineteenth of January 1967 dawned as cold and overcast as any London morning in the first month of the year, but the atmosphere inside De Lane Lea Studios was warming up fast.

Beck arrived on time for the session, but he was already having second thoughts about stepping in front of the microphone – that was why he brought Rod Stewart along. But Mickie Most was having none of that nonsense. Beck was the star name, and it was his name that was going on the record label. Stewart, on the other hand, was an utter unknown, and when Beck protested Most simply shrugged. "Mickie just said 'I've got to go where the money is,' and that's it. He didn't want to know about Rod Stewart." He was making a record with Jeff Beck – and that meant Jeff Beck had to make the record.

Even Most had to admit, however, it was not going to be easy. The first problem came as Beck read through the lyrics. He'd seen them before, of course, but they'd been an abstract then, just words on paper. Now he was actually going to have to voice them, and his toes curled with embarrassment as he scanned the page.

They remain chillingly bland. In 2004, Ozzy Osbourne sat down to record a cover of the song, during the sessions for his Prince Of Darkness box set, and he was still in shock a year later. "(Those) are the worst lyrics I've had to sing in my life", said the man who sat through some pretty dodgy Sabbath songs. "It took me ages to do, because I was laughing so much. 'Flies are in your pea soup baby, and they're waving at me...' Who would sit down and write such a mind-shattering lyric? What the fuck does that mean? I don't know how half these guys survived, with the lyrics they came up with."

Beck's performance echoed his own sentiments. "Jeff's singing really wasn't that good", Most later acknowledged. "It was a bit of a struggle with the vocals – in fact, I'm singing most of the chorus of "Hi Ho Silver Lining", and I'm not much of a singer myself, so between us we almost ruined that record." Stewart joined Most in the backing choir (although he was scarcely audible in the finished mix), and eventually they nailed the performance as firmly as they were likely to. But Beck had another apparent frailty up his sleeve when it came time to record the guitar solo.

In his mind, he envisioned pulling off what would, at that time, have been a milestone of sorts, the first double-tracked guitar solo ever to appear on a British rock record. But he needed time in which to get it right – time that Most was not prepared to grant him. "I had all these little inflections in the first take that I couldn't copy", Beck shrugged. "Everything is slightly off... (it) sounds like two guys playing. I was actually trying to get it right (when) Mickie said 'that'll do.' He was one of those guys who always said that: 'Next! We've got (someone else) coming in."

Still the recording was completed, and with Most having already agreed that the nearly-year-old "Beck's Bolero" should be dropped onto the B-side ("Mickie never cared about the B-sides", Mud's Les Gray once vouchsafed. "He recorded the hits. You could do what you liked on the other side, so long as you let Mickie have the production credit"), "Hi Ho Silver Lining" was scheduled for release in March. Beck, Most smiled, might like to start thinking about what he wanted to wear on TV.

In fact, Beck was now having serious misgivings about the entire situation. He really wasn't happy with "Hi Ho Silver Lining" as either a song or a performance, and especially not as the launch-pad for his solo career. The whole pop-star notion had lost its sheen; now he found himself itching to simply get back out on the road again, and play the music he wanted to play – blues, rock'n'roll, Gene Vincent, whatever.

There was so much going on in London now, and Beck wanted to be part of it. Jimi Hendrix might have been an over-rated huckster, but he was still one of the most exhilarating entertainers Beck had ever witnessed and, twice over the next week, Beck caught the American playing live, at the Marquee and the Saville Theatre. Twice, therefore, he saw how a great guitarist, with a pretty good band, could win over an audience with a show that was firmly built upon the twin peaks of excitement and technique.

Other bands were already rising to meet Hendrix's challenge – the Who were putting on some of the best live shows beck had ever seen them play. Co-billed with Hendrix at the Saville, in fact, they came close to shading every group he'd ever witnessed. Cream, too, had shaken off the dour-faced seriousness of their earliest performances, and were getting into the swing of Swinging London. Clapton was even sprouting an Afro now and, much as Beck disdained it ("I don't know why he's grown his hair that way," he tutted. "He doesn't need it. The short crew-cut, Levis with paint on them and sneakers were always his scene"), he at least applauded the energies that prompted Clapton to such tonsorial extravagance.

There was an entire vanguard of new bands, new sounds, new music exploding out of the club circuit, obscurely-named combos with names like the Incredible String Band and the Pink Floyd; and a vast audience filing out to idolise them. And how was Beck welcoming this brilliantly bold new future? With a song that only Amen Corner could love.

There was no point talking to Mickie Most, of course. Beck had made his bed (or, at least, signed his contract), and now he had to lie in it. Peter Grant, however, was more understanding. If he had learned anything from his years as a road manager, it was that the music industry attracts two sorts of people – those that understand music and musicians, and those that understand records and hits. Grant was in the first camp, Most was firmly in the second. The point, therefore, was to let Most worry about the hits, while Grant and Beck got on with the music, and the moment that Most realised that the music was capable of doing as well as the hits, then everything would come together.

It was not, however, going to be easy. While Most was happy to let Beck get on with forming a band for live work, he remained less than tolerant over the guitarist's choice for lead vocalist. It was not that he disliked Stewart himself, or that he didn't rate the boy's voice. It was the business side of things that rankled, the fact that, just as he had during his days with Steampacket and Shotgun Express, Stewart insisted upon retaining Rowlands and Wright as his management, which meant that absolutely every decision concerning the 'Jeff Beck Group' needed to be run past another pair of ears, and drawn up into a separate agreement, before it could be acted upon – even things as simple as TV and radio broadcasts or recording sessions.

It was inconvenient, but more than that, it was divisive, as Peter Grant later explained. "What it meant was, Rod would see more money from the group than anybody else. He could basically name his own fee for everything he did with the group, so right from the start we knew that there would be problems further down the road. But it was what Jeff wanted, he wanted Rod in the band; so I squared it with Mickie and we just crossed our fingers." In later years, Most would insist his reluctance to record Rod Stewart was down to Beck's own insistence – "Beck didn't want us to record Stewart in case he became popular." If that was the case, however, why did Beck even want him in the band? Assuming, that is, that the band ever even came together – something that a lot of observers were privately beginning to doubt.

Neither surprised nor especially disappointed by Harris' departure, Stewart suggested Beck call up Dave Ambrose, the bass player with Shotgun Express, and ask him if he'd be interested in playing. Ambrose agreed – he was, in fact, on the verge of committing himself to the latest incarnation of Brian Auger's Trinity, but he had a few spare weeks ahead of him and, with Viv Prince still hanging onto the drum seat, the Jeff Beck Group made their live debut at London's 100 Club on Oxford Street at the end of January 1967.

With a live set heavy on blues covers and the odd Yardbirds number, it was a raw, raucous and absolutely tentative venture – not one of the players seems to recall anything about the show beyond the fact that it took place, and press coverage for the barely-announced event was zero. But *Record Mirror* described the gestating quartet as the latest arrival in the post-Cream supergroup stakes (once Baker, Bruce and Clapton got going, every new combination of known names was going to get saddled with that epithet) and, in early February, London journalist Valerie Wilmer (writing for the American *Hit Parader* magazine) found Beck in determined mood.

"I'm prepared to work hard (and) I'm entitled to make a joke of it", he said of the new band. There would be no more static statues standing around, plugging their latest record. The Jeff Beck Group – whomsoever it should ultimately comprise – was aimed at entertainment first, commercial acceptance a distant second. "There's nothing I hate more than standing on stage playing my latest disc. I hate the thing that it stands for. I want to do something more that."

But he also told *Beat Instrumental* that he intended to keep live performance to a minimum, and replace them with performances in a whole new arena. "I think the best way to publicise a group is through films", he declared. "We could go and do the long slog around the well-known ballrooms, being paid next to nothing for appearances, but that's not how I want to do it." He was quick to assure readers that he was not going to go down the same route as the Monkees – his movies, he insisted, would "go out as B films. They're not being made with TV in mind." And he wasn't ruling out all concert appearances. "From the film group, I'm hoping to form a new group for live performances." But he was adamant that he'd already done the round of pubs and clubs once. There was no need to do it again.

Theoretically, it was not that outlandish a route to take. Music and movies had enjoyed a healthy relationship from the moment technology actually permitted them to conjoin; the first major "talkie" ever was Al Jolson's *The Jazz Singer*, while it was through the auspices of the teen rebellion flick *Rock Around The Clock* that rock'n'roll itself was first ushered into the entertainment mainstream.

Since that time, and particularly since the Beatles swung into celluloid, the addition of a name band had boosted the hopes of any number of films, and even unknown performers (as Ron Wood's Birds discovered) could push a project forward. Fired by the success of the Yardbirds' slot in *Blow Up*, however, Beck's ambitions aimed higher than simple cameos. He intended his band to take centre stage throughout, which was another reason why they needed to look good. The film would revolve around their activities, be it a fictional adventure or a reality-based recreation, their music would score the action, their name would be top of the bill.

Furthermore, Beck was in the heart of an organisation that had already taken its first steps in that direction – late in 1966, filming began to *To Sir With Love*, a racially-charged schooldays drama that co-starred Sidney Poitier and Beck's RAK Management colleague, Lulu, and whose title theme would soon be landing the latter a US chart-topper.

Unfortunately, there were considerations that Beck did not take on board as he sketched out his ambition. Andrew Loog Oldham, at the helm of the Rolling Stones, had already discovered just how difficult it could be to take a movie treatment from paper to production, and he was overseeing one of the biggest groups in the world. The idea that the somewhat less-well-known Jeff Beck Group could succeed where the master of the hustle had already failed, was a pipedream even before Beck sat down to discuss its practicalities with Peter Grant, and discovered that, even if they could surmount all the other hurdles, there was one that would take an awful lot of leaping. Mickie Most.

Most hated pop musicals – or, at least, he hated the absolute lack of control that they represented. And control was the name of Most's game. The producer recalled, "Mark London and Don Black were asked to write a (title) song and, as part of her appearance in the film, (Lulu) would sing (it). They played it to me and I wasn't particularly knocked out. But... that's what we had to do." He wasn't happy about it, though, and he was absolutely adamant the song would not be released on single, a decision that reduced Lulu – who loved the song as much as Most despised it – to tears.

"All the time I was at Decca", she says, "I was always suggesting songs I wanted to release as singles, and they always turned them down." One of the reasons she quit the label and linked with Mickie Most was the belief that he would allow her more independence. Now here he was pulling the same stunt. Control.

"I could very rarely get Mickie to release the things I wanted. He didn't think 'To Sir With Love' was a single. I remember crying because I couldn't believe he wouldn't let it be the A-side." Instead, Most offered only the most one-sided of compromises, telling Lulu he would place the song on an American B-side, the Stateside issue of her comeback UK hit, 'The Boat That I Row.'

"Because 'The Boat That I Row' had been a hit in Britain, and because my American singles always tended to mirror the British ones, Mickie saw no reason to change." US DJs, however, felt otherwise. While a modicum of airplay helped 'The Boat That I Row' to Number 115 on the chart, 'To Sir With Love' would jump into the Top 100 in early September, and keep on jumping until it was Number 1. "And when it did so well", Lulu laughs, "Mickie was absolutely thrilled. He had no pride."

He did, however, retain his stubbornness. Without so much as putting it into words, he made it very clear that Beck could forget the movies idea. In fact, what was he doing, wasting time thinking about any of this? When it came time to promote the record, Most would let him know. In the meantime, he ought to relax. The next few months were going to be very busy.

Beck decided to agree with them. The Jeff Beck Group that played the 100 Club had already disbanded. The Prince/Ambrose rhythm section, while undoubtedly redoubtable, was only ever a temporary measure; now Ambrose was off to the Auger band, and Prince... he was just off, to subsume himself even deeper into legend. Leaving Stewart in London to fend for himself, Beck announced that he was going on holiday, a short jaunt around Europe during which he would leave as few forwarding addresses as he possibly could.

His idyll was to be very short-lived. He'd been gone for less than two weeks when Peter Grant tracked him down in Brussels, Belgium, and called him back to London. Had he got anywhere putting a band together? If not, he might want to pull his finger out. RAK had set him up a tour, and the first date was barely a fortnight away.

The outing that was to serve as the world's introduction to Jeff Beck, Solo Star, was a two-week package that, in the spirit of a music business still trying to escape the tug of the old vaudeville days, lined up one of the most disparate bills imaginable. Top of the bill was balladeer Roy

Orbison, one of the few survivors of the pre-Beatles rock era to still be enjoying regular British hits – "Too Soon To Know", went to Number 3 in summer 1966; "There Won't Be Many Coming Home", climbed to Number 12 at Christmas. Now "So Good" was poised on the eve of release, and the Big O was over in person to promote it.

The psych/Mod hybrid of the Small Faces, newly invigorated by their switch to Immediate, were next, the remainder of the bill spread between the grinning folk of the Settlers and the beat boom hold-over Rory Storm, the Ryan Twins and Sonny Childe & TNT. How Beck would fit into this all-encompassing mélange was, of course, a complete unknown. But, with only the now imminent "Hi Ho Silver Lining" single to judge from, Mickie Most's murmured vision of transforming him into the "Engelbert Humperdinck of the guitar" was probably as good a guess as any.

The clock was ticking. There was no question who would be the new group's vocalist – Rod Stewart, of course. The perennial problem of the rhythm section, however, remained, as the pair wracked their brains to think of players who they not only liked but who were actually available. The list was appallingly short, even before Beck threw in his own unbendable insistence that whoever it was needed to look good. There'd be no dour Entwistles or Wymans in the Jeff Beck Group, no anonymous Samwell-Smiths or Peter Quaifes. He wanted a character. And then he thought a little more. He wanted Ronnie Wood.

"He looked great, and he was a great laugh", Beck reflected. Unfortunately, he was also a guitarist, but that didn't phase Beck. "I stuck a bass around his neck and made him get on with it. Poor bastard. But I know people who preferred him on bass to guitar. He used to play these really gutsy, almost childlike bass solos, which really were so great. No-one else could touch him; he used to do these twangy Duane Eddy kind of bass solos. Amazing!"

Wood was not stepping into absolutely unknown territory. The youngest of a brood of brothers who were already music crazy, Wood grew up in a house that was littered with musical instruments and, once his elders took over the downstairs back room to serve as a practise space, the eight year-old Ronnie would wait until he had the house to himself, and then lay siege to "a showcase of instruments – drums, woodblocks, tea-chest bass, kazoo, comb and paper, cornet, clarinet, harmonicas, banjos, guitar and trombone." He might never have mastered the majority of them, but he was fearless in the face of the unknown.

He also had a good role model to follow. Four months earlier, Jimi Hendrix had pulled much the same trick on another lead guitarist, Noel Redding, as he pieced together what was to become the Jimi Hendrix Experience. Redding explained, "I actually went to audition for Eric Burdon and the New Animals, but they'd already found someone, and I was about to leave when Chas Chandler, God bless him, walked up to me and asked if I could play bass? I said 'No, but I'll give it a go,' so I was handed this bass guitar, and introduced to these other guys, other musicians, who were in the studio. So we started jamming, played these three tunes with a keyboard player, Mike O'Neill; a drummer, Aynsley Dunbar; and this American gentleman wearing a funny raincoat.

"Then afterwards, the American gentleman asked me if I wanted to go down the pub, and of course, musicians always say yes to that. So we went down the pub, and he was asking me all about the English music scene, I was asking him all about the American music scene, then he asked if I'd like to join his group. And that was Hendrix."

Like Wood, Redding had never played bass before. "Never in my life. What I did, being a guitar player, I just withdrew the top two strings and thought about the four that were left. Chas gave me a few little learners, a few pointers, and after that, I had it sussed. It was very quick; we were working within two weeks. We only rehearsed for something like three days."

Wood followed Redding's example to the letter, utterly unflustered by the prospect of, essentially, learning a brand new instrument on a stage in front of some of the largest audiences he'd ever faced. "I don't mind playing bass with Jeff. He's a very good blues guitarist and I expect we will be playing blues – with a difference." Besides, Wood continued, "I'd seen the Yardbirds a lot at the Crawdaddy, so I picked up a lot about bass from Paul Samwell-Smith. But I also learned from sticking with Jeff's licks", and Beck, for his part, "used to just let me go. He could've got a few bass players, but they weren't very inventive." They may not have enjoyed hearing themselves reverberating back through a 200-watt amplifier, either. Wood, however, loved it and so did Beck. In any case, it was only a temporary arrangement. Once the tour was over, and the band had a chance to relax a little, Beck insisted they would recruit a "real" bassist, and Wood could switch back to rhythm guitar.

In fact, the only drawback to the entire arrangement was that not only did Wood not own a bass, he was so broke that there really didn't seem to be any way of procuring one. Not by honest means, anyway… Visiting the Sound City Music shop on London's Charing Cross Road one day, Wood spied a Fender Jazz Bass hanging unsupervised on the wall. He took it. "Five or six years later, when I was in the Faces, I went there and told them, 'I'm the guy who stole your Fender Jazz Bass and I've come here to pay you.' They were delighted."

One down, one to go. The first show of the tour was just a week away when Beck made his final call – to Ray Cook, the drummer he'd worked so well alongside in the Tridents. Cook leapt at the opportunity. Since the demise of the Tridents, he had been playing with a Kent-based band called Sands that was scarcely going anywhere. Beck's offer was a once in a lifetime opportunity and, even more thrillingly, the drummer's 19th birthday would be falling on 4 March, the second day of the tour.

Just as he had with Woody, Beck had only one requirement – Cook would need to acquire a new drum kit. But the option Wood chose was not open to Cook; instead, he borrowed the money from his parents, and plonked down £400 for the required set-up. Then all he had to do was sit by the phone, awaiting his first summons to Beck's latest rehearsal space, the tiny Studio 19 on Gerrard Street.

There, the quartet put together a set list that essentially echoed the 100 Club repertoire – a couple of blues guitar showcases for Beck (Buddy Guy's "Stone Crazy", Howlin' Wolf's "I Ain't Superstitious"), an old Temptations chestbeater for Stewart ("I Know I'm Losing You"), "Jeff's Boogie" from the Yardbirds days and the first of the handful of originals that Beck and Stewart would credit to the mythical Jeffrey Rod, "Let Me Love You". At least, it was original until you heard Buddy Guy's prototype version.

"Remarkable, innit?" Beck laughed when journalist Charles Shaar Murray mentioned the resemblance. "We just slowed it down and funked it up a little with a Motown-style tambourine. There was a lot of conniving going on back then; change the rhythm, change the angle and it's yours." Copyright law may have been on the group's side, but time emphatically was not.

CHAPTER
TWELVE

With just five rehearsals under their belt, and with everybody aware that they were nowhere near ready for the public, the Jeff Beck Group turned up at the Finsbury Park Astoria Theatre on 3 February, with more crossed fingers than confidence. The group was scheduled to play two sets that night, walking on stage in their newly acquired band uniforms – white jackets for Rod, Ray and Woody, plus a dark one for Jeff to mark him out as the leader. So far, so good. They got through the first song without mishap as well. And then the electricity went off.

"It was bloody awful", Beck shuddered. "Everything went wrong. Someone was looning around with the amps, the drummer lost his timing and I was trying to be manager, agent and instrumentalist all in one go. I left. Somebody fucked around with the power supply on our first number, we didn't even get through the second number. Rod's mike went dead, we walked off, it started howling and whistling, we came back on... we gave it two shots, then I pointed at the guys and said 'fuck this, let's get off.'"

The band members immediately blamed the Small Faces – even today, Beck swears "I still think it was something to do with the Small Faces' management not wanting us to do any damage, because we were red hot and ready to go. But that was a nasty trick to play, and I don't even care if it wasn't intentional, it just looked like big trouble on that tour."

Stewart agreed. "Jeff decided that this was the end of the day, he wasn't going to stand any more of this, and he walked off the stage. Then I looked down and saw I hadn't done up my fly. The curtain came down and nearly knocked Woody over because it was so hefty; I caught him and we both did a sort of watusi off the stage."

According to the reviews, the second set was no better. "They played badly and created a very poor impression", grumbled *Melody Maker*. "It was a sad occasion and an object lesson in relying too heavily on past reputation... It was obvious that they had not rehearsed sufficiently, and Jeff seemed to have difficulty even playing a good solo."

Record Mirror concurred. "Beck's act was full of sound gimmick and a stack of noise" they said, while *Disc* merely fumed "(he) looked unhappy and sounded diabolical. It's hard to believe he's a guitarist praised to the heavens for his talent." And so on...

The stage had not even been packed up for the night before Beck and Peter Grant were deep in conference; by the time the tour buses left for the next show in Exeter, it was clear the Beck Group would not be travelling with them. (PP Arnold, who shared the Small Faces' roost at Immediate, joined the tour three days later in his place).

"A lot of reasons contributed to me calling off the tour", Beck said the following week. "All these things seemed to come to a head on the opening night. It's not worth appearing on a bill starring such names as Roy Orbison and the Small Faces. Frankly, I would never tour with such artists again... I'd rather top a ballroom tour." More recently, he confirmed, "To be honest, we didn't really feel like we fitted there. We were more into boozy barroom places, and it worked out fine because that's where we ended up playing, in all those boozy barroom places, dodging bottles and things."

For Simon Napier-Bell, however, the Finsbury Park show was the end of the road. Thrilled to be involved with what he believed to be the greatest guitarist of the age, Napier-Bell had seen nothing but success written in the stars. "What I hadn't allowed for was that Jeff didn't rehearse his group properly. I thought they couldn't go wrong. (Instead) it all went wrong. It was a dismal concert and I couldn't snap my fingers and come up with a solution; I was the same age as them and felt too intimidated by them to tell them what to do. I couldn't say 'you lazy cunts,' like Peter Grant would have done." So he walked away instead – away from Beck and, once John's Children fizzled out a few months later, away from management altogether. His half-share in Beck's management, of course, was passed directly to RAK.

For all the bad reviews, however, not everything that went wrong at the Astoria could be laid at the door of their own performance, a point that the same quartet would prove just two nights later. Scrambling to restore the musicians' confidence, Peter Grant pulled strings to squeeze them onto the bill at Brian Epstein's Saville Theatre, sandwiched between New Orleans R&B legend Lee Dorsey, and the youthful Pink Floyd – like Beck, newly signed to EMI's Columbia imprint. (Though Beck had, been contracted to that label as a Yardbird, a solo contract wasn't signed until February 1967.)

Throughout 1967, Sunday Nights at the Saville ranked among the capital's most avidly attended rock shows – Beatles manager Epstein was just moving into the final 12 months of a three year lease on the Shaftsbury Avenue building and, having barely tapped its potential over the past two years, early 1967 saw him go hell-for-leather to make a splash. The first of the Sunday night concerts, on 23 January featured the Who and the Jimi Hendrix Experience; a fortnight later, there was a near riot when house manager Michael Bullock lowered the safety curtain during a Chuck Berry concert to foil a couple of stage invaders.

Bullock was sacked, only for the National Association of Theatre and Kine Employees to threaten a nationwide strike unless he was reinstated. Epstein resisted their pressure at first, refusing to bow even when the Union threatened to take away the Saville's license – "I shall simply move the shows to another theatre", he responded. But, when a second Berry concert the following week passed off trouble-free, Bullock was reinstated in time for the Lee Dorsey show.

Unfortunately, while Bullock was able to celebrate the resumption of his career, Beck again found himself staring oblivion in the face. With no excuses to fall back on, no jealous roadies or bitter saboteurs to blame, the band's performance was another wash-out, a clatter of noise that could not compete with the swirling magic of the ever-improving Floyd – and the unabashed good-time noise of Dorsey. Backstage after the show, Beck announced that he was retiring the group from live performance and handed Ray Cook his walking papers.

It was not an easy decision for Beck to make. As Cook's mother, interviewed by *Melody Maker* a few weeks later, pointed out, Beck had known Cook "a long time... Jeff was a friend of the family." To make matters worse, "Ray had his 19th birthday the day after the tour opened. What a marvellous birthday present. I don't know how or where he'll pick up again; (he) has had such a raw deal. Now he faces a very grim future with no job, and a very heavy debt incurred by (the) new drum kit. I can't understand why Jeff should do this to Ray."

Well... As Stewart told *ZigZag* in 1971, "(Ray) froze." Beck, too, was keen to defend his ruthlessness. "I just made a mistake, and I feel I'm entitled to make just one mistake." He reiterated the haste with which the band had been put together; "I couldn't go on (the tour) and do a Donovan. I had to get a group together." He simply dragged together the first one he could.

Now he had to drag together another. Two days after the Saville debacle, the Jeff Beck Group was scheduled to record their maiden appearance on BBC Radio One's *Saturday Club* and, having seen all their other schemes for the band go so horribly awry, Peter Grant and Mickie Most could only sit back and hope that this time they would finally get their act together.

Cook was replaced for the occasion by Mickey Waller, a seasoned hand who could certainly handle five songs in the studio. "Rod knew Mickey from his Steampacket days", Beck explained, "and that's how we got him, on Rod's recommendation." Beck himself was not immediately certain that the newcomer was suitable. "He didn't have the heavy-metal attitude I wanted. But he was very good. Very classy sounding drums." Nevertheless, the afternoon got off to a bad start, as the musicians arrived at the Playhouse Studio and discovered that, not only did their contract still name Ray Cook as drummer, but it omitted Rod Stewart altogether – a side-effect of Stewart's separate management agreement, apparently – and producer Bill Bebb had set up the studio for the Jeff Beck Trio.

Thankfully, the session itself went a lot smoother than any of the group's previous engagements. Five songs were taken from the live repertoire, beginning with a dramatic take on "Let Me Love You" that still haunts listener Bernie Tormé's memory. "I had a completely different uptempo, riffy version of "Let Me Love You" that I recorded on my not very trusty Grundig from *Saturday Club*. What a band, they did totally different versions of the same song. I wish to God people still did that."

Next up were a reprise for "I Ain't Superstitious", a magnificently crunchy, guitar-heavy "I Know I'm Losing You", a powerful rendering of "Stone Crazy", with Beck and Stewart trading verses, and finally an airing for the song that would, within the fortnight, hopefully be appearing on radio all the time, "Hi Ho Silver Lining".

A choppy rhythm guitar (presumably overdubbed by Wood, whose rudimentary bass is an unmistakable anchor around the song's neck) underpins the performance; Beck's own guitar blisters, and the backing vocals are as joyous as they ought to be. Indeed, it's a sensational performance, one that simply confirmed Beck's own opinion of the new line-up, voiced to *Saturday Club* host Brian Matthew that same afternoon. The original group, he lamented, "weren't powerful enough. So I've completely reformed the group. I've got a couple (sic) of new members, so it sounds better now."

With Waller still on board, the newly reconstituted quartet made its live debut with a 5/- (25p)-a-head show the Worthing Pavilion on 23 March; "Hi Ho Silver Lining" was in the stores the following day, a date originally scheduled to coincide with the final nights of the Roy Orbison tour; and with the release of the Attack's rival version.

The first indication of the Beck version's supremacy arrived with the reviews. The Attack single scarcely got mentioned; Beck's was heralded as a more-than-spectacular debut from the man who even Jimi Hendrix was proclaiming "Britain's best guitarist." "A worthwhile solo debut from the ex-Yardbird", enthused the *NME*. "He dual-tracks in uninhibited style, belting in a harsh drawl which I think the girls will find strangely appealing. It builds to a whistle-able happy-go-lucky chorus that's a real blues chaser."

Beck disagreed. With passionate vehemence. "Hi Ho Silver Lining" was still fresh on the shelves when he admitted to *Disc And Music Echo*, "I don't like the song. It was made before I got my present group together, and is nothing like our stage act. In fact, I get very embarrassed when I have to play (it) on stage, and tend to try and ignore it." He was determined that his next single would be somewhat more in keeping with his reputation. "I never do anything twice as far as my guitar playing goes", he told *Melody Maker* journalist Peter Jones. "So I'm sure it'll be the same for my singing." He even had "some ideas (already) kicking around" for that follow-up.

"I'm delighted the single is in the charts, but the singing is an embarrassment to me", he continued. "It's even more of a joke when you realise that I left the Yardbirds to concentrate on guitar work, and we have a really great vocalist like Rod Stewart in my group, who does nearly all the vocals on stage." Only when it came time to perform the hit single did Stewart step aside.

At the same time, however, he was also aware of the benefits that "Hi Ho Silver Lining" might confer. "The point is this: 'Hi Ho' was aimed at the people who don't know me. It was just a commercial record. People who knew me before were surprised at it, but it did the trick. (It) may be a bum record for Jeff Beck, but it's been good in other ways. It's in direct opposition to all that publicity I got about being a fantastic guitarist, only concerned with my music. I don't want to be put in one bag, or labelled."

Indeed, talking with the *NME* at the end of May, he seemed almost gleeful to note that Jimi Hendrix, still less than nine months into his London sojourn, had already been firmly trapped by his reputation. Right now, Beck explained, "he's the guv'nor. (His)... trouble will come when he wants to get off the nail he has hung himself on. The public will want something different, and Jimi has so established himself in one bag that he'll find it difficult to get anyone to accept him in another." Of all the myriad comments that Hendrix inspired during 1967, Beck's words would turn out to be among the most prescient – although it was Hendrix who ultimately tired of the bag, not the public.

Of course, Beck's disdain for his first solo single was scarcely to dent the record itself. Don Arden's *Mr Big* autobiography recalls doing "what I had to" to guarantee radio play for the Attack record. But RAK, apparently, were doing even more. "As the publisher of both records, I got the sales figures back for both of them and, sure enough, for the first week, they showed we were comfortably outselling Beck version. But it was the Beck version that was higher in the charts. I put more money behind it, but the second week it was the same deal. On paper, the Attack were outselling Beck by nearly 2-1, but he was the one shooting up the chart. Clearly, even more money was being put behind the Beck record. At that point, I threw in the towel."

In fact, the Beck single's progress up the chart was not quite so remarkable as Arden remembers; indeed, although he proudly claims to have thrown a party to celebrate "when Beck's version went to Number 1 and stayed there for what seemed like an eternity" (for, as publisher, he would indeed have profited grandly from such a feat), in the real world "Hi Ho Silver Lining" did not even crack the Top 10, and the only apparent eternity involved was, the length of time it took to climb that high. Though the single entered the lower reaches of the (then-"official") *Record Mirror* Top 75 in the week of release, it was the beginning of May before it gnawed the Top 20. Then, having risen to Number 14 – and stayed there for an admittedly remarkable three weeks – it began its decline. By the first week in June, it was out of the chart.

The record fared considerably better on the pirate radio charts. Radio London, too, dropped "Hi Ho Silver Lining" into its Fab 40 in the week of release and, by mid-April, it stood at Number 4, out-performing the Move, Jimi Hendrix and Lulu. But the London chart was never the most reliable barometer of public taste; if it was, "Hi Ho Silver Lining" would not have dropped off the listings altogether the very next week.

Grant and Most had long enjoyed a friendly relationship with the so-called pirates, the independently-owned radio stations that set up on the fringes of British waters and broadcast a non-stop diet of pop music in glorious defiance of the BBC's legal monopoly of the radio waves. Most recalled sailing his yacht out to both Radio Caroline and Radio London "to try and plug our records", and both he and Grant acknowledged that sums of money did change hands as a part of the process.

Unlike the charts operated on behalf of the BBC and the music press, Radio London's Fab 40 was calculated not according to sales but by some mysterious combination of the station staff's own predictions and preferences. Big L personally liked to describe its chart as some six weeks ahead of the mainland, a testament to the hit-picking abilities of its resident disc jockeys. Unfortunately, the chart was also tainted by the suspicion that advertisers, sponsors and record pluggers had at least as much influence on the listings as the DJs – all the more so since certain record labels and management agencies never seemed to have any problem placing records on the Fab 40, regardless of their performance on other charts.

RAK were proudly numbered among this coterie, as Grant explained when asked about the Beck record's precipitous decline. "What do you think? We stopped paying for it to be in the chart. Mickie decided that it was more important to have a big hit with Lulu, rather than medium hits with everyone, so we channelled all the money we'd have spent on Jeff and Terry (Terry Reid's "The Hand Don't Fit The Glove" had just entered the chart at Number 37) and pumped it into 'The Boat That I Row' – which then went straight to Number 1."

No matter. Today, few people recall either the Lulu or the Terry Reid songs. "Hi Ho Silver Lining", on the other hand, remains one of the best-known, best loved, and most insanely catchy songs of all time, sweeping the British disco scene and setting itself up as the ultimate party record. Beck himself has described the record as "like having a pink toilet seat hanging round my neck for the rest of my fucking life", but he also sees the funny side of that. "The police in England love that song, because every time I get nicked for speeding they tell me so. Then they give me a ticket."

The British police aren't the only people. Travel to those Spanish coastal resorts where British tourists are packed tighter than sardines in a can, and "Hi Ho Silver Lining" (up there with "Y Viva Espana" and, strangely, Typically Tropical's "Barbados") still fills the dancefloor.

With the record's American release set to follow the UK by just a few weeks, Beck flew to California in early April, to handle some advance publicity for the single (and, of course, spend some time with Mary Hughes). He then returned home on 9 April, his head filled with fresh ambition.

All of Los Angeles, it seemed, was talking about the pop festival that John Phillips and Lou Adler were staging in Monterey in June, and the rumour mill was swirling with suggestions of who would be playing there. Beck wondered if he might be among the clutch of British acts that would certainly be invited to appear, but even if he wasn't he at least hoped to attend the event.

Even more exciting, however, was the glimpse he'd received into a possible future direction for his own music. Visiting the Galaxy, a club on Sunset Strip, he caught a pair of performances by Iron Butterfly, a band that was just beginning to break through onto the local mainstream but who already had great swathes of their future renown in place, including the show-stopping "In A Gadda da Vida."

On record, that song would devour an entire side of their first LP. On stage, Beck was astonished to discover, it occupied an entire concert. "I wouldn't go round handing out gold-plated posters about them on the musical side, but what knocked me out is that the whole of their second appearance was devoted to just one number. They spun it out for around 35 minutes. That's why I liked them so much, just for being able to do that. From that admiration grew the seeds of an idea of his own. Mickie Most had not even begun to think about a Jeff Beck LP. But Beck himself had already decided what he wanted to do with one, a side-long "guitar concerto" that would allow him to stretch in the same directions as the Iron Butterfly.

"I really thought that would work", he explained years later, "and it might have, if I'd actually put anything into it. But there was so much else going on at the time, that there was never the time to do anything about it, and Mickie probably wouldn't have been keen, and Rod and all the others. So it never happened and, when you think about it, it's probably just as well."

CHAPTER
THIRTEEN

The high spirits with which Beck returned from America were not to last. The group had undergone another rupture in his absence, as Mickey Waller upped to join the Quotations, the British session group hired on as the Walker Brothers' regular accompanists – their own latest UK tour kicked off on 31 March, in the company of Engelbert Humperdinck and Jimi Hendrix.

A new drummer, Rod Coombes, was hastily procured. Destined to become one of the foremost players of the 1970s with Juicy Lucy, the Strawbs, Stealers Wheel and John Entwistle, Coombes was a total unknown when compared to his bandmates, but he gelled well enough for Beck to finally come through on the pledge he'd delivered to Wood at the outset, and shifted him over to rhythm guitar. For bass duties, he returned to Dave Ambrose, the bassist who'd filled in for Jet Harris three months earlier. Again the arrangement was intended to be nothing more than temporary. But Beck hoped that might change as things developed.

Early rehearsals seemed to bear out his instincts. The band took over the Granada cinema in Kennington and, within days, were sounding so good that Beck happily invited *NME* journalist Keith Altham down to hear them.

What Beck wanted to hear, he explained, was noise. "Disgusting heavy-heavy-heavy stuff. I wanted sacks of cement being dropped either side of me." And it sounded like he'd found it. "We've got a great group together now, and I'm hoping to be able to communicate with my own material for the very first time."

On 11 April, the Jeff Beck Group played their first major London concert since the Astoria disaster, headlining the London Marquee. They were well aware that this time there could be no mistakes. The entire music press would be in attendance, with their pens specially sharpened for the occasion, but a thousand or so other fans were there as well – so it was fortunate indeed that, from the moment the band plugged in, it was clear that all previous problems had been ironed out.

Reflecting back on past mishaps, Beck mused, "in a way, (the bad reviews) drew attention to us. I'm not knocking the papers, but it's true that people nowadays don't believe exactly everything they read in the press. They want to come along afterwards and make up their own minds. So I pulled in, with the boys, 1,000 at the Marquee soon afterwards, and we were able to put matters right." Only a handful of reviews and dissatisfied voices backstage lowered the tone of the evening, but Beck took encouragement even there. "We got trashed because Rod couldn't be heard over all the noise. Perfect!"

Two nights later, the Group (or the Jeff Beck Sound, as the local promoter mis-billed them) were at the Worthing Assembly Hall, the following night "Jeff Beck and His Group featuring Rod Stuart" played St George's Ballroom in Hinckley. But, with what was becoming infuriating regularity, this latest line-up was doomed to an early demise.

While Woody has since recalled "We realised that two guitars weren't going to work", he also remembered how the chemistry between Beck and Ambrose was constantly misfiring – nothing serious, nothing major, just little niggles that kept Beck out of sorts. "Jeff couldn't take (Dave), so he asked me 'would you mind switching (back) to bass?' I accepted – I loved the challenge." With a week to go before the group's next scheduled show, Ambrose departed, this time to join Mickey Waller in a new band being put together by London singer-songwriter Cat Stevens.

Rod Coombes received his marching orders at the same time, although this split was apparently amiable. "The way I remember it", Peter Grant recalled, "Rod and Jeff had been trying to get Aynsley Dunbar to join the group from the very beginning, but he was never available. And then one day he was, so he joined."

Beck had indeed been eyeing the Liverpudlian drummer for some time, ever since he first made his presence known aboard the Mojos, one of the crop of Merseybeat bands that exploded forward with one great single in the wake of the Beatles' breakthrough ("Everything's Alright"), and then slipped back into obscurity. Dunbar himself moved on to John Mayall's Bluesbreakers, playing alongside Peter Green in the Hard Road line-up, while he was also present at Jimi Hendrix's first ever London jam sessions, laying down the rhythm while Noel Redding came to grips with the bass. His time with Mayall, however, had finally come to an end, and Beck pounced.

Beck's interest in Dunbar, the guitarist readily admitted, was the fact that there simply wasn't another drummer on the scene who sounded like him. "He has this strange technique. It's like the rhythm of the chain-gang workers in the deep Southern States in America. That sort of thing." The new line-up had still to make it through more than a couple of rehearsals, but Beck told *Record Mirror's* Peter Jones, "(it) could be very good."

Back to a quartet, the Group returned to action on 21 April, with a show in St Albans. The sequence of increasingly confident shows the band played over the next week, however, came to an abrupt halt on 27 April, after Beck made his solo debut on television's *Top Of The Pops*, with Rod Stewart nowhere in sight. The single was now pushing its way into the Top 20, and an entire nation's worth of pop fans who had never heard of Beck before "Hi Ho Silver Lining" came galloping into view. Now they were prepared to descend upon any concert hall in reach, to catch a glimpse of their new idol.

Problem was, they were never going to get what they expected. "Hi Ho Silver Lining" was in the band's repertoire, of course. But so was a host of utterly unfamiliar, and utterly un-pop-like blues and rock workouts, all bellowed into their ears by an odd-looking guy with a big nose and a raspy voice. Two nights after *TOTP*, the Beck Group headlined Cromer's

Royal Links Pavilion, where they encountered a crowd that had no interest whatsoever in Howlin' Wolf and Buddy Guy covers. The night didn't simply end in a riot, it was transformed into an all-out brawl. Peter Grant readily recalled a number of other shows that walked a similar line between chaos and carnage as audiences not only demanded to hear the hit, but made it plain that that was all they wanted to hear.

Neither was Mickie Most at all averse to compounding Beck's discomfort by pointing him in what Grant described as "ever more bizarre directions". Over the last couple of years, the likes of footballer George Best and actor Michael Caine had started earning hundreds of extra-curricular pounds doing nothing more than standing around looking good, while wearing, eating, or whatever-ing some hot new product. Knowing that Beck was never going to gracefully agree to some of the more conventional hoops that a bona fide pop star needed to jump through – opening supermarkets, that kind of thing – Most hit upon modelling as a new way of widening Beck's public appeal.

"I told Mickie, he's never going to go along with that", Grant laughed, "which of course got back to Jeff and more or less guaranteed that he would do it." In early May, Beck posed for a session with fashion photographer Nicholas Wright, and then set up a meeting with theatrical agent Kenneth Pitt to discuss Beck's entry into the world of male modelling. Pitt – a man whose client base, over the last decade, had stretched from Judy Garland to Crispian St Peters, and from Manfred Mann to the young David Bowie – turned him down. Beck's modelling career was never mentioned again.

On 7 May, the Jeff Beck Group were a more-or-less last minute addition to the *New Musical Express'* annual Poll-Winners concert at the Empire Pool, Wembley – and a last minute no-show as well. The gig itself was an opportunity for the past year's most triumphant performers to line up and thank their fans... Beck was intended to join Cream, the Beach Boys (who'd just launched their second UK tour), Love, Cat Stevens, the Troggs, the Small Faces, Dusty Springfield, Paul Jones and Lulu.

Behind the scenes, however, the event's organisers found Beck in extraordinarily recalcitrant mood and the following week's *NME* could only mumble mysteriously about the impossibility of meeting his "backstage demands" – one of which, apparently, was an assurance that he should not be expected to include "Hi Ho Silver Lining" in the two- or three-song set he had been granted. Naturally, the organisers thought otherwise and, when Beck refused to bend, that was the end of the argument. The concert went on without him, and the Beck Group departed without playing a note. Mickie Most, who'd pulled in a number of favours in order to arrange Beck's inclusion, was not pleased.

"It was a constant battle between Jeff and Mickie", Peter Grant sighed. "Mickie was doing everything he could to press his agenda forward, and Jeff was doing everything in his power to derail it. They could both be incredibly stubborn, and I was sitting in the middle trying to look at things from both points of view and help them just get through the day without swiping one another."

Grant admitted that his sympathies lay totally with Beck – "He was such a creative musician, but he was very highly strung, and Mickie didn't understand that. As far as he was concerned, a musician was there... not even to make the music, but to front it. Peter (Noone) was Mickie's ideal artist, because he didn't argue, he went along with everything. Lulu and Don (Donovan), they were easy-going as well. But Jeff... sometimes, he'd suggest something to Mickie and, if Mickie agreed, Jeff would immediately have second thoughts about it. 'Well, if you think it's a good idea, it can't be'. So then Mickie started doing the same thing back to him.

"That's why the group never did anything that whole first year they were together, because the only work they'd actually agree to were the little nuts and bolts things that I was able to sneak in under the radar, things that Mickie didn't pay any attention to because they weren't worth his while looking at."

On 12 May, the Jeff Beck Group made their debut before the newly-emergent hordes of London's psychedelic community as they descended upon the Chalk Farm Roundhouse for the grandiosely titled Two Day Light Show. In the six months since the first 'American-style' hippy happening was introduced to Britain – again at the Roundhouse, in December – the building had shed many of its early characteristics; holes in the walls had been patched up, toilets had been installed, a decent electric supply had been arranged. But still the place could not be compared to any other concert venue in the land – built to accommodate a vast Victorian railway turntable, then converted into a warehouse for Gilbey's gin, the very air inside the building remained thick with the odours of its past uses and the dust of a century's worth of storage.

But the stage had already creaked beneath the weight of some of the year's most significant bands, and live shows that were once regarded as one-off events were now becoming a regular fixture. This particular weekend, Beck's Friday-night show was to be followed by a Saturday headliner for Simon Dupree and the Big Sound; and, if that sounds a curious billing (Beck had a hit single, Dupree was still six months away from his first), it was smart as well. Just about every hip head in the city would be on the other side of the river the next night to catch Pink Floyd's Games For May at the Queen Elizabeth Hall. The best Dupree could hope for was to soak up the stragglers who couldn't get in.

The Beck Group's live set had solidified into a driving R&B behemoth capable of swinging from the soulful extremes of the Four Tops' "Loving You Is Sweeter Than Ever" and the Drifters' "Some Kinda Wonderful" to the rock solid blues of "I Think I'll Be Leaving This Morning" (a work-out that eventually metamorphosed into "Blues Deluxe") and "All Night Long" (BB King's "Rock Me Baby" as it bled into Beck and Stewart's own "Rock My Plimsoul") – a barrage that was gaining the group a reputation for unprecedented dynamism and, maybe, just a hint of unpredictable dishevelment.

Listen back to the handful of live recordings that have survived from the earliest months of the Beck Group's lifetime and, over and over again, one truth is inescapable. The band could play like demons. They just hadn't figured out how to stop playing, and so almost every number just clattered to a halt. 'A bit more togetherness would have helped'. *Disc And Music Echo's* condemnation of one show holds true for many others. "Beck… (played) a lot better than he ever did with the Yardbirds. But the rest of the group ought to organise themselves and realise that an audience is worthy of more professionalism."

Even from the depths of disgust, however, critics couldn't help but marvel at the strength of the chemistry between Beck and Stewart. Songs like "Let Me Love You", "Stone Crazy" and "I Ain't Superstitious" were excellent vehicles for Beck's talent, and most people catching the band in concert noticed that side of things first Beck could torment his guitar through the most unearthly sounds without ever losing sight of the song they were playing.

But then Stewart would step out of the bossman's shadow, with "I've Been Drinking", the group's rearrangement of Dinah Washington's "Drinking Again", or Jimmy Hughes' "Neighbour Neighbour", and suddenly the focus of the entire show would change as a second virtuoso competed for attention. Beck, however, knew that there was a lot more volatility to the relationship than simple showmanship.

Looking back on his years with Beck, a generous Stewart reflected, "I was playing with great musicians and playing something that meant something – we were updating Chicago blues. Jeff, in some ways, moulded my voice, because I had to learn to fill in the holes that he left. There was only one guitar, bass, drums… so there were plenty of holes for me to sing in. With Jeff being such a wonderful guitar player, and so fluid, we bounced off each other. It was the ideal combination – great music, great style, great visual." In fact, the only thing that was lacking was trust.

"It turned out, even while Jet and Viv were with us, that Rod had plans of his own", Beck moaned. "He didn't know what I was doing… I didn't know what I was doing… but it suddenly became very evident that I'd better start finding out, better watch out what was going on.

"The thing about Rod was, he was already familiar with the live circuit we'd been playing, which was something I hadn't really got into. He was doing blues circuits with Steampacket and Shotgun Express, he was much more au fait with that kind of deal, and he knew other players who were great. And then Rod and Woody… I think Woody was getting frustrated not being allowed to play guitar, and I think Rod saw the first cracks in the structure very early on, so he and Woody paired off like a couple of girl guides and I was left out in the cold."

Wood agreed. "Those two had a thing of not talking to each other, and I got on so well with Rod that I joined in the fun as well." He insists that his respect for Beck, for his "more or less purist approach to being a great manipulator of his guitar" prevented him from taking the "joke" as far as Stewart did, but Beck was feeling the estrangement regardless.

He and Wood had been very close in the past; Stewart, however, became closer "and put a block between me and Ronnie." From the very beginning of the band, Beck realised, "Rod had designs on moving somewhere else." And later in the band's life, as that ambition solidified as Stewart's sole motivation for getting up in the morning, he seemed to somehow blame Beck for the fact that it hadn't yet transpired. "He hated me so much, for some strange reason which I can't explain. I only offered him his career on a fucking plate. It was just a shitty time."

But, as Mickie Most discovered and Peter Grant confirmed, Beck himself was not an easy man to work for. *NME* writer Keith Altham met with Beck at the BBC's *Top Of The Pops* studio in May, and reported, "Beck gets a perverse satisfaction from having a 'wicked' reputation in the pop business. At his best, he is a talented guitar-perfectionist with a pleasant, conversational manner. At his worst, he's an obstinate, uncompromising character who avoids doing things he dislikes by the simple expedient of walking out on them." Or forcing them to walk out on him.

A hard taskmaster, Beck never tired of letting his bandmates know that they were expendable – indeed, throughout the Jeff Beck Group's 18-month existence, Rod Stewart was the only member not to be given his marching orders at least once, while Woody was in and out of the band three times. And then there was the drum seat. "There were (people) coming and going, but they just didn't do what I wanted", Beck later complained. "They were argumentative. 'You, OUT. Fuck off. I know what I want'."

For now, things appeared to have been settled down. For the first time since the Jeff Beck Group formed, Dunbar's reassuring presence allowed them to string together days, even weeks' worth of live shows, with the only interruptions coming as "Hi Ho Silver Lining" continued to make its own demands on Beck's time – a solo appearance on Dutch TV's *Moef-Ga-Ga* in mid-May, another bash at *Top Of The Pops*, with the studio orchestra and a trio of backing singers to accompany him, a few days after that.

Beck also found himself drawn into a BBC-TV expose on the groupie scene, within the weekly *Man Alive* series. The 28-minute *Ravers* was actually headlined by the Beck Group's companions at the Two Day Light Show, Simon Dupree and the Big Sound. As that band's Peter Flaherty recalls, "*Man Alive*... spent a week on the road with us", concentrating their cameras on the inter-action between the musicians and the girls who flocked to meet them. "Today", Flaherty acknowledges, "it would be considered a rather tame programme, but in 1967 it was pretty risqué. The producer was pushing the BBC's rules on censorship."

Beck's comments, filmed at the RAK offices, were essentially a re-run of thoughts he had revealed in an interview with the *Sunday Mirror's* Jack Bentley back in March, and which he would reiterate in 1969 for *Rolling Stone* magazine's famous "groupies" issue. Recalling his encounters on the Yardbirds tours, both at home and abroad, he explained, "It was all a teenybopper scene then, with all these screaming chicks who would just come for the music, mainly, and just scream. That's all they did, mainly. And sometimes, older women – strange chicks in their 30s – would try to pull us."

Since then, however, "The scene has changed completely. Completely." Once, as Eric Clapton put it, "they were just chicks who wanted to look after you when you were in town. If making love to you was going to make you happy, they'd make love. If you were tired and didn't want to make it, they'd cook you a meal and make you feel at home. They were really 'ports of call'." Now they were voracious head-hunters – except they weren't just collecting heads, as Beck discovered on his first trip to Chicago with the Yardbirds.

The Plaster Casters, two girls who cast and collected plaster models of their conquests' genitalia, were originally set on their way by a High School homework assignment. Cynthia Plaster-Caster explained, "the art teacher said take a plaster cast of something solid. I had never seen a penis before, but I heard they got solid. So I couldn't wait to meet my girlfriend downtown and tell her about my homework assignment." Their first subject was Mark Lindsay, of American beat band Paul Revere and the Raiders.

The operation itself was simple – a few minutes of fellatio, then the subject's erection would be plunged into a mould filled with dental alginate. The mould would then be filled with plaster and a cast, lifelike in every veined and pimpled detail, would be the result. "It didn't take long at all for word to get around. Roadies started picking us up and bringing us the rock stars' rooms from word of mouth. They would see the logo on our suitcase and yell 'bring up the Plaster Casters!'"

Beck was one of the first English musicians the Plaster Casters ever encountered. Cynthia recalled, "we ran into Jeff Beck... when he saw us with the logo on our suitcase, he jumped around and began screaming at a teen party where you could meet rock stars. It was such pandemonium. The ushers thought it was girls getting hysterical over the band, but it was the other way around." Indeed, she credits Beck with earning her her first piece of mainstream news coverage. "I was mentioned in the *Chicago Tribune*. They said there was... a girl who made a plaster cast of Jeff Beck's third leg. And I went 'right on!'"

Beck's opinions had apparently changed since then. "Groupies use groups", he snarled. "Groupies use groups. Not the reverse, the way it might look. It's all for their own egos. It's got very little – very, very, very little – to do with giving or sharing, so far as they're concerned. It's saddening, really. They have this nasty kind of cunning way of seeping inside your sleeve and into your life, when really you don't know them at all." They were thieves, he swore. He had lost "nearly a dozen lace shirts" to sundry nocturnal souvenir-hunters, while one LA lady made off with a pair of expensive sunglasses. "She just fucked off with them, and I never saw her again. They're like that. You've got to watch everything you own."

Groupies, he concluded, were one of the reasons why, when touring,

"I cannot wait, cannot wait, to get home." Still, he had some useful pointers for any musicians who might want to avail themselves of their services. "Derby and Nottingham are good scenes. In those areas, girls will follow groups within a 50-mile radius, and the message is always the same – have sex, will travel. The West Country is pretty useless, so it's a favourite to take a girl with you when you're going to Exeter or Plymouth." And of course, no amount of homegrown comforts could hold a candle to the girls in the States – and, if they did, no prizes for guessing what would happen to that candle. "I had to get away before I became a sex maniac", Beck concluded. Viewers of *Ravers*, however, might have wondered whether it was already too late.

"Even the women who wept when Valentino died might find it hard to grasp what it means to be a raver", cautioned the *Radio Times* in the run-up to the show's broadcast. "Today the girls who follow the pop groups start young – and, once started, there is no stopping them. They come from every kind of background. The only things they share in common are their youth and their idols... (and) a world where... the girls have become the hunters, the boys the hunted."

Peter Flaherty continues, "We were away from home the evening it was shown, so we arranged to watch the programme on the hotel's television before the gig. We had no idea what the show would be like; they had filmed ten times the footage that they needed. When the show was over, it was funny as a fight to see some of the guys rush to the hotel's pay-phone, explaining to partners their actions. One of their partners even left home and went to live with her mother for a while!"

Beck, too, had reasons to be circumspect in his conversation – if circumspect he was. His relationship with Mary Hughes, back in California, was over now; back in London, he'd met and fallen in love with model Celia Hammond. The last thing he'd have wanted to do, so early in their relationship, would be to throw it away for the sake of a throwaway sentence or two – although it probably wouldn't have mattered. Over the next close-to-two decades, Beck and Hammond would become what the tabloids like to describe as the "success stories" of showbiz romance, with Hammond herself mapping out a career that proved at least as wilful as anything Beck would come up with.

Already established among the most striking figures on the modelling scene when she met Beck, Hammond was also emerging as one of the most controversial, a vocal opponent of animal cruelty at a time when such concerns were still regarded as the province of eccentric old ladies with a houseful of cats.

A vegetarian since her teens (Beck followed suit, shortly after they moved in together), the *Vogue* cover girl was motivated to take her stand after seeing a news report on the annual Canadian seal cull – at a time when, she shuddered, "I was the top model for fur. Then I saw footage of the so-called seal cull... I saw the horrific gin traps, and here I was promoting fur."

Photographer Norman Parkinson once remarked of Hammond, "Celia has tremendous imperfections, yet I think these add up to her attraction because other women feel that, if they tried really hard, they could look as good as she does." For a short time, it looked as if those imperfections included biting the hand that fed her – interviewed a few days after watching that show, Hammond mentioned her revulsion at what she'd seen in an unscheduled, unscripted outburst that stunned the entire fashion industry, her own regular employers most of all.

Others, however, leaped to her defence, including Lady Dowding, of the then little-known charity Beauty Without Cruelty. It was she who asked Hammond to fly to the Gulf of St Lawrence, to act as the charity's official observer at the cull; Hammond agreed, and was so affected by what she witnessed that she loudly, and publicly vowed never to model fur again.

More than that, she set about encouraging her fellow models to follow suit – Donovan's "Celia Of The Seals", a song from his 1971 album HMS Donovan, celebrated Hammond's stance, while Hammond herself would continue fighting for animal rights throughout the remainder of her modelling career, and thereafter. She is still involved today, heading up the Celia Hammond Animal Trust, a London-based charity that offers low-cost neutering and vaccination for pets. (Beck was among the star attractions at a Hard Rock Café benefit for CHAT in 1988.)

CHAPTER
FOURTEEN

Early June saw the Jeff Beck Group enter the studio for the first time, to cut the much-anticipated follow-up to "Hi Ho Silver Lining". "Tallyman", like so many of the Yardbirds' best-loved early records, was a Graham Gouldman composition, as the young Mancunian songwriter maintained a stranglehold on the charts untouched by anyone beyond the Beatles-Stones axis. The trilogy of Yardbirds hits that made his reputation was followed by a pair for the Hollies ("Look Through Any Window" and "Bus Stop"), while Cher, the Shadows, the Downliners Sect and Friday Browne had all recorded his songs. Herman's Hermits' mid-decade success, meanwhile, was all but built upon Gouldman's pen.

As Peter Noone recalls, "Graham wrote 'No Milk Today', 'Listen People', 'East West', 'Ooh She's Done It Again', he was just a phenomenal songsmith. I mean, everything he played to me, I loved. And it's the construction. We turned down Carole King songs and Neil Diamond songs, but we never, ever turned down a Graham Gouldman song, and I, still to this day, say, 'why didn't I get him in Herman's Hermits?'"

Gouldman himself was a confirmed Beck fan. "The first time I saw (the Yardbirds) was with Eric Clapton, and that blew my head off", he recalls. "But then I saw them with Jeff Beck, and that was unbelievable; he was better, he looked better, I liked the guitar he used better." Still, he was surprised when Mickie Most declared that Beck's next single would be his own "Tallyman".

The song itself was as alluring as any of Gouldman's past compositions, an ode to the old-time debt collectors who went from door-to-door, picking up the shilling-or-so a week payments that their clients owed. But it was no better suited to Beck's reputation and talents than its predecessor, and was at odds with "Hi Ho Silver Lining" as well – few of Gouldman's songs ever beat their hookline to death; few even boasted what one would describe as a singalong chorus, or anthemic demeanour. They clung, instead, to timeless melodies and evocative imagery: a song like "It's Nice To Be Out In The Morning" can make you feel homesick for Manchester, even if you've never been there.

But Mickie Most loved the song, Beck didn't hate it, and the arrangement even allowed him to pull off an astonishing slide guitar solo. In fact, the only sourness at the entire session came when it was time to put down the vocal. Beforehand, Beck had convinced himself that Most had agreed to let Rod Stewart sing the lead. Most, on the other hand, had no recollection whatsoever of such a conversation, and simply repeated the mantra he'd devised back in January. He was making a Jeff Beck record. Which meant Jeff Beck would be making it.

He did allow for a modicum of compromise, at least allowing Stewart to share the two-part harmony, but that was far as he'd go.

"It's basically a hit song", Beck told *Rave* magazine shortly after the session, "but after the last one, I don't know what it'll do. That was a pretty bad record. It was like giving someone a lousy car to win a race with – well, I got a lousy song to prove myself with." More recently, Beck described "Tallyman" as the best of all his 1967 solo records. "'Tallyman' is a great song. It's not a bad-sounding record, that."

Reviews agreed with him. "I didn't like 'Hi Ho'", Penny Valentine told *Disc & Music Echo* readers, "(but) I like this... (it) is so much better sung and produced... (and) Jeff's guitar does high-pitched moans." *Melody Maker*, too, was impressed – "Jeff's guitar is sounding more 'human' every day", while *Record Mirror* declared, "the voice comes through well." There were some harsh words, however, from the Hollies' Graham Nash. The record got better as it went on, he declared, and though Beck "hasn't got the ability to sing... he's getting there. I just wish he'd stop spending so much time commiserating himself and get down to some really hard work. That's what he needs, man."

Rod Stewart agreed. Years later, he would look back on the sheer schizophrenia of the Beck Group's first year together, and confess that he never quite figured out exactly what was going on, why Beck – "a great guitarist, a great musician" – was so willing to record such patently unsuitable material. "I just couldn't understand him."

In fact, Beck would have liked nothing more than to get down to some hard work with some suitable material, and the addition of "Tallyman" to the band's repertoire only heightened the absurdity. As the new single commenced its own rise towards the Top 30, now the pop kids had two fab faves to howl for, and the Beck Group's travels that July only amplified the divide that was yawning between what they wanted to do and what they found they had to.

Mickie Most, however, knew exactly what was going on. "Those records were what was keeping the Jeff Beck Group alive. Somebody had to pay their weekly wages, so it kept them working." And the constant work was what allowed them to hone their attack to the perfection it would so swiftly attain.

Throughout 1967, Beck's own eyes were firmly on the United States. "Hi Ho Silver Lining" had been a hit there, and the grapevine was constantly buzzing with reports on just how desperately the country awaited Beck.

Alan Merrill, guitarist with the Left Banke (and, five years on, with Arrows, a glam-pop band that had its own hitmaking relationship with Mickie Most and RAK), recalled his own impatience. "I'd been a fan of Jeff Beck back in his days with the Yardbirds. Although I was mainly a 12-string folk-rock player, I even bought a Fender Esquire in 1966 and tried to play it like Beck did... to no avail, no matter how much I practiced."

"Tallyman" did nothing in the United States, but it impacted all the same. Merrill continued, "I was playing down at the Cafe Wha? and there was another group, Kangaroo, whose guitarist, Teddy Spelios, could actually do the Beck vibrato and do it on a Fender Broadcaster, with the highest, most obnoxious action on a guitar I've ever seen. It was more like a bow than a guitar.

"One day I came in to the Cafe Wha? with an import of 'Tallyman'. There was a DJ there so I had him put it on. Teddy instantly made me a ridiculous offer for the single, which I accepted. Then, while we were playing our set, Teddy took the Beck single back to his flat and learned it, with drummer ND Smart and bassist John Hall. Kangaroo's next set started off with 'Tallyman', and it was note perfect."

Beck, meanwhile, was making his own obnoxious guitar statements. On 2 July, opening for Cream at the Saville Theatre, he played a couple of numbers with his 12-string Telecaster tuned to the then-unfathomable depths of D. It was, he celebrated, a revelation. "No-one had ever done that. It was very low and gritty, a real fuck-off sound. It was like a bloody 10-piece orchestra, it was so powerful, and so absolutely happening. (Pete) Townshend was watching, and he was wetting himself; he came back and said 'The best thing about tonight was the sound of your 12-string Tele'."

Beck agreed, not only about the sound but also with its effect on his bandmates. "That would have been the perfect flavour, I thought, for Rod, because he sang perfectly to the key of that thing. Unfortunately, we never got much on tape with it, but that could have been really good."

Despite this, the Saville show was not a triumph. With the media keyed up to expect (and receive) a classic Cream performance, opening performances by Rod Stewart's old pals Jimmy Powell and the Dimensions, John Mayall's Bluesbreakers and Beck were on a hiding to nothing from the get-go, with *Melody Maker* reviewer Nick Jones condemning "the Bluesbreakers playing the blues like they've always played the blues... (Beck) also playing yesterday's blues, only a bit louder..."

Cream, on the other hand, "obliterated (all) that had gone before, from the first quiver of 'NSU'..." while the closing number in the set, "I'm So Glad", swept the landscape even cleaner, as Cream ushered Beck, Mick Taylor (the now-departed Peter Green's replacement in the Bluesbreakers) and the Dimensions' Red Godwin onto the stage to join Clapton for a "freaking... four-guitar feedback finale."

The Saville Theatre show also marked the end of yet another era for the Jeff Beck Group. Aynsley Dunbar – already uncomfortable with Jeff Beck's pop star games – had long ago gained the reputation of a dyed-in-the-wool blues purist, fiercely denouncing anything that compromised the integrity of the music he loved. He had accepted "Hi Ho Silver Lining" and "Tallyman" as necessary evils, but went ballistic when he arrived at the Saville to discover his bandmates were now dressing the pop-star part as well. "It was the peak of flower power", as Stewart put it, "and the band decided to reflect all the sartorial extravagance that fashion demanded. Beck was bedecked in a green floppy hat and a fur coat, Wood and Stewart were armed with "flowers and kaftans and no trousers. Did we look a state! Aynsley was really insulted – this wasn't the blues!" The aggrieved drummer served immediate notice of his decision to quit – something that could have come as no surprise to Beck. Another drummer bites the dust.

In fact, Dunbar's departure had been a real possibility from the moment he joined the Jeff Beck Group. He'd quit the Bluesbreakers, after all, to pursue a solo career, and never hid the fact that his latest berth was simply a stop-gap while he formed his own band. Neither would there would be any hard feelings after he'd departed. As Stewart later reasoned, "he... really got the band together", a point that was confirmed the following week when, working out his notice, Dunbar joined the Jeff Beck Group on the BBC's *Saturday Club*. Although they performed just three songs, the energy level went through the roof, an electrifying "Tallyman" headlining the session, before airings for its B-side, the "Rock My Plimsoul" revision of BB King's "Rock Me Baby", and, finally, a new song, the luxurious blues-guitar showcase "I Think I'll Be Leaving This Morning".

"I think the Aynsley period really was the highpoint of the band," Peter Grant reflected. "It was the only time that everybody was working together towards a common goal, even if you could argue that, really, everybody had their own completely different agenda – Aynsley was planning his band, Rod was dreaming of going solo, Woody was looking to get back to playing guitar again and Jeff was just being Jeff." Indeed, those divisions were never far from the surface, as Stewart was about to prove.

His solo career, so far, had been little more than a minor distraction around his obligations to whichever band he happened to be singing with at the time; had, in fact, been laid to rest when Columbia dropped him the previous year. Over the past few weeks, however, Stewart had been spending time with the Small Faces' Steve Marriott (who was married to one of Stewart's ex-girlfriends, Jenny Ryland), just as he and Ronnie Lane began easing themselves into a new role as in-house songwriters at Immediate Records,

It was a role that Mick Jagger and Keith Richard had already delineated; they wrote (and Jagger produced) Immediate's first ever Number 1, Chris Farlowe's version of the Stones' "Out Of Time". Now Marriott and Lane, too, were writing for Farlowe, and fellow Immediate acts Apostolic Intervention and Pat 'PP' Arnold ('The first lady of Immediate', as the advertising slogan insisted), and were soon offering to pen songs for Stewart as well. "Marriott wrote some incredibly commercial things for me to record," the singer recalled and, although nothing would ever come of these particular collaborations, label manager Tony Calder was sufficiently intrigued by the possibilities to suggest a Rod Stewart solo single.

The original plan was to link Stewart with Arnold at a session overseen by her former paramour Mick Jagger. Keith Richard was along on guitar and bass, Nicky Hopkins delivered piano, and a few onlookers have since declared Ron Wood was there as well, perhaps playing bass but probably just watching. The session, however, was doomed. Despite having just two songs to record, Carole King's "Come Home Baby" (recently covered by Wilson Pickett), and Lee Dorsey's "Working In A Coal Mine", Jagger and Stewart completely failed to hit it off.

"There was a row in the studio," Geoff Wright, Stewart's manager, recalled, "with Jagger saying that Rod could not hit the right notes, and that his voice wasn't right for the song." And, with that, Jagger apparently packed up the master tape and walked out of the studio. Just weeks later, the Rolling Stones and Andrew Loog Oldham parted company for the last time. The session, which Jagger apparently paid for himself, was permanently shelved.

Stewart would, however, wring a single out of his association with Immediate. Among the other artists involved with the label, and constantly on the look-out for fresh talent was Mike D'Abo, the songwriter whose "Handbags And Gladrags" had recently given Chris Farlowe a major hit, and who was now looking for someone to voice a new song, "Little Miss Understood."

He agreed to give Stewart a go, but like Jagger, was soon regretting it – the singer later recalled D'Abo halting a take to ask, "Can't you get rid of that frog in your throat?" It took several goes before they finally arrived at a take that D'Abo could live with, and it was duly released as a pleasant, but scarcely distinguished single later in the year.

More intriguing was another loose combination that Stewart threw himself into as the summer drifted on. Aynsley Dunbar was just weeks away from unveiling his new group, Retaliation, when Clifford Davis, a booker at the Gunnell agency, called to ask if he'd be interested in another project entirely. Peter Green had left the Bluesbreakers by now, and was likewise preparing to debut his new band, Fleetwood Mac. Before he did so, however, all the industry talk about supergroups had got Davis thinking. Green and Dunbar were already a proven partnership. Who, if the entire musical universe was their oyster, would they choose to complete one of their own?

Jack Bruce, of course – for what musician did not dream of playing alongside him? And, to complete the quartet, a singer that both Green and Dunbar had worked alongside, Rod Stewart.

One session produced three recordings: two versions of the Beck Group live favourite "Stone Crazy", and one of "Fly Right Baby", with Bruce forsaking bass for piano. 'I think Brian Auger was there as well,' Peter Green later remarked. 'I think he came in and did a guest organ. But we just did the session,' Green continued, 'just did the two tunes, and that was it. Everyone just mucked down to it. It was good.'

However, any hopes that the session's successes might be the blueprint for a bright future were doomed to disappointment. A veritable army of concerned managers, bookers, accountants and lawyers were grumbling back and forth the moment they got wind of proceedings. And they still grumble. Although one of the versions of 'Stone Crazy' did eventually turn up on a Blue Horizon retrospective LP during the 1970s, where it was credited, strangely, to Dunbar's Retaliation, when Vernon tried to include both Crazy Blue numbers within 1997's Blue Horizon Story box set, he was stymied by what he diplomatically described as "problems of a legal nature." "I heard one of the other guys didn't want them coming out", Peter Green explained. "So he stopped it. A shame."

There simply was no time to explore the quartet's possibilities any further as the four musicians had their own immediate futures to take care of, each scheduled to appear with their regular bands at the following month's (long-windedly rechristened) National Jazz, Pop, Ballads & Blues Festival in Windsor.

Staged over the mid-month August Bank Holiday weekend, the festival packed a line-up that seems almost impossible to imagine today. The Small Faces, the Move, Tomorrow and Marmalade were highlights of the first, Friday, night. Dunbar's Retaliation would make their public debut on the Saturday, alongside the Nice, Paul Jones, Arthur Brown, Zoot Money, Ten Years After, Amen Corner and Timebox; and, to wrap it all up on the Sunday, Cream, Beck and Fleetwood Mac were scheduled alongside John Mayall, PP Arnold, Alan Bown, Chicken Shack, Donovan, Denny Laine, Blossom Toes and Pentangle.

For all that, the three-day event was not to prove wholly successful. The following Monday's newspaper headlines were consumed with reports of the near-riot sparked by the Crazy World of Arthur Brown after fans took his invocations of 'Fire' too literally and set a pile of rubbish ablaze – and then threw bricks and bottles at the firemen who attempted to extinguish the blaze.

Musically, too, the festival had its problems. WEM, who provided the venue's PA, supplied what was amounted to a state-of-the-art set-up, capable of emitting a then-staggering 1,000 watts. Yet that was meaningless when pumped out across a crowd of 20,000 people, as *Melody Maker* – having arrived anticipating a cornucopia of guitar-playing genii – angrily pointed out. "A host of guitarists like Peter Green, Eric Clapton, Jeff Beck and David O'List (of the Nice), had their sound reduced to a near-pathetic level." Indeed, it was an indication of just how atrocious things sounded from out front that, when the reviews came in, Ron Wood's decision to take the stage in full Native American garb received almost as many press plaudits as the performance itself.

An audience tape exists of part of the Windsor performance, horribly distorted and crude in the extreme but capturing five songs that, in turn, illustrate the Beck Group in full flight. Elmore James' "Talk To Me Baby" is the standout, a positively filthy bass line squelching beneath Beck's lascivious slide, while Stewart's vocal floats through his entire emotional gamut. The slow blues "I Think I'll Be Leaving This Morning" and a defiantly scrappy "Rock My Plimsoul" both suffer from the low guitar volume the reviews mourned, but the opening "Some Kind Of Wonderful" indeed lives up to its title, despite Stewart's opening warning "you've heard it all before" and regardless, once again, of that all-enveloping bass mix.

But proving that Beck's distaste for "Hi Ho Silver Lining" was not shared by even his most dedicated fans, the biggest roar of the proceedings was reserved for the moment when, as Stewart puts it, "it's about time he took the microphone and gave us...." The fact that Beck himself sounds like he'd prefer to be doing anything but singing the song doesn't detract (his enthusiasm reaches its nadir with the flies in your pea-soup lyric – he actually ignores the next line altogether); the backing vocals are as joyous as you could wish, and the minimalist guitar solo is at least intriguing. The audience cries of "turn it up", however, testify to the atrocious sound quality that marred the entire weekend.

CHAPTER
FIFTEEN

By late July 1967, the members of Pink Floyd were beginning to finally realise that something was going seriously wrong with Syd Barrett, the frontman, songwriter and lead guitarist who had propelled them through two hit singles, an incredible debut album and a firm roost at the top of the psychedelic tree.

The band had already cancelled their own spot at the Windsor festival, citing Barrett's "nervous exhaustion" – according to drummer Nick Mason, "they sent poor Paul Jones on instead. Paul had recently split from Manfred Mann and was enjoying a successful solo career singing R&B. He mounted the stage to a cry of 'Do you like soul music?' A roar of 'NO!' came back, along with a hail of love beads and beer cans."

Now Floyd were facing a monthful of further cancellations, as the ailing Barrett was despatched for a few weeks' rest on the Mediterranean island of Formantera. Problem was those cancellations included a pair of very important German television dates, *Music For Young People* and *Beat Club*. If only they could find a stand-in, those shows at least could be salvaged.

Beck himself was in Germany at the same time, handling some promo work for "Tallyman". To this day, nobody seems sure whether it was wishful thinking on behalf of one or other act's management, a miscommunication across two languages and an ocean, or simple journalistic invention. But, according to the American trade paper *Billboard's* 12 August issue, "Jeff Beck replaced an ailing Syd Barrett when the Pink Floyd flew to Germany for a TV date."

"No I didn't", responded Beck when he was asked about it 30 years later; no he didn't, echo the rest of Floyd – in fact, according to Mason, when it did come time to replace Barrett permanently, some six months after that German visit, Beck's name did come up in conversation. "But I don't think any of us would have had the courage to make the phone call."

Compared to the promotional workload he'd faced last time around, "Tallyman" was occupying very little of Jeff Beck's time; indeed, it was already becoming apparent that the single was not going to repeat its predecessor's chart performance (it peaked at Number 30), and Mickie Most was now casting around for Beck's next single. "I've just heard the demo," Beck told *Record Mirror* a few days after the Windsor show. "It's a great and solid number. The writer is completely unknown. It's not even recorded yet." Nor, apparently, would it be. Between now and the end of the year, almost every waking moment for the band would be spent on the road.

Perhaps unsurprisingly, the only other drummer who'd ever lasted any kind of course with the band, Mickey Waller, replaced Dunbar in the Jeff Beck Group. He reacquainted himself with their repertoire over a few rehearsals at Studio 19, but even he was surprised at just how little the group's vision had changed in the months he'd been away. Long John Baldry recalled a conversation he had with Waller "sometime in the very late 1960s, where he told me how much he hated being in that band. They were fighting with each other, they were arguing with Mickie and Peter, and it was never over anything that actually mattered. They just niggled one another, like 'Why are you wearing those shoes? I hate them.' Every day."

Once, Beck himself had overflowed with grandiose visions. Now he barely even spoke of anything that wasn't immediately apparent. That glorious dream of using movies to supplant live work had long ago been punctured; so had all the other plans and dreams he'd floated over the past months – even his hopes of getting back to California to catch the Monterey Pop Festival were shattered. And while the likes of the Who, Hendrix, Janis Joplin and the Jefferson Airplane all secured their berths in rock immortality across a sun-drenched weekend in northern California, the Jeff Beck Group were playing on the Isle of Man.

Scrapped, too, was any notion of recording an album this year, as Mickie Most, reluctant to relinquish the reins of power for a second, found his own schedule simply too cramped to make the time Beck was demanding.

1967 was the year of the grand statement. From the Beatles' Sgt Pepper (which Beck, unique among his peers, did not even bother listening to… "it's not my type of music at all, so I'm not interested") on down, through the ranks of the Pretty Things, Pink Floyd, the Who, Cream, Hendrix on and on and on, it was as though the bar for artistic accomplishment was being raised every week.

Beck knew he could equal it; had, in fact, already thrown down a gauntlet of sorts when he announced that side-long guitar concerto back in April. Just weeks later, however, RAK apparently dismissed such ambitions by insisting, via a news story in the *New Musical Express*, that "Jeff Beck's first solo LP is likely to be recorded live before an audience of about 250 of his fans. His recording manager Mickie Most is currently looking for a suitable venue for the session. The album, complete with audience reaction, is being planned for late summer release by Columbia."

From a grand guitar concerto to a simple in-concert recording – it was astonishing how swiftly ambition faded (or was allowed to fade), and Beck was painfully aware of every last implication of that. "I feel as if I've been dropped", he complained. "Hendrix and Clapton have reached the same point as I have (as guitarists) and they've been accepted. But so many things went wrong at the beginning of my career, including the release of 'Hi Ho Silver Lining'." While his peers were soaring off into the stratosphere, granted free rein in the studio to indulge their every whim, Beck was being offered… a live album? And now, even that carrot had been snatched away.

Many commentators have remarked how unfair it was that, throughout a year of unbridled creativity and musical madness, the Jeff Beck Group was effectively sidelined. "I'd like to make an LP," Beck moaned on more than one occasion. "But Mickie doesn't think it's time. He doesn't want to spend a lot of money on an album until we've decided what we're going to do."

The strange thing is that, with the benefit of lashings of hindsight, Most may have been correct – at least so far as the British market, the one Most best understood, was concerned. To a United Kingdom bathing in the gentle pastures of The Piper At The Gates Of Dawn, Sgt Pepper and Disraeli Gears, the Jeff Beck Group's brutalisation of the blues would simply have been too much, too soon. It would require the correspondingly brutal universal comedown of the new year, and the attendant realisation that petals and flowers had not made a blind bit of difference to anyone outside of the florists' shop, to legitimise the group's music in the eyes of the general public.

In the meantime, then, the Beck Group churned on round the clubs and ballrooms, from Rugby to Malvern, Lowestoft to Hartlepool, Folkestone to Dunstable, and breaking cover only to slam their mutant moods in the face of audiences that expected to be treated a little more gently. They played second fiddle to Manfred Mann when Winston Churchill's old home at Blenheim Park was opened up for a Sunday-afternoon concert on 23 July (PP Arnold and the Nice and Simon Dupree and the Big Sound completed the bill), and shook the old pile to its foundations. A month later, across the final weekend of August, they were equally disrespectful to the ghosts of Woburn Abbey at the last of the summer's great love-ins, His Grace the Duke of Bedford's Festival of the Flower Children.

Staged over three days, with live music through until sunset, and then non-stop records and tapes through the night (hence the organisers' promise of 72 non-stop hours of sounds), the festival erred more on the pop side of psychedelia than the underground events staged elsewhere. The Jimi Hendrix Experience headlined the final Monday evening, as they conducted their own super-exhaustive scouring of every stage in the land; behind them, the Small Faces, Eric Burdon's Animals, Dantalion's Chariot, Family, Al Stewart, the Bee Gees, the Alan Price Set, Zoot Money's Big Roll Band, Marmalade, Tomorrow, Blossom Toes, the Syn, Tintern Abbey and Breakthru completed the line-up

The weekend had already enjoyed its fair share of drama, beginning with the arrival of a balloon from which thousands of flowers were dropped onto the arriving crowds. Things became even more dramatic, however, when Marmalade – still comparative unknowns, without a hit to their name – decided to hand sparklers out to the audience as they completed their set. The crowd hung onto them for a while, but then began tossing them back towards the stage, the occasional throw lifting the still-smouldering sticks way over their target and onto the cloth canopy that overhung the stage. The next band on, Tomorrow, were still early in their set when somebody noticed the inevitable – the stage was crowned in flames.

There was no serious damage, and no injuries – indeed, the event was deemed such a success that it was staged again the following July with several of the same participants. Nevertheless, Tomorrow's set was cut dramatically short, and the tabloids had a field day to the exclusion, more or less, of any real coverage for the rest of the festival. Neither do any of the other key participants seem to recall the event with any particular clarity: "Woburn... Woburn... that was the one where they had the fire, wasn't it?" Hendrix bassist Noel Redding recalled 30 years later. "We were playing so many of those outdoor things, though... I'd need to check my diary. I remember Beck, though. Jimi loved that band. He always said they reminded him of being back in New York, checking out some mad R&B group in Harlem. And Christ, they were loud!"

"What I want to do, what I'm trying to do, is produce the white equivalent of coloured music", Beck told *Record Mirror*. "I really hate white music. When you take good white records, and there are some – for example, 'A Whiter Shade Of Pale' and 'Groovin'', the reason they're good is because they sound coloured."

One could probably argue that point... "A Whiter Shade Of Pale" sounds like a lot of things, but "coloured" is not one of them. Yet Beck was not to be deflected. "I've studied Negro music, by listening to it a lot. And I have records by coloured musicians dating from the 1920s right up to the present time." Constantly listening to them, constantly learning from them, he was now constantly trying to update them to capture "the same feeling in my playing, not just an imitation of the coloured sound but real soul." Other guitarists pursued similar goals, but aimed for authenticity. Beck demanded originality as well.

"We used to take things like John Lee Hooker and Muddy Waters and all the great bluesmen, and play them our way, which is the way to do it," Stewart reflected, while Beck continued, "we were trying a lot of covers of less well-known songs off the Stax label, Otis Redding things, anything to break out of the blues mould. We were doing things like 'Neighbour Neighbour', some Jimmy Ruffin stuff, stuff that we could take and supercharge a little. It was a very minimalist feel, but it suited us, and although we did get a lot of shit thrown at us, that just made us all the more determined to do things our way." Indeed, Beck occasionally appeared to go out of his way to encourage the shit-throwing... captured on a live recording of a Marquee show in September, is Beck's response to Stewart telling him to "play the blues". He launches into the main theme from *Bridge Over The River Kwai*.

The Marquee was to become one of the Beck Group's most reliable stomping grounds as they made their way around the club circuit during 1967 – they appeared there four times during the year, and the survival of a full, 11-song tape of their third visit, in September, offers up the closest approximation we could hope to hear of the now aborted live album – and, perhaps, the most pertinent reason why that album didn't emerge.

Ollie Halsall, guitarist with the opening Timebox, once remarked, "the only thing I remember about that night was the noise Beck was making – he was probably playing better at that time than he ever did again, in terms of seeing what he could do with the guitar."

Authors Christopher Hjort and Doug Hinman, in their voluminous chronology of Beck's entire career, *Jeff's Book*, agreed with him. "Where many of (Beck's) 1967 colleagues strive to forge a smooth sound, Beck seems intent on throwing aesthetics out of the window in favour of a pure yet dirty tone. The poor guitar twists and turns in Beck's hands, squeezed to uncontrolled feedback, as he bends the strings in either big, swooping lines or in sudden outbursts of energy." Indeed, it is hard to imagine (let alone locate) any other band of the age putting on quite so destructive-sounding a performance – even Hendrix, who was certainly no stranger to torturing his instrument, alleviated the impact with his showmanship and flash.

Nine months ago, Beck had so feared the impact that Jimi Hendrix might have on his freedom to play his own style that he all but contemplated giving up, mortified to discover that tricks he'd made his own over the years, visual flourishes and sonic assaults alike, needed to be reconsidered, redesigned, revamped. That fear was still there – some nights, Beck would find physically fighting against his own instincts, desperate to pull out some kind of grand statement but holding back, just in case Hendrix had already done the same thing the night before. But it also gave him new strength, power and, above all, a menacing presence that, once seen, was never forgotten.

Beck scarcely moved on stage, except to emphasise the effort he was putting into wringing his instrument's neck. And, though the band certainly donned their share of period costume (offstage, Beck was especially fond of a wolverine fur coat), there, their concessions to anything remotely resembling the Summer of Love abruptly ended. In another year's time, the Stones and the Who would fancy themselves as cheerleaders for a new revival in dirty old rock'n'roll, returning to their earliest roots to revisit Cochran, Chuck Berry and so on again. The Jeff Beck Group had been there all along.

"There weren't too many people doing what we were doing", Beck recalled. "There was a half-dozen of us in a sort of circle around the London area" – the Jeff Beck Group, the Jimi Hendrix Experience, Cream, the Who, the dying embers of the Yardbirds – "keeping tabs on one another. You were more interested in what the others had to say, not outdoing one another. You wanted them to fail, but you would have died if they had."

Indeed, on the one occasion Beck did seem to dismiss his peers' latest activities, the firestorm of protest that his words invoked forced him very swiftly, and very publicly, to back down. Remarking how Eric Clapton remained "the greatest blues guitarist in the country, and always will be", Beck then suggested that that was all he was. "As far as I'm concerned, the wild sounds of Jimi Hendrix and the Cream are finished. The latest albums by both of these groups (Axis Bold As Love and Disraeli Gears) were not at all sensational. Nothing new in them."

A week of howling protest later, Beck was denying he'd ever said those words. "What I said was, if they didn't look after their public in this country, they might lose their tremendous popularity. The actual sounds, the music they make, are fantastic." Nevertheless, it was apparent that Beck did not necessarily relish the wild experimentation and manic artfulness that was passing for music at the time. In much the same breath, after all, as he now praised Clapton, Hendrix and Townshend – "I'd love to play with (the Who) – the guitarist is fantastic" – he was also extolling the guitar-playing ambitions of his dog. "Pudding is a born guitarist. The only trouble is that (he) chews up the neck of any guitar that I give him."

For all their refusal to espouse the values of the summer of love, of course, the Jeff Beck Group had no problems filling the various Temples of Hippy; in fact, just a month after the Woburn Festival, they were racing back to London from an evening show in Dartford to headline UFO, long transplanted from its original basement home to the Chalk Farm Roundhouse. There, Beck would be joined on the bill by two alternative media attractions, the lights and sounds of Mark Boyle's New Sensual Laboratory – UFO regulars and pioneers of the lightshows that would come to dominate the 1970s rock landscape – and the luscious charms of the Contessa Veronica, the actress/dancer best remembered today for her role in the psychedelic sci-fi sex romp *Zeta One*.

Fears that the Jeff Beck Group might somehow appear at odds with such surroundings, however, were readily disqualified the moment they caught sight of the evening's opening act. Alvin Lee's Ten Years After was a band whose name meant little outside of the hardcore blues circuit, but was destined to help rewrite the blues rulebook.

There was a little sniping before the show, naturally. Despite their youth, Ten Years After had already pushed their debut album onto the shelves, an eponymous behemoth produced by blues supremo Mike Vernon, and the impression that Beck had been sorely misused (nor to mention under-rated) when he was passed onto Mickie Most was never so pronounced as when those two bands shared the stage. For Beck matched Ten Years After in every department – not because he was the headliner, or because he was the "star", but because the his group weren't simply coming from the same place as Lee's, they had essentially built it for them. TYA were just lucky enough to reap the immediate rewards.

As Beck himself has said on numerous occasions, it is pointless playing 'what if' with his past history. But still it's impossible not to wonder what might have transpired had the Beck Group been signed by Decca, recorded in West Hampstead and been produced by Mike Vernon.

Of course we'll never know. But it might have sounded a lot like the BBC session that the Jeff Beck Group taped at the beginning of November. The previous month had seen the band return to the BBC to record a three-song session for the newly-launched Radio One's *David Symonds Show*, and "Rock My Plimsoul", "Let Me Love You" and an instrumental jam called "Walking By The Railings" were as dynamic as the Beck Group had sounded all year. But even that performance was crushed when the band turned out for John Peel's *Top Gear* on 1 November.

The band recorded under the supervision of producer Bev Phillips – the man who also wrung career-best performances out of Cream and Hendrix, when they dropped by the BBC, and who John Peel once credited among the truly motivating forces when it came to turning Radio One on to underground rock: "In the teeth of opposition from middle management, much of what went on in the early days of Radio One was due to Bernie and... Bev Phillips, his right-hand man and engineer."

Having loosening up with a fiery romp through "Beck's Bolero", Phillips led the Jeff Beck Group through five songs, "Ain't Superstitious" and "You Shook Me", Stewart's stupendous version of "Loving You Is Sweeter Than Ever", and "You'll Never Get To Heaven If You Break My Heart", all packing a punch that vindicated all of Beck's ambitions for (and Jimi Hendrix's descriptions of) their sound.

Unfortunately, it was not necessarily the quest for musical perfection that could render the Jeff Beck Group's sound so perfect, at least according to Peter Grant. "The one thing about that band, that I thank God never witnessed with any other, was this. They played best when they were at each other's throats. All you needed was for one of them to turn up pissed off about something, and they would play like their lives depended on it."

Right now, it was Ron Wood who was pissed off. Six months had passed since he last strapped on a rhythm guitar, six months during which Beck constantly reiterated his promise to start auditioning bass players "soon" – and not one had passed through the rehearsal room doors. Maybe it was time, Woody decided, to force the issue once and for all. After all, if Beck didn't want him to play guitar (or not play bass – he was never quite certain which it was), someone else was bound to.

In early October, Wood took his first step outside the Jeff Beck Group to guest alongside the Crazy World Of Arthur Brown at the recording of their debut BBC session. Still some months away from igniting fame with the chart-topping "Fire", the Crazy World were nevertheless regarded among the most promising, and insistently intriguing bands on the London underground, their repertoire a combination of spine-chilling band originals and butchered swamp blues covers – "I'm Your Witch Doctor" and "I Put A Spell On You" were both coerced into this maiden BBC broadcast, alongside Brown originals "Time", "Nightmare" and "Devil's Grip" (the group's recently released debut single). Songs arranged for the group's traditional line-up of vocals, organ and drums, but opening up anyway to accept Wood's slashing, simmering guitar.

It was a joyous experience, an eye-opening excursion. No less than his bandmates, Wood had enjoyed sneering at the psychedelic traces that draped so many other group's music like the fashionable baubles and streamers they were. But now he came to actually try his hand at playing them, he found they really weren't so bad... were rather challenging in their own funny way, and a helluva lot more rewarding than simply banging away on a bass all night. So, when Kim Gardner called him a few nights later to ask if he was busy, Woody was tempted to tell him, "no, not at all."

Since the demise of the Birds, and the non-starting possibility of linking with Wood in the Beck Group, Gardner had joined the Creation, a band that modern history now justly ranks among the crop of mid-1960s bands who bridged the musical gap between R&B and Psychedelia – Freakbeat, as modern ears term it – and made possible a lot of what was to follow.

Certainly they'd pumped out a string of borderline classic singles over the past year, and they were more or less established as superstars in Germany. But line-up changes constantly wrinkled the group, and in late 1967, one more departure left them in desperate need of a guitarist on the eve of their latest tours of Germany and Switzerland. Drummer Jack Jones told Creation biographer Sean Egan, "We had to find a guitarist and we had to find one quick. Of course Kim knew Ronnie Wood... (he) said 'Ronnie's not doing anything. He's talking about going to America with Jeff Beck, but that's not going to be for a year – and, if it works out, he could stay with the band. Why don't we try Ronnie?' So Ronnie came down, we got it together and it was fine..."

In fact, Wood turned down the Creation's first approach, but started regretting it almost from the moment the words were out of his mouth. He made amends, though, when they came back to him a few days later, despairing over the hastily recruited replacement they'd picked up in his stead.

He could make no long-term promises. He'd play the Swiss and German dates, and think about the future when they got to it – as Jack Jones continued, "He's a good lad, Ronnie, but... I don't think he was ever one hundred per cent committed. You always (got) the feeling that, if Jeff Beck gave a call, then Ronnie would be gone."

Gigging with Beck through November and December, Wood initially did a remarkable job of juggling his Beck commitments with his Creation workload. But he was absent from the group's next recording session, at Abbey Road in December, as pianist Nicky Hopkins recounted.

"The whole thing with the Beck Group that surprised me was (that) there wasn't actually a group. It was Jeff and Rod, plus whichever drummer they hadn't managed to piss off lately, and Woody floating around, pretty much playing when he felt like it, and not turning up if he had something else to do." Hopkins was quick, too, to pick up on the friction that constantly sparked between Beck and Stewart. "I remember looking over at Madeleine (Bell, backing vocalist at the session) and we were both thinking the same thing: 'Can you imagine being stuck in a room with this pair all the time?'"

Although Hopkins remembered playing on "two or three songs" on this occasion, the session actually produced just one finished take – a raw version of "I've Been Drinking", characterised by what Beck describes as some "shit hot" singing from Stewart, "good" playing by the rest of the band, and a "fucking terrible" kazoo-shaped guitar solo he still wishes would disappear. "I hate that tone." One development that he would want to explore further, however, was the addition of a new member. He'd always enjoyed having Nicky Hopkins as a friend. Now he wanted him to have him as a bandmate as well.

Indeed, over the next few weeks, Beck and Hopkins seemed to run into one another everywhere they went , around the clubs at night and in the studio by day. They were reunited early in the New Year, at a session for Paul Jones' next B-side, "The Dog Presides": Peter Asher, one half of the Peter & Gordon singing duo, was producing; Mike Vickers, another former Manfred, was handling the arrangement, Paul Samwell-Smith was on bass, and Asher's sister Jane's boyfriend, Paul McCartney, was playing drums. "I remember hoping Paul was going to sing," Beck recalled of the session three decades later; he didn't, but Beck and Hopkins enjoyed themselves egging him on and, when Beck met with Mickie Most a few days later, to discuss the session for his own next 45, he asked that Hopkins be included in the party.

Most, who had already lined up Clem Cattini, a female choir and a full orchestra for the occasion, nodded. The record already had the figurative kitchen sink in place. There might as well be a piano in there.

CHAPTER
SIXTEEN

The Eurovision Song Contest has never really been about songs. Local politics, yes. Pretty faces, yes. Eye-catching dance routines and silly bing-a-bong choruses, yes. But songs?

Vicki Leandros certainly didn't think so. When the nations of Europe lined up in readiness for the 1967 event, only one song out of all the contestants seemed guaranteed victory – her own performance of "L'Amour Est Bleu", a beautiful sentiment, a haunting melody, a gorgeous refrain. Nobody could believe it as the evening's votes mounted up, and "L'Amour Est Bleu" slipped further and further from any chance of victory... of the runners-up position, of even a closely-run third. "L'Amour Est Bleu" finished in fourth place, Leandros' Luxembourgian associates were horrified and, across Europe, lounge acts and pianists hung their heads in despair. They'd spent weeks perfecting their own versions of the song – but who would want to listen to them now?

A lot more people than anyone expected. "L'Amour Est Bleu" may have tanked at Eurovision, but long after the winning British "Puppet On A String" had been forgotten, and the French and Irish entries consigned to that dark place where all losing Euro-numbers go, "L'Amour Est Bleu" remained on people's lips. First, Leandros' version began rising up sundry national charts; then, when French orchestra leader Paul Mauriat rearranged it for aching strings, he scored the biggest hit of his life.

A British release for the Mauriat rendition was scheduled for late January 1968, and nobody doubted that it would prove as monstrously successful in the UK as it had across the continent. Nobody, that is, apart from Mickie Most. He, too, agreed that "Love Is Blue" would be a hit. But he'd said that about "Hi Ho Silver Lining" as well, when he first found out that the Attack would be recording it. The song itself was a hit. But who would the lucky performer be?

In the event, Beck's version would come in a merely honourable second in the race for the top; while Mauriat's rendition reached Number 12 in Britain and topped the American chart, Beck climbed no higher than Number 23 at home, although he did enjoy by far the more inventive promotional campaign. "For Valentine's Day", the adverts declared, "you still have time to send Jeff Beck's 'Love Is Blue' instead of a card."

But, of the two, it is Beck's version that is best remembered by his own fans, with an embarrassed squirm, if not admiration.

Neither history nor Jeff Beck himself have ever revealed the guitarist's reaction when he first heard what Most had in store for him. Part of him, he later agreed, was absolutely horrified: "Mickie Most was a recording producer. He didn't care tuppence about the music, he just wanted me on the Columbia label, and he wanted hit after hit under his control. It was a very dodgy Mickie Most move, because he normally comes up with original material. But he found this crap cover of a French love song... and I don't even remember making that record."

But part of him found the entire gesture so perverse that it was difficult not to admire it. "It really was the Plan 9 From Outer Space of a Jeff Beck record, the equivalent of that. It was junk. But, now I think, what would life be, without Plan 9 From Outer Space every so often? I'm becoming softened to those records. I've got used to them. Because if they've annoyed other people as much as they've embarrassed me, I think there's a happy balance there." Besides, as he told *Disc & Music Echo* at the time, "the fantastic thing is, I really like the melody."

He also argued that, in some ways, the record reflected his own ambitions, the prospect of abandoning conventional rock altogether and producing "guitar concerts – using a large orchestra to back me. Just as a singer gives a concert, I'd like to do the same thing with my guitar. And I think that releasing a record like 'Love Is Blue' is a step in that direction."

He didn't, he insisted, want to be the "Engelbert Humperdinck of the guitar" that Mickie Most still liked to suggest. "But I'd like to have the sort of successful career that Engelbert and the Shadows enjoy." What, after all, "do the fans want from me? I know blues is my scene, but everybody's doing it."

In some ways, he continued, he was spoiled for choice. "When I was with the Yardbirds, I was restricted so badly that I used to be like a naughty boy and play all these weird things all the time. Now I've got my own band and it's like being in my own field." He compared his predicament to "a little child, (being given) a piece of ground to play in, a huge 20-mile field, and told 'play.' He has all the space to play in and he'll probably just sit down and do nothing. There's so much (I can) do that it is really difficult (to decide)."

He was not, of course, proposing to abandon the Jeff Beck Group itself. "In fact, we've just changed our name to Jeff Beck's Million Dollar Bash, and we've started using a rock'n'roll pianist as well. So that scene will obviously carry on for a while." But he was also open to the possibility that the band might never lift itself out of the live circuit and onto vinyl, and that it was vital he keep all his other options open.

Nicky Hopkins – the "rock'n'roll pianist" in question – had not, in fact, joined the band at the time; was merely mulling over the offer he'd been made. Although he recalled rehearsing a few times with the full band around this time ("although it might have been later... I was doing a lot of things during that whole period, hard to keep them all straight"). Neither had the Jeff Beck Group changed its name. In fact, with Wood back on board in early February, his Creation vacation apparently at an end, the Jeff Beck Group simply picked up where it left off before Christmas, on the road again.

As before, too, the majority of the shows were on the same old bread-and-butter circuit, but hindsight, at least, allows a few to stand out. On 9 March, the Jeff Beck Group touched down at Middle Earth, the hippy hideaway in London's Covent Garden, to top the bill over Marc Bolan and Steve Peregrine Took's Tyrannosaurus Rex. The duo had just recorded their second session for the BBC, and work was now beginning on their debut album. But Bolan was brimming with confidence regardless, later telling manager Tony Secunda, "even when I started, I had an audience – we blew Jeff Beck and Rod Stewart off stage."

Another memorable night, so far as the support group was concerned, came when the Group visited Hull a week later. Opening tonight were the Rats, a deeply blues-drenched local band whose lead guitarist, Mick Ronson, was a confirmed Beck fanatic. "Before the show, I went up to Jeff and we were talking, and I asked him about 'Jeff's Boogie,' how he did (a certain part)", Ronson recalled 20 years later. "So he showed me, in the dressing room before we went on."

Days later, "Jeff's Boogie" was incorporated into the Rats' live show, alongside another number they heard that night, Tim Rose's "Morning Dew". "Benny (Rats vocalist Benny Marshall) recorded the Beck Group's entire show, and we learned all the songs, all the licks", Ronson confided 20 years later. "The next time we played, we had 'Morning Dew' down as well."

"Morning Dew" was a relatively recent arrival in the Beck Group's live set, implanted there by, of all people, Lulu. She herself first encountered the song during 1967, and brought it along to a recording session, insisting that it would be her next single. Mickie Most, however, disagreed and, though the song was recorded (it later brought Lulu a minor American hit), so far as she was concerned, it was a dead issue – until it turned up in Beck's repertoire. "I bet I was the one that suggested it", she speculated. "I was mad about Tim Rose."

In fact, Beck and Stewart swiftly joined her in his fan club; the American was gigging regularly around the UK now (with a backing band that included drummer John Bonham), and the pair caught his show whenever they were able. Indeed, there was talk of Rose composing further numbers for the Jeff Beck Group, but though he delivered a few, "unfortunately, we didn't get any more 'Morning Dews'."

It was in the midst of this latest spate of live shows that the Creation came calling for Woody again. A handful of recording sessions were looming, together with what looked like a very lucrative Spanish tour. Beck's immediate itinerary, on the other hand, involved a whole lot of nothing, broken only by more club gigs grinding up and down the UK and a low-key hop across to the continent. Wood weighed the merits of both in his mind, then took the only option that promised to be enjoyable. Beck would have to find himself a new bassist.

He settled upon John 'Junior' Wood, formerly of Tomorrow, and now one half of the duo Aquarian Age, with that same (now shattered) band's drummer, Twink. But any enthusiasm and excitement that surrounded this new beginning – at last, a "real" bass player! – was to be savagely undone over the course of the next few weeks.

The continental dates opened in Chur, Switzerland, on 15 April before moving on to Denmark, Sweden and France for a two-week outing that divided the local press even more furiously than the hit singles had splintered Beck's home audience. Night after night, audiences reeled home disappointed, shocked not by the volume and violence of the live show, but by the sheer unprofessionalism of it.

"It is sad when your old idols fail to deliver," groaned Gothenburg's *Tidningen* following the first Swedish date, and it was being polite. The rival *Posten*, on the other hand, was pulling no punches whatsoever.

Beck was bad enough, as his guitar ran the gamut of "funny sounds", from "an air alarm (to) a big dog." But Rod Stewart was even worse. "To sing the blues is not to scream and moan. This combination of young white musicians and blues is not ideal." Even worse, the taped evidence (the following evening's show in Stockholm was recorded from the audience) bears out these criticisms, and then some. The entire band sounds half-hearted and haphazard, with Beck and Stewart seemingly playing from entirely different songsheets.

A performance at the Brondby Pop Club in Copenhagen was no less tense, as the Jeff Beck Group found themselves sharing a bill with Ten Years After, the local Baronets, and the Tages, a Swedish band whose local renown exceeded every other group on the bill. Vocalist Tommy Blom later remembered Beck seriously considering surrendering his headline slot to the Tages – with two hits on the Danish chart, the Swedes were the main reason why much of the audience had turned up.

In the event, Beck did close the show, but he would quickly come to regret it as the band turned in a performance that tapped lows they'd never even come close to before. And the worst of it was, they didn't seem to care – only Beck, surveying the post-show wreckage of his fans' expectations, seemed to comprehend precisely how badly they'd let the audience down, and he rushed to make amends; the Jeff Beck Group would return to Copenhagen in a week's time, to play another show. It would be his way of apologising for this evening's shambles.

It was clear that Junior Wood wasn't working out. Even though he could scarcely be blamed for all the flaws and faults that bedevilled the European dates, it was obvious to all that the Jeff Beck Group was lacking something... someone. By the time they returned to England in early May, Wood had already passed back to the Aquarian Age and Ron Wood, himself home again, was invited – if not physically begged – back into the fold. And, though his initial response was to turn down the entreaty, he didn't, for at long last Beck had something concrete to offer him. Two somethings, in fact. First, Mickie Most had finally consented to an album; and second, they were going to America.

Wood quit the Creation on the spot, as Jack Jones recalls. "One day he walked in and said 'I'm sorry, lads, I've always wanted to go to America and Jeff's putting a band together. I'm going to have to leave." He played his last ever gig with the band on 18 April 1968, within the strangely salubrious surroundings of the John Lewis department store on Oxford

Street, London – the shop's owners had clocked the growing fad for putting on live bands in the hipper discotheques and decided to grab some of the action for themselves. It was a lesson that Mickie Most was also about to learn.

"Mickie really didn't give a shit about touring America because that wasn't his stomping ground", Beck explained. "He had more of a control over Europe and England, (but) Peter Grant recognised a twinkle in my eye... we met across a crowded room, and I said 'Let's get the fuck out of here, and go tour America. Because there are big things happening there.' I was saying 'What the hell are we doing grinding up and down half a dozen shitholes in England, when we could be doing two million shitholes in the States?' And Peter said 'Let me look into it.'

"In the States at that time, there was this serious underground thing going on, with Steppenwolf, Vanilla Fudge, Blue Cheer, Paul Butterfield, all that stuff. In Britain, the blues were everything; straight, unadulterated, faithful blues, which we simply didn't play. We wanted to mess with them a bit, and anything would go in the States, they were ready for anything. They were expecting it. They didn't particularly want us to play blues, they wanted progressive rock. So we let them have it; we went over there and we completely flattened New York on our first ever appearance."

Grant could not, however, take all the credit for arranging the tour. His partner, too, had a sizeable say in the matter, but it was not Grant's powers of persuasion that made the difference. It was the news that the Yardbirds were breaking up. Although their work with Most – the Little Games album and a clutch of decidedly un-Yardbirds-like singles – had never recaptured the band's glory days, they remained a fair attraction in the United States, not only on record and on the road but in the Epic Records boardroom as well. The split was still more or less unspoken, but Keith Relf and Jim McCarty were clearly pulling in one direction; Jimmy Page and Chris Dreja in another. The group's remaining lifespan could surely be measured in months now, if not weeks, and Most knew that their demise would leave a sizeable hole in his American profile. Who better to plug it than the Jeff Beck Group?

Beck knew this, but still he credited Grant with a lot more than simply acting as a buffer-cum-go-between betwixt himself and Mickie Most. Most managers are only there when it's time to share in the glory. Grant, however, would be around for the bad times as well, mucking in as a roadie when the band was on the road, and stepping in as extra muscle when the occasion called for that. Promoters always thought twice about short-changing an act when confronted with the full force of Man-Mountain Grant, and even the most leech-like hangers-on could easily be dislodged once Peter set his mind to it.

Of course, he could be a hard task-master for his own charges if and when he felt the need – when Simon Napier-Bell warned him that the Yardbirds could sometimes prove a handful, Grant simply laughed "I'll just hang them out the first floor window." "He would have as well," Napier-Bell confided.

But Grant was more than mere brawn. Beck continued, "We brought Peter Grant in to oversee everything. People talk about the band's musical influence, but if I have anything at all to do with the development of heavy metal, I apologise." Where the Jeff Beck Group made their greatest contribution to the future of rock'n'roll, he insisted, was on the other side of the business table.

"Until we came along, nobody had any control over what was going on. Managers didn't – they barely knew where we were playing, half the time. And roadies knew who to go to, to get the money from, but very often, they never got it – 'Sorry chaps, the promoter's fucked off to Florida for the weekend.' Peter Grant was one of the first guys to start shouting the odds, and get them – and if I have anything to do with musicians having control, with them not getting ripped off all the time, and managers coming in who actually care about their artists, I'm pleased, because up to that point, managers were running away with money, promoters were running away with the money, the band was the underdog left high and dry."

America promised more than fair play, however. Despite the income generated by Beck's own three hits, the Jeff Beck Group itself was not making money in Britain; indeed, Rod Stewart later revealed, "We were literally down to our last crumb. We had nothing left. But Peter Grant was smart enough to see (what was) happening in America, where bands were making it without being seen on the surface – newspapers, records, none of that. So he said 'I'm gonna put you out there.' It was a last-ditch thing to keep the band going."

CHAPTER
SEVENTEEN

The Jeff Beck Group's first American tour was originally scheduled to kick off in Boston, at the legendary Tea Party, on 28 May. The Yardbirds would be into the final stretch of their own latest tour by then; the two parties would then meet up in New York in the middle of June, at which point Peter Grant would wave goodbye to the Yardbirds, then head back out on the road with the Beck band.

Somewhere down the line, however, somebody (Grant said it was Mickie Most) realised that it would work out a lot cheaper to simply employ the same road crew for Beck as was already worked with the Yardbirds rather than have to hire two crews to essentially do the same job. Just cancel the first 17 days' worth of Beck shows, and they'd save a small fortune.

Grant agreed, the scheme made sense. The only problem with that scenario was, somebody would have to break the news to Beck that, little more than a year after he'd last blown off an American tour at the end of his own time with the Yardbirds, he was about to do it again. Most, however, simply smiled. They'd just have to come up with something to take his mind off it. And before he said another word, Grant knew exactly what he intended.

"Jeff could be a bit of a broken record sometimes", Grant laughed. "Make an album, tour the States, make an album, tour the States. And Mickie just didn't see the point. He was having hits, but nothing so huge that it demanded an LP. Mickie didn't like making LPs to begin with – he did them with the Animals and Herman, because the American label kept asking for them. And he did them with Donovan, because Don was a songwriter, that's what he did. But the Beck Group was just something Jeff did in between the hits. It wasn't a 'real' group, to Mickie's way of thinking. It was more like a hobby. But he knew Jeff would be furious about cancelling the American shows, so he threw him an album as a consolation prize."

Most had another agenda as well, however. For more than a year now, he'd sat and listened to Beck and his band complaining about the sort of music they didn't want to be recording – the "Hi Ho Silver Lining"'s and "Love Is Blue"'s of the world. Now was their chance to show him what they did want to do. And faced with such an unequivocal moment of decision, the quartet had to admit – they didn't have a clue.

"We had a great sound," Beck says, "but nobody had written any songs. We needed a writer, but we didn't have time to mess around writing songs. We had to go on the road and do something."

Stewart, Beck acknowledged, would occasionally put pen to paper. "But Rod wrote folk songs then, he was into Dylany-type lyrics, 'If I

Were A Carpenter' type lyrics, which wouldn't really have worked out for us." All they could do was what they'd been doing all along, "playing a lot of blues, and trying to rework them in an interesting way. We were obsessed with Motown, but we knew we couldn't write anything as good as that."

It would have made all the difference, he admitted, "if someone had invested in a week of time scouting for some writers, and made us listen"; it might even have helped if they'd actually been given some warning about the imminent sessions, and a few weeks in which to try and prepare. Instead, Beck told journalist Charles Shaar Murray in 2005, "we came straight off the road and into Abbey Road, set up the gear and just performed a set."

At the same time, however, "we didn't want to simply regurgitate our live show, because we'd already been playing that for six months. So we encouraged each other to come up with off-the-wall suggestions."

It was that decision which ensured great swathes of what was now a phenomenal live show would be left by the wayside – "Stone Crazy", "Talk To Me Baby", "I Think I'll Be Leaving This Morning", "Bye Bye Baby", "(I Know) I'm Losing You", and "Oh, Pretty Woman" were all abandoned. Another live staple, Stewart's showcase "(I Know) I'm Losing You", would remain unrecorded until the singer taped his third solo album.

In their stead, however, came performances that remain legendary today. A dramatic and uniquely brooding version of "Old Man River", says Beck, was one of Stewart's ideas. "At least, I think it was. I really can't imagine that I'd have gone into the studio and said 'Rod, sing "Old Man River"!' Rod loved Paul Robeson." And it showed. Although Beck acknowledged that the performance could – should – have been even more powerful, still he could not fault Stewart's performance. "Great singing, really splendid. Bloody brilliant. We just needed choral voices sitting on top of it, to justify that classical timp sound. I really hear an angelic churchy choir, and then guitar solo for days on the end of it." The timpani, incidentally, was delivered by Keith Moon... "You Know WHO", as the original album liner notes punned.

The inspiration for a gorgeous instrumental version of the traditional "Greensleeves", on the other hand, came from Mickie Most. "Mickie had a J200 Gibson, I think it was, and I was playing around with it, and just went through "Greensleeves". And he says 'That's great, that's going on the record.' I said 'Alright, let's do it then,' and he said 'You've already done it. I had everything on tape, thanks very much'."

The most amazing aspect of that, however, was that Most himself spent very little time at the studio. Faced with having to divide his production skills between the Jeff Beck Group's album and a new Donovan project, being recorded on the other side of London at Olympic Studios, he opted to leave Beck in the hands of engineer Ken Scott. "Ken was an ex-BBC guy who knew how to work a desk properly", Beck laughs, "and I just pushed him left and right and up the middle and whatever I could get out of him." Most, on the other hand, "was yachting in Cannes and just generally swanking about the place. Technically, he probably doesn't know one reel of tape from another."

Scott impressed Beck from the outset. "Our first day there, I said 'do you mind if I touch these controls? Because if you do mind, you can go now.' And he was 'go right ahead.' Unfortunately, we were only in there for a very short time, but I think he was learning as much as I learned about what we were doing, and what we could do, because we couldn't go anywhere near what, say, Jimi Hendrix was doing, with wild left-right panning and fancy sounds, we were just a blues band with rock overtones."

Stewart, too, was happy to see the back of Most. "As far as I was concerned, what we were doing didn't need producers, and I remember telling Jeff this. So I really don't think, with all due respect, that Mickie Most had much to do with producing the Jeff Beck Group. It was done by the four blokes in the band." And Ken Scott.

It was Scott, Most himself remembers, who came up with one of the most revolutionary effects on the entire record, the strangled roar which erupted out of Beck's guitar. "I said to Ken... 'I'm just going over to Olympic and I won't be long, so I want you to get a nice heavy guitar sound for Jeff." He came back to find Beck's amplifier locked in a cupboard, with a microphone standing outside.

There were so many highlights on the album: "Let Me Love You", which made up with pyrotechnics all that it lacked in lyrical finesse; the rip-roaring "Blues Deluxe"; and a couple of savagely transformed Willie Dixon staples, "You Shook Me" and "I Ain't Superstitious". There was also a murderous rendition of "Morning Dew" (one of two songs Nicky Hopkins would appear on), but the key to the album was a revision of the Yardbirds' "Shapes Of Things".

The band had already incorporated "The Sun Is Shining" and the guitar improvisation "Jeff's Boogie" into their live show; now they turned their attention to one of the Yardbirds' biggest hits. "That was another idea of Rod's", Beck acknowledged. "He loved the Yardbirds, and thought I was mad to leave them – he used to say he was thrilled to bits to be almost replacing Keith Relf, because the outfit we put together around ourselves was not dissimilar to the Yardbirds. So I said we'd do the song, but only if I could rearrange it, so I did that – slowed it down half a tempo, turned it into more of a grungy, rocky thing."

Armed with his Sho-Bud steel guitar, Beck transformed the song into what he still proudly describes as a slab of "dirty... evil" sound – "we were always messing around with other instruments, to see how they'd work", he recalled, singling out his wah-wah technique on "I Ain't Superstitious" as an example of how, though others had already introduced the pedal to their recordings, the Beck Group still marched fearlessly where none had dared to tread.

The wah-wah pedal made its bow on the British rock scene in early 1967 – Jimi Hendrix imported the first, Eric Clapton (in New York with Cream, that February) brought over the second, and immediately pressed it into action on "Tales Of Brave Ulysses", a cut destined for the group's then-gestating second album. Hendrix followed through with "The Burning Of The Midnight Lamp" and, where the masters led, countless others followed. But still Beck could describe "I Ain't Superstitious" as an "early wah-wah novelty. I liked the Cry-baby pedal (that those others utilised), but it was bloody irritating after a while. Clapton and Hendrix were using (wah-wah) differently, I wanted it more like a war club, so I found the holes for it. I put slap echo on it to accentuate the edge."

With the cancellation of the American dates, RAK arranged a bunch of British club dates to keep the band fresh, then slotted in recording sessions in between the gigs. It was a madcap schedule that meant what became Truth "took two weeks to record." But, said Beck, "it was a delight. We were so ready to record, because we'd been on the road for eight months, ten months at that point. I think we cut the basics in about four days, then we fiddled around. We added John Paul Jones on bass in a few places, some timpani on "Old Man River"... I stuck "Beck's Bolero" on there, to fill it up a little more..." When Mickie Most came round, asking where the next single was, everybody grinned guiltily, and admitted they really hadn't thought about such things.

The final album sessions fell at the end of May, as a few final numbers were recorded (the unreleased "Long Blues" among them), the existing tapes were mixed and, as if in remembrance of the abandoned live album, some canned applause was added to "Blues Deluxe" – "for ambience", Beck insisted. "A spacey blues at this tempo needs something to give it some arena-type space. So we had great fun with a sound effects album, (although) I think we overdid it a bit."

They found time, too, to finalise a cover that, in itself, was to become as influential an icon as the music itself. The wild psychedelics that had characterised the previous year or so's LP sleeves had fallen far from fashion in recent months, and the multi-textured, super-detailed likes of Sgt Pepper, Satanic Majesties and Disraeli Gears already resembled relics from an ancient past.

The watchword now was simplicity – the unadorned party-invite the Stones would choose for Beggars Banquet (after Decca rejected their original vision of a heavily-graffiti'd toilet stall), the old-time tobacco tin of the Small Faces' Ogden's Nut Gone Flake, the plain white-on-white of the Beatles' eponymous double.

Truth would beat them all to the punch, a jet-black vista into which South African-born Stephen Goldblatt, a 22-year-old photographer at the Sunday Times, dropped a tiny but stunning portrait of girlfriend Celia Hammond. The only other intrusions were Beck's name (and Beck's alone – the Group did not get a look-in), and the album title. (Goldblatt would go on to become a successful cinematographer, with credits ranging from The Cotton Club to Lethal Weapon and on to Batman Forever).

Once the album was complete, it was back on the road... but not any old road this time. At last, the Jeff Beck Group was heading for America, for an eight-week outing they already knew would change their lives.

But still, according to Stewart, they packed light. "We had just one set of good clothes that had to last us the whole tour."

Peter Grant and Jimmy Page were waiting for them in New York. One pitfall of the delay in kicking off the tour was the fact that a fortnight's worth of low-key shows had perforcedly been cancelled, and the opening night was now what had once been a highlight, the Fillmore East in New York City, on 14 June.

Page had news for them – the Yardbirds had finally broken up, shattered by the rigours of touring behind an album (Little Games) that they really didn't believe in, and disillusioned by the band members' own sheer apathy towards a follow-up. The Yardbirds final recording session in New York on 2 June even saw them falter when presented with Page's "My Baby", a song that would soon be developing into the classic "Tangerine". Three days later, the group played their last ever American show, in Alabama; everybody knew that the clutch of British dates that awaited them upon their return home would be the end.

Beck was not shocked by the news – more shocking, to his mind, was the fact that the Yardbirds had even survived this long. "When I heard "Goodnight Sweet Josephine" I thought 'Boy, have you made a good move to get out of that!'" He was pleased, however, to find Page bubbling with enthusiasm for his next venture, whatever that might be, and thrilled to know his oldest friend would be watching as the Jeff Beck Group played its American debut.

San Francisco entrepreneur Bill Graham opened the Fillmore East in early 1968, the logical counterpart to the original hometown Fillmore within which the entire American psychedelic underground movement was fostered.

The new venue did not immediately prosper. A 60-year-old former movie theatre and meeting hall on Second and Sixth, on the Lower East Side, the place took weeks to get up and running, as years of neglect and water damage were repaired. Finally, 8 March 1968 brought the big opening – Big Brother, Tim Buckley and Albert King – but, though that night sold out, other shows weren't so fortunate and the Fillmore East was making a loss for months... all the more so, said Bill Graham, after Martin Luther King was assassinated on 4 April.

The Lower East Side was a predominantly black area; the Fillmore's target audience was white. Fear took a big bite out of the Fillmore's audience, that weekend and for several more to come; and, as if that wasn't enough, other problems benighted the fledgling venue, including the radical political groups around New York who seized upon the Californian philosophy of free love and free music, and translated that into the notion that they shouldn't have to pay for anything. The Hell's Angels moved into view for a time, the police and the unions were constantly breathing down Graham's neck.

Still, the Fillmore East was already as much a part of the American music scene as its Western counterpart, and though audiences remained tentative, they were no less demanding... maybe even more so. The Fillmore West was Hippy Central – Cream made their debut there in

August 1967, and Eric Clapton marvelled, "When we played the Fillmore for the first time, the band was in the light show. If you were in the audience, you didn't know who was playing. Not at all. It was a sensory thing."

The Fillmore East had its own light show, an even grander, more impressive one as well. But audiences were less likely to simply bliss out in the stalls, and let the music carry them wherever. They wanted action, they wanted edginess, they wanted... if not violence, then at least its musical equivalent. The bands that went down the best in New York were those that came closest to translating that ideal into action, with the Who (who played there at the height of the April unrest) at the very top of the pile.

Rod Stewart was scared to death. The Grateful Dead were headlining; the Jeff Beck Group was in the middle of the bill, and as they waited backstage, they could hear the audience filtering in, taking their seats, and rippling politely for the opening band, the electronic raga rock of Buzzy Linhart's Seventh Sons. At least, they rippled politely for a moment or two. Then they started booing – sporadically at first, but growing louder and more vociferous the more the hapless Sons went on.

In the dressing room, the Jeff Beck Group was working out an opening routine that would, Beck declared, stop everyone in their tracks, "two numbers in a segue, finished with a big RRRARRHHHH!" Stewart, however, was hardly listening. His ears were pinned exclusively to the noise outside, as the audience's outrage finally overwhelmed the opening act, and the performers beat a hasty retreat. By the time it was time for the next act – his act – to take the stage, Stewart could not control his panic.

He knew that Jeff Beck – the great Jeff Beck, the ex-Yardbird Jeff Beck – would not suffer the same fate as Buzzy Linhart. But what about his bandmates? Did anybody care that they were there; did anyone even want to hear him sing?

Stewart had encountered partisan Beck fans before, the glowering youths who would stand in front of the stage and stare, worshipping everything the guitarist deigned to do but merely mouthing threats and slurs when Stewart started to sing. That was in small English clubs, where a thousand-strong audience was regarded as huge. How many people were out there tonight? Two thousand? Three? This was America, after all. How many of them had guns? And how many would use them? The opening "Let Me Love You" was not even underway and Stewart hadn't simply lost his nerve. He was sure he'd lost his voice as well. So he did the only thing he could think of. He grabbed the little red bag in which he'd stashed a bottle of brandy before the show, wrapped himself up in his mackintosh and hat and ducked behind Beck's amplifier.

He still held the microphone. Out of sight of everyone, he opened his mouth. Astonishingly, a sound came out. He kept singing. Nobody shot at him. Okay, maybe this wasn't so bad after all. Just as long as he stayed tucked away, maybe he could get through the evening.

"Rod was hiding for about the first 15 or 20 minutes", Beck remembered. "I told the audience, 'in case you're wondering, I'm not singing. There is a singer behind my amplifier.' And he came out at the end of about four or five numbers, and they went berserk. We were crying, we were tearful, it was wonderful, and Rod just poured out this emotion. I'd never heard anything like it, he sang like I'd never heard him before. The blues, he just had everybody jumping in the air, and from there on we got great reviews; it was really quite emotional."

The *Village Voice* newspaper picks up the thread. "The Jeff Beck Group caused something like a mild furore... Arriving without a fanfare of advance publicity, their full-grown English hard rock, driving and together, caught everyone off-guard... They're going to be one of the hottest groups around."

The *New York Times*, too, was overwhelmed. "The group's principle format is the interaction between Mr Beck's wild, visionary guitar against the hoarse, insistent shouting of Rod Stewart", wrote critic Robert Shelton. "Their dialogue was lean and laconic, the verbal ping pong of a musical Pinter play... an auspicious beginning for an exciting group." And so on and so forth, a review so glowing that Peter Grant simply cut it out of the paper and had it messengered over to Epic Records.

As with every other RAK production of the age, Epic had first dibs on the unreleased Truth, but so far hadn't even mentioned it. Now they couldn't talk about anything else. By the end of the business day, the label hadn't simply agreed to release it, they'd already scheduled a rush-release. The album would reach American stores at the end of July (the UK wouldn't hear it until October), although Beck doubted whether his American label were ever quite certain what – or, rather, who – they'd signed.

That was confirmed the night the label bosses descended en masse to see the band play, then cornered Stewart backstage to voice their approval. "Hey Jeff, you sang great! Fucking good guitar player you got in the band as well."

CHAPTER
EIGHTEEN

O f all the plaudits that rained down upon the Jeff Beck Group, those that awaited Rod Stewart were loudest of all. Beck himself, after all, was already a known quantity, while the rhythm section... well, who really pays attention to the rhythm section? Stewart, though, stunned everybody – where had he been hiding all these years?

Alan Merrill was at the Fillmore for the Jeff Beck Group's second show; so, he says, was every other guitarist in the Village. "No one was sure what to expect. Would he be singing? He had solo hits as a singer. Would he be doing Yardbirds songs? It was an odd crowd, because the Grateful Dead were headlining. So there were Brit-rock Anglophiles and hardcore stoners all mixed in one hall.

"Beck took centre stage and played a riff. Then a guy with high rooster hair started to sing way up in a woman's testator, but with grit and balls! I had never quite heard anything like it. You could literally hear the entire audience's breath go out in shock and amazement. Rod Stewart was a totally new sound to us, and he was so powerful and controlled that I couldn't believe my ears.

"I focused on the bass player, a very young and shy Ron Wood, and he played bass in a busy and musical way, looking down all the while. Mick Waller hit the drums in a jazz-rock fusion style, way ahead of his time. I remember he wore National Health glasses, and looked out of place alongside the three rockers. But they were a very tight and professional outfit. If Beck played any bad notes, I didn't hear them. He was as perfect as a rock and blues lead guitar player could be. He did a cheeky version of "Jeff's Boogie" that was better than The Yardbirds' recorded version. "Rock Me Baby" and "You Shook Me" were surreal.

"I'm running out of superlatives. It was that good, one of those shows that were an epiphany to see and hear. I felt sorry for the Grateful Dead having to follow that. If memory serves, Phil Lesh didn't even try. He simply put down his bass and let it feed back. As I was leaving the Fillmore I saw Kangaroo members Ted Spelios, John Hall, and ND Smart walking out, shaking their heads in disbelief. We were all speechless. It was a show that raised the bar in what rock music had to be from that day on."

Later in the tour, in San Francisco, Stewart himself caught a Janis Joplin and Big Brother show, and came away so overwhelmed that, he said, he completely lost confidence in his own singing abilities. But he had no need to fret, and he knew it. Writer June Harris covered the Fillmore East show for the New Musical Express, and raved, "Stewart far surpasses 100% of the lead singers who have been passing through New York of late. America has never seen a team like Jeff Beck and Rod

Stewart. The only possible description of their two-fold dynamite would be to suggest it's like watching the brilliance of Jim Morrison teamed with Eric Clapton...."

It was all, Beck joked, a very long way from "our annual gig at the Nottingham Rowing Club. I only came over to America to do some shopping, really, and I was in New York and it started to rain, so I went into the Fillmore to take shelter. The next thing I knew, I was up on stage. But seriously, it was very breathtaking to go down so well on our debut. We didn't expect the sort of reaction we've been getting. We're enjoying ourselves immensely at the moment."

New York was to remain the Jeff Beck Group's base for the next week; their next performance, however, arrived without warning, the day after the second Fillmore show. They'd been expecting to rest that day – and they needed to; following the exertions of the previous evenings, Stewart's voice was completely wrecked. But then the Grateful Dead cancelled their headlining spot at Staten Island's Daytop Music Festival on 16 June, and the Jeff Beck Group were slotted in as replacements before the musicians themselves were even aware of the fact.

It promised to be a tentative show, then, and a far cry from the triumph of the previous evenings. But any rough spots that the Jeff Beck Group might have been fearing as they prepared to take the stage were ironed out when Jimi Hendrix appeared, hungry to perform but bereft of his own band members.

Wood and Waller promptly volunteered to accompany him, jamming through three numbers while Beck watched from the side of the stage. Finally, he'd seen enough. "I'm not really in favour of jamming", he mused. "But I heard three numbers and just stood there aghast – and then I had to play. So I leaped onstage and we all jammed together. Jimi was fantastic, and it sounded as though (the audience) approved of my guitar-playing." They certainly did; as the *Village Voice's* Annie Fisher wrote afterwards, "They jammed long and loose, feeling each other out, bringing off a few really remarkable moments, (before) finally breaking into 'Foxy Lady' to finish it off. Dynamite!"

Hendrix was in the midst of recording his third album, Electric Ladyland, at the time; and, having now connected with the Jeff Beck Group, he stuck to them like glue. Over the next week, with the band headlining the Scene Club, on 8th and West 46th Streets, Hendrix would make a point of dropping in every single night to have a jam. Eric Clapton, whose own latest US tour with Cream had just wrapped up, popped in as well and Beck's Scene residency got off to the most improbable start imaginable as both Clapton and Hendrix joined the Beck Group onstage.

A couple of evenings later, Alvin Lee and Buddy Miles (a drummer who picked up a guitar for the occasion) joined Beck and Hendrix for a furious succession of favourite oldies – "Good Morning Little Schoolgirl", "Hey Joe" and "Wild Thing". Another night, Hendrix picked up the bass to accompany Beck through a seething version of "I Ain't Superstitious" – which they interrupted midway through by throwing their instruments to one another, carrying on without missing a beat. "Jimi used to come in towards the end of our set", Beck recalled, "and he'd just get up on stage. No-one else could have done it. You would've said 'Hey look, man, once is enough.' But with Jimi, you felt part of something massive, history."

The resentment he once felt towards the American had dissipated. "He and I became sort of drinking partners in New York, playing together a lot, and I realised that if he could say he enjoyed what I did, that was enough for me." It no longer mattered, Beck decided, what the public grumbled, whether one was ripping off the other by simply doing what came naturally. What did matter was, they knew what they were doing. "So it was kind of with his blessing that I carried on."

The Scene shows, legend insists, also included some of the best performances that the Jeff Beck Group itself ever gave. But, coming so soon after the Fillmore and festival triumphs, Beck himself wasn't so certain. "When we played big places, it was fine. But then we had to go and play this piss-hole club for six nights, where people could scrutinise us from about two feet away, and it kinda took the magic away."

Another New York-based musician, keyboardist Al Kooper, was likewise unimpressed by what he saw of the Scene shows – which, admittedly, wasn't much. "I had to leave after three numbers. The band was blowing changes, the bass player was losing time, Beck was uncomfortably and bitingly over-volumed. It didn't make a lot of sense to me."

Nor, it transpired, to Beck. According to Peter Grant, "Jeff once said the worst thing that could have happened to them was to start out like they did, with the Fillmore shows, because it meant suddenly Rod didn't think he needed to work any more. Then Woody and Mickey Waller picked up on that, and suddenly Jeff was having to carry the band every night."

The first serious blow-up came when the Jeff Beck Group played their rescheduled Boston show in front of a capacity crowd of 750, all well-versed in the reviews of the New York shows, and all expecting to witness the Second Coming. Instead, they got what Beck described as a shambles, as promoter Don Law recalled. Backstage after the show, he stumbled upon Beck taking Wood and Stewart to task. "He was really chewing them out. You'd never hear that from a West Coast band."

Audiences were less aware of the flaws that were infuriating Beck. Future Aerosmith guitarist Joe Perry remembered, "I'm down the front, watching Jeff in total awe. No-one who was there ever forgot those early Jeff Beck shows." And the *New England Scene* magazine was equally stunned, not only by Beck's musicianship, but also by his insistence on involving the audience in the show.

There was a point in one of the performances when Stewart tried to lure the audience into a singalong. They refused, so Beck took over as ringmaster instead, "by having them clap a rhythm. He then proceeded to use the audience as a drum, working guitar phrases and runs around the tempo. Unlike Clapton, who rarely changes an expression... Beck laughs and defies the image of the tough, esoteric rock musician whose only source of meaning and pleasure comes from his music."

The tour rolled on, with word of the New York show constantly travelling just a little ahead of the band. Three nights at the Grande Ballroom, Detroit were followed by four at the Shrine Auditorium in Los Angeles... "The underground scene is really big in the States", Beck told a UK journalist during a telephone interview. "(At home) it only means Mile End tube station."

The Detroit shows were booked by Russ Gibb, a schoolteacher in his mid-30s who fell into the music industry after a visit to San Francisco in 1966 introduced him to the Fillmore West. He returned home convinced that Detroit required its own Fillmore and, armed with a pocketful of phone numbers collected from Bill Graham, contacted bands, managers and, most important of all, the company that supplied the Fillmore's strobe lights. Bare months later, on 7 October 1966, the Grande Ballroom was up and running, a 1930s-style ballroom stripped bare and reconstructed around all the key accoutrements of the psychedelic experience.

That first night, headlined by Detroit's own MC5, attracted 60 paying customers. But there was twice that many the following night and, before long, the Grande was selling out every night. It didn't matter who was playing... like the Fillmore West that inspired it (and the Fillmore East that would follow), the name possessed a cachet that out-ranked even the greatest headline band.

The Beck show was not originally scheduled for the Grande but the considerably smaller Dearborn University. Ticket demand, however, quickly pushed the promoter to seek an alternative venue – and he wound up at the Grande, with a supporting bill that included the cream of local talent, Charging Rhino of Soul, Gold and Frost, the hard-hitting outfit that gave the world future guitar hero Dick Wagner (alongside Steve Hunter, the soul of Lou Reed's 1970s live band).

Even amid a month that also promised shows by Fleetwood Mac, Pink Floyd and the Who, the Beck gig was an event, and the city poured out to witness it – then went home to emulate it. Beck himself was equally impressed. "Of all the cities on that first American tour, it was Detroit that I kept hearing about when I went back there, people who'd been at the show and formed a band afterwards, or joined a new one, and they all wanted to play like Beck. That whole psychedelic blues thing that came out of Detroit, it all came out of those first shows at the Grande.

"Detroit the other night was outrageous. Everyone was really enjoying themselves, and there were about 30 or 40 people grooving away on stage. It was a great atmosphere... amazing and overwhelming. We spent a long time planning our American tour, getting things just right, and it was worth it."

A live tape from one of the Shrine shows, meanwhile, survives to give modern audiences a taste of the action. A raw medley of "You Shook Me" and "Let Me Love You", opens the show, a three-song Yardbirds sequence rounded up "The Sun Is Shining", "Shapes Of Things" and

The Yardbirds at their blueswailin' best - though their Beck-Page twin-guitar attack was short-lived.(Jorgen Angel - www.angel.dk)

Beck in contemplative mood at the Reading Festival, 1968.
(Ray Stevenson/Rex Features)

The Beck Group in classic pose: from left, Rod Stewart, Aynsley Dunbar, Ron Wood, Jeff Beck. (Dezo Hoffman/Rex Features)

Jeff's fellow Yardbird Jimmy Page (right) went on to superstardom with singer Robert Plant in Led Zeppelin. (Jorgen Angel - www.angel.dk)

"Jeff's Boogie". "Blues De Luxe" and "I Ain't Superstitious" served up another taste of Truth, before the show ended with "Bye Bye Baby" and "Rock My Plimsoul".

It was a devastating set, all the more so for its comparative brevity. The spring of 1968, after all, was the peak of improvisational playing, as an entire generation of bands picked up on Cream (and, to a lesser extent, Hendrix)'s flair for extended soloing. The Jeff Beck Group, however, had no time for any such indulgence.

Occasionally, Waller would be granted a short drum solo, while the band itself would sometimes lurch into jam territory when a song, or an audience demanded it – a tape from the show at LuAnne's, in Dallas, captures the live premier of "Mother's Old Rice Pudding", a new song that Beck introduces as one that "has never been heard before because we've never played it. And we're gonna jam so, you know, groove along." And they do, while Beck burns through what still sounds like a medley of every great guitar riff he never found a home for.

Such moments were the exception, however. Rather than plough one furrow for what sometimes felt like hours on end, Beck was far more likely to go the other route entirely and litter his performance with throwaway riffs and motifs – that same Texan tape sees everything from the theme to the *Beverly Hillbillies* to Matt Murphy's bluesbasher "Steppin' Out" thrown into the brew, while he was also prone to regular airings for the signature swirl (but only the signature swirl) of "Over Under Sideways Down" and a battery of old rock'n'rockabilly riffs.

At every show, the band received an ovation; in every review, the writer insisted that the Jeff Beck Group had blown all-comers off stage... "put (them) to shame", as the *LA Free Press* insisted. Both Moby Grape and Sly and the Family Stone took a stab at topping the bill over Beck in San Francisco – neither would make that mistake again. Nobody would.

Truth was released in America midway through the LA Shrine residency, and it hit hard. With radio already primed by advance copies of the record, and "Ol' Man River" receiving so much attention that it was briefly scheduled for release as a single, Truth entered the *Billboard* chart on 24 August, buoyed by a crop of genuinely enthusiastic reviews. Truth, declared Robert Christgau, was "the best thing from England this year, with the exception of Traffic. Deluged by British blues bands, they said it with a rock'n'roll difference, a good record characterised by new sounds and a respectable tour."

Even Al Kooper, so dismissive of the Scene shows a few weeks before, described it as "a classic in much the same way (as) the Clapton/Mayall album", and Beck should have been thrilled. A great review in *Rolling Stone* was something to be proud of in those days. But he didn't need Al Kooper to tell him what he already knew. "From the articles of his I've read, he talks out of his arse. He came to see us play and said 'I admit I was wrong,' but I didn't care. I'd rather he had stuck to his guns...."

With several days at their disposal in Los Angeles, the Jeff Beck Group became a regular sight around town. For Rod Stewart, however, their stay would prove one of the most monumental few days of his life. After years of struggle, years of trying and years of cutting flop solo singles for labels that didn't care who he might be, he was finally being courted by a real record-company man.

The band was based at the Continental Hyatt House hotel, and Stewart was just passing through the lobby when someone called his name and hustled over – Lou Reizner, the London-based American who headed up Mercury Records. He'd been at the Shrine show the previous evening, and the performance blew him away... Rod's performance blew him away. Had the singer ever thought about making a solo album?

Stewart tried to stay cool, not because he disliked the idea but because he was sure that, if he started jumping about, Reizner would clear his throat and make his excuses... "I'm sorry, I thought you were somebody else." Instead, it rapidly became apparent that Reizner was the one who was trying to control his excitement. He really wanted to sign the boy.

They agreed to speak again when both arrived back in London, at the beginning of August – but even before then, Stewart was on the phone to his managers (his real managers, as he liked to refer to them, as opposed to the babysitters at RAK), Rowlands and Wright. Rowlands rang Reizner the first chance he got, and caught the man just as he set out for his hairdresser. "We did the deal walking from Chester Street to Grovesnor Square," Reizner later revealed. Stewart would receive a £1,000 advance and he was adamant that he wouldn't take a penny less.

Later, he told Reizner why he'd stuck to that figure – £1,000 was the price of the D-I-Y Marcos "build your own sports car" kit he'd had his heart set on ever since they came on the market. That was also why it would take him so long to actually make his solo album. He had to build the car first.

CHAPTER
NINETEEN

T he Yardbirds played what was intended to be their last ever concert on 8 July 1968, at Luton Technical College. Somehow, however, it seemed that news of the group's final demise had not quite filtered into Peter Grant's mind – even as the band was preparing to deliver their final performance, he was arranging a Scandinavian tour for September, with further dates in Japan, Australia and the US awaiting his final confirmation.

Keith Relf and Jim McCarty shrugged. Their own project, Together, was already underway – the day before the Luton show, in fact, they linked up with Nicky Hopkins, Tony Meehan, folk guitarist Jon Mark and producer Paul Samwell-Smith to begin work on the new group's debut single. So far as they were concerned, there was no going back.

Page and Dreja were less dismissive. Neither had given much thought out to precisely what they intended doing next, beyond the vague possibility of trying to start up a new band together. Advising Grant only to revise the Scandinavian contract somehow, to make it apparent that the Yardbirds themselves would not be touring (he opted to rename the band the New Yardbirds), they began casting around for suitable members, beginning with a singer to succeed Keith Relf.

Page's first choice was Terry Reid, whose solo career under Mickie Most's auspices continued to struggle. Critically, Reid was regarded among the greatest vocalists around, and the two albums he'd cut with the producer contained some of the most far-sighted music of Most's entire career, But the public simply wasn't biting... yet. Reid remained convinced that he was on the right track, and turned Page's invitation down. He did, however, know another singer Page might want to look at; and, when it turned out to be the same Birmingham-based vocalist that the Move's old manager, Tony Secunda, had already suggested he check out, Page, Dreja and Peter Grant made arrangements to travel north.

There, within the distinctly unglamorous surroundings of a Birmingham teacher training college on 20 July 1968, Page caught sight of Robert Plant for the first time, a singer who was so good that Page was convinced there had to be something very wrong with him as a person. Nobody this great could still be labouring in the obscurity of a band called Hobstweedle.

Page decided to take a chance, however, and, no sooner had Plant accepted the awestricken trio's offer than he was pushing forth one of his own friends to make up the numbers, John Bonham, another Brummie, who'd played in one of Plant's earlier bands, but was now touring the country for £40 a night in Tim Rose's group. Page had already been turned down by the drummer he first dreamed of playing with, Procol Harum's BJ Wilson. Maybe he should give Bonham a go.

In early August, the New Yardbirds – Page, Dreja, Plant and Bonham – had their first rehearsal, running through a clutch of old Yardbirds songs beginning with the highly appropriate "The Train Kept A Rolling." But though the afternoon went well, and the band was sounding good, Chris Dreja knew it wasn't for him. His heart just wasn't in it; he simply didn't have the energy to be starting a new band all over again. "I wanted to be independent, and not have to rely on loonies."

He wasn't sure how he expected the others to react to the news – the Scandinavian tour, after all, was less than two months away. Page, however, was quick to assure him that it didn't matter. He already had a replacement lined up, and when he told Dreja whom it was, the bassist's jaw hit the floor almost as hard as Page's had when he first heard of the new recruit's interest. It was John Paul Jones, and Page was still in shock as he delivered the news to Dreja. "John Paul Jones is unquestionably an incredible arranger and musician – he didn't need me for a job."

Page himself recalled the conversation occurring at sessions for Donovan's "Hurdy Gurdy Man" single; "I was working at (the) session and John Paul Jones was looking after the musical arrangements. During a break, he asked me if I could use a bass player in the new group."

In fact, according to Jones, who booked the band, Page was never actually at that particular session (Alan Parker contributed the signature guitar lines). Instead, the fateful comment was delivered at sessions for another singer entirely – Keith De Groot, an exciting new discovery from producer Reg Tracey – backed up by a positively stellar gathering of musicians. Page and Jones were joined by Nicky Hopkins, Albert Lee, Big Jim Sullivan, saxophonist Chris Hughes and drummer Clem Cattini, all letting rip across a glorious barrage of rock'n'roll oldies. But while the ensuing album (De Groot's No Introduction Necessary) did nothing, the conversation between Page and Jones was to have lifelong consequences.

If Page was astounded by Jones' enthusiasm for a new, unknown band, he readily understood his reasons. Like Page in the years before he joined the Yardbirds, Jones had spent his entire career playing what other people told him to. It was time to begin expressing himself, "and he thought we might be able to do it together. He had a proper musical training, and quite brilliant ideas. I jumped at the chance of getting him."

Dreja, meanwhile, gracefully and happily stepped aside, turning instead towards a new career built upon his long-time love of photography. One of his earliest commissions would be the band photograph that bedecked the back cover of the new band's debut album. The New Yardbirds were complete, and there wasn't a single 'old' Yardbird in sight.

British audiences received their first taste of the returning Jeff Beck

Group on 10 August, the second day of the National Jazz and Blues Festival. Relocated now to Kempton Racecourse in Sunbury, following Windsor's objections to the previous year's bash, the festival nevertheless retained its reputation as the crowning glory of the British rock year, a chance for established bands to confirm their success and for new bands to tilt at their thrones. The previous year, both Fleetwood Mac and the Nice had joined the Jeff Beck Group in emerging from the festival as superstars-in-waiting, with the Nice confirming their ascendancy this year by co-headlining the second evening of the three-day festival, alongside the chart-topping Crazy World of Arthur Brown.

Joe Cocker, Tyrannosaurus Rex, Ten Years After and a tumultuous percussive performance from Ginger Baker and Phil Seaman were also scheduled to delight the hordes that same evening. There was also a completely unknown new band called Deep Purple who were buried so deep within the running order that they were barely even noticed by the majority of onlookers (and were, in any case, doomed to disappoint everyone who did catch them).

For many of the thousands gathered in the field that afternoon, however, the true highlight of the day would be the Jeff Beck Group. The British music papers were full of tales of their American success, and everyone seemed to know somebody who'd heard a copy of Truth; Columbia wouldn't be releasing it in Europe until October, but a handful of import copies had already made it over the Atlantic and at least one club DJ in London had been spinning it.

Neither was the band to disappoint. "There is no doubt", *NME* reviewer Keith Altham wrote, "that this group have come back from the States with a harder sound and a much more together act – particularly enjoyable is the vocal/guitar play between Beck and Stewart."

For the first time, Nicky Hopkins was on stage with the band. "Jeff called me a few days before and said they were still thinking about adding keyboards, but only if I would play them. So I said I'd do Sunbury and we'd see how it goes – and it was great. Then somebody leaked it to the press that I was joining and, after that, I didn't really have a choice!" In fact, the leak got at least one of its facts wrong – it stated that Hopkins would be present on the band's Swedish tour at the beginning of October when, according to the pianist himself, there was never any intention of him joining until they returned from that jaunt to prepare for their return to America.

Much of September 1968 was the band members' own – there was one outstanding club date to play, the Manor House's Bluesville 68 on 6 September, and a pair of BBC sessions later in the month. The second of these, for Radio One DJ Stuart Henry, was cancelled for reasons unrecalled; but the first, for John Peel, which went ahead as scheduled on 17 September, saw the group already looking beyond Truth.

Alongside "Rock My Plimsoul", "You Shook Me" and "Shapes Of Things", the band also turned in a beautifully bluesy "Sweet Little Angel", then followed through with the still-forming "Mother's Old Rice Pudding", a song that started life as a simple jam through a succession of riffs but which had been utterly transformed by its live experiences to emerge a stunning funk-based extravaganza surely modelled upon the Group's recent exposure to Sly and the Family Stone.

Ever since the band opened for them in San Francisco in July, Beck had been loudly proclaiming them among his favourite American bands of all time. And, while "Mother's Old Rice Pudding" might still have been somewhat more free-form than the super-disciplined-despite-appearances Family Stone would have permitted (and no way could Ron Wood hold a candle to Sly's bassist Larry Graham), the influence was palpable all the same. Furthermore, though it would be another six months before the Jeff Beck Group even considered writing any further new material, the dishevelled lope of "Mother's Old Rice Pudding" would prove a blueprint.

In the meantime, though, there was the European debut of Truth to deal with, and the Scandinavian tour that would be occupying the band's time as the album finally hit the shops. The first reviews were already in, and Beck was pleased to see that most of the critics simply took their cue from the American press. Although the *NME* did hesitate in proclaiming Truth anything more than "competent" ("the whole LP lacks atmosphere and becomes mildly boring"), others greeted it for what it was – a snapshot of the British blues as they were slowly transformed into something fresher, louder and more experimental than they ever had been before.

Rolling Stone's claim that it represented as great a step forward as Bluesbreakers, the Clapton/Mayall album of two years before, was echoed in several places, but the British press noticed one major difference. Truth was undiluted blues, but it was blues squeezed through a wringer of countless other notions – an incendiary blast of noise that eschewed the gospel according to Mac, Mayall and Ten Years After and rewrote the rule book from the groundfloor up.

Yet when the Jeff Beck Group arrived in Scandinavia, it was to discover the entire region buzzing not over the prospect of seeing Truth in person, but over the debut, three weeks earlier, of the New Yardbirds, a half-dozen shows through Denmark and Sweden that, though the group was absolutely unknown and untried, nevertheless left nobody in any doubt as to its awesome potential.

Photographer Jorgen Angel, a 17-year-old student from Copenhagen, caught the band's opening night in his hometown, and spoke for many in the club when he recalled, "As for these 'New Yardbirds', I didn't expect much. Not long before the concert actually began, there was still a lot of talking on whether they were going to play under the name of 'The Yardbirds' or under the name of 'The New Yardbirds', and how people would react. Because in the club magazine, they were billed as 'The Yardbirds', with a photo of the Yardbirds, not of Bonham, Plant, Page and John Paul Jones.

"Plus, in these days, when you saw a band turning up with the word 'New' in its name, you knew that something was murky, that it wasn't the same group any more. Can you imagine a group called 'The New

Beatles'? Of course not, you would be disappointed even before hearing a single note. So before these New Yardbirds even went on stage, I remember I was annoyed. I wanted 'the real thing.' But, as soon as they began to play, I was hooked!"

In keeping with their name, the group's repertoire was firmly grounded in a variation on the Yardbirds' final set, although that in itself offered plenty of clues as to the new group's future. The showcase "Dazed And Confused" was already in place, albeit under its original title of "White Summer", while the band members' shared love of blues introduced "Babe I'm Gonna Leave You" and "How Many More Times" to the brew.

Casting around further, Page seized upon the Stax churner "The Hunter", a delirious stand-out in the live repertoire of London blues band Free (the two bands, Free and the Yardbirds, shared the same publicist, Bill Harry). But, if there was any single song in the New Yardbirds' arsenal that was to set the tone for the next year of relations between Jimmy Page and Jeff Beck, friends from before they even joined their first bands, it was "You Shook Me" – the same "You Shook Me" the Jeff Beck Group had included on Truth; the same "You Shook Me" to which John Paul Jones had gifted an immortal organ line.

Right now, of course, Beck knew nothing beyond the fact that the New Yardbirds had left an indelible impression on the ears and eyes of everyone who saw them – a lot of whom would be coming back for more once the Jeff Beck Group hit town.

With Grant by their side, the Jeff Beck Group's first dates took place in Stockholm, Sweden, where they were among the headline attractions at a nine-day long British "Week" – Paul Jones, Chris Farlowe and Jethro Tull were among the other stars of the season, with Tull then scheduled to peel away from the capital to support the Jeff Beck Group on the remainder of the tour.

On paper, it was a great match. A far purer blues band than their subsequent reputation would ever let on, Jethro Tull were essentially the vehicle for guitarist Mick Abrahams, as the band's newly released This Was debut album made clear. Tensions between Abrahams and vocalist Ian Anderson were already mounting, however (the guitarist would quit just two months later), the awkwardness only exacerbated by their proximity to the constantly rowing headliners.

Neither did the bands' itinerary serve to calm their constitutions. A clutch of public appearances around Stockholm culminated with a performance at a fashion show, where the band took the stage at 2pm, during a break between the modelling displays. Janne Schaffer, of the local band Sleepstones, caught the performance, and recalled they looked as if they were at the wrong place, wrong time... so wrong, in fact, that much of Stewart's performance was obscured by a curtain. But the music was good."

Nevertheless, by the time the end of the tour finally hove into view, both groups were desperate to return home as early as possible. Which might well explain what happened next.

On 5 October, the Beck Group's show at Copenhagen's Brondby Popclub would go down in history as one of the worst they ever played – even worse than their last-but-one appearance in what was surely an ill-starred city for them. One of the arguments that forever rent the quartet had taken place before the show – but rather than getting worked out in the dressing room, it continued on once the band got on stage. It was simply the audience's bad luck that they'd paid to witness it.

A clattering mess of untuned instruments, out-of-sync rhythms and barely-competent vocals, the performance was a shambles even before Beck apparently decided that, if the rest of his band couldn't be bothered to play properly, neither would he. Instead, he simply soloed for the sake of it... "a cold and technically incoherent show-off", as the local *Extrablade* magazine put it.

Offstage at the end of the night, Beck's temper had not improved. Back at the hotel, he trashed his room; then, with Peter Grant having already picked up the Group's earnings from the tour, he announced that they were all going home. Two shows still remained to be played, at Copenhagen's Star Club and Roskilde's Fjordvilla, but Beck had had enough. The band checked out of their hotel, then made their way to the airport and bought tickets home.

Promoter Arne Worsøe knew, of course, that Beck was unhappy – "I spoke with him late Saturday night and he was very disappointed by his performances." At that time, however, Beck assured him that he intended making amends over the next two shows. Instead he had fled and Worsøe was not going to let him get away with it. He called the police as soon as he figured out what had happened; the law arrived at Copenhagen airport just in time to prevent the band and their entourage from boarding their flight.

Peter Grant was arrested, and the rest of the Group were taken into custody until the situation could be resolved with Worsøe. The cancelled gigs would remain cancelled, Beck was adamant about that. But Grant agreed to refund at least some of the money he'd already picked up – enough, at least, to refund the audience's tickets, and pay off the staff who'd been employed for the night – and the musicians were finally released.

Yet even with this unscheduled break in their itinerary, still the Jeff Beck Group had just three days to spare before departing for the US again – and that was nowhere near enough time to settle all the arguments that had blown up in Scandinavia.

Neither did their routine – a three-week tour that kicked off in Chicago on 11 October – offer any chance of a respite. Last time across America, after all, the Jeff Beck Group was still merely something to be anticipated, coasting entirely upon the rumours and reports that skipped ahead of the tour bus. This time around they were the undisputed headliners, superstars in waiting. When they hit Cleveland, Ohio, the local Cleveland Press announced that Truth was the fastest selling album in the city.

The band played the first of the American shows as a quartet; Nicky

Hopkins finally joined them in New York, during the few days break before their return to the Fillmore East. "I really, truly must be one of the luckiest guys to have Nicky in the group", Beck marvelled in an interview that weekend. "He's going to help write songs and put them down in a true musical way, which I can't put over to the others. It's going to be an entirely different group, I think."

Hopkins, too, declared that "Jeff brought me in for the songwriting", and he admitted that it was that, rather than the opportunity to sit in a tour bus and grind around the world, that most appealed to him. He was never, after all, short on offers to join one band or another; just a couple of months earlier, in fact, Jimmy Page had invited him to join the New Yardbirds, to add the keyboards that John Paul Jones, behind his bass, would necessarily be unable to perform.

"I was tempted, but only in as much as it was work. It sounds odd to say it, but I couldn't see a future in it. John would still play keyboards in the studio, the whole band was writing, John and Jimmy were both great at arranging. Really, what would be left for me to do?

"Whereas with Jeff... the one problem with Truth was that even the group's originals were rewritten or rearranged versions of other people's songs – which wasn't a problem at the time, a lot of people were doing that. But Jeff also knew that if the group was to really make an impression, they needed to get away from the covers and into writing their own great originals...

"Looking back, listening to the things that Rod and Woody went on to do with the Faces, it always puzzled me that they had so little to say for themselves while they were with Jeff. Those songs of Rod's didn't just appear out of nowhere – he had the ability all along, and he was writing while he was with Jeff. But the problem was that Jeff didn't pay any attention to them, it was 'Ah Rod, another Dylan cover?' when he should have been encouraging him, and working with him."

In fact, the real stumbling block, as Hopkins himself would later discover, was that nothing was good enough for Beck – not on stage, not in the studio, and certainly not in the form of a demo that he might listen to once and then dismiss as worthless. It was a failing that would irreparably damage the Group as it worked through the next (and final) nine months of its life.

Hopkins' immediate impact was largely confined to a distributing a few frills around the edges of the existing set, mapping out a handful of rearrangements and taking the lead on one "new" song, a sweet instrumental take on the Gerry Goffin/Carole King classic "(You Make Me Feel Like A) Natural Woman" – so sweet that Stewart himself would retain much the same arrangement for his own version of the song, six years later during his Smiler album sessions.

The problem with that, of course, was that it then left Wood and Waller wondering why they didn't have showcases of their own – complaints that now saw "Mother's Old Rice Pudding" enlarged to allow them their own moments in the sun, soloing around Beck's increasingly demented wah-wah work. It wasn't always a successful performance –

the incoherence that had always rendered the song either a brilliant showcase or an embarrassing indulgence was only heightened now, and for a few days Hopkins campaigned actively to get the song either dropped from the show or at least rearranged. He gave up, though, once he became aware of another of the band's fatal flaws. It wasn't that they didn't like to rehearse; the fact was, they steadfastly refused to.

From New York, the band zipped down the coast to Alexandria, Virginia, to open for the singer who had so terrified Stewart when he caught her in San Francisco, Janis Joplin. Today, however, he was more relaxed – a consequence, perhaps, of the tomfoolery with which he and Wood had occupied themselves earlier in the day.

Seated in a restaurant before the show, the pair spotted a stationery railway locomotive on the tracks behind the building. Trains had always fascinated Stewart; he couldn't resist wandering over for a closer look. And when they realised there was nobody around, "we hopped aboard", said Wood, "and proceeded to release the brakes. The thing just started moving. We jumped off yelling and zoomed back into the restaurant. (Then) we hid in there, while this giant locomotive rolled uncommanded into the sunset."

CHAPTER
TWENTY

Whereas the Jeff Beck Group's last American visit had seen them constantly on the move, this time around they decided to base themselves in as few towns as possible, then make 'day-trips' to surrounding shows. On the east coast, New York became their home from home, and they were back there the following day to greet a surprise visitor – Mickie Most was no stranger to America, of course, but he was a rare guest indeed at a Jeff Beck Group concert. He was here now, though, to celebrate the American triumphs of no less than three of his acts: Donovan and Terry Reid were in town as well.

Of them all, however, it was Beck whose progress excited him the most. Travelling up to Boston with the Jeff Beck Group to take in the first of their four-night return to the Tea Party venue, Most enthused "it looked as if the Marquee had been planted in Boston." The city had always been strong Yardbirds territory, and the success of the group's last appearance only heightened the locals' love for Beck. Hours before the gig itself, a furiously partisan local audience was waiting outside the club, amusing themselves by (among other things) scrawling "Beck is God" on the venue's walls.

Beck repaid their devotion with brilliance. The Massachusetts Institute of Technology's *The Tech* newspaper enthused, "Beck says and does more things on a... guitar than can easily be believed." Local journalism student John Donovan was one of the first to stake his place at the front of the stage. "The thing I really remember about that show isn't so much the music, but Beck's attitude. The MC introduces the band, the crowd is giving him a standing ovation and he hasn't played a note.

"His sidemen go on first, then Stewart comes out in a baby pink velvet suit and frilly white lace shirt, camping it up big time for the audience. Finally, Beck casually saunters out. He has to walk to the opposite side of the stage to get to his amps. He has his ox-blood Les Paul slung over his shoulder backwards like a rifle, holding it by the neck. At the first sight of him, the audience goes even crazier. He's ignoring everyone. He gets to the middle of the stage, stops, and stands there peering at the crowd, as if to say, 'What's the fuss? Did the Beatles just walk in?'

"He heads to his spot on stage and plugs into his stacks, which are next to where Nicky Hopkins is sitting at a spinet piano, the only amplification being several mikes running through the PA overhanging the keys. Beck takes one look at this set-up, laughs, and hits the volume pot on his axe, sending a wall of feedback washing over Hopkins. Later in the show, they're doing a slow song, can't remember which, Stewart is going over the top with extravagant vocal stylings and Beck is looking bored and pissed off – so he cranks up his amps again and stomps out the vocal. Obnoxious, sure, but I thought it was cool...."

Even the loss of his favoured Les Paul guitar, shattered when one of the roadies dropped it, could not hold Beck back in Boston. Dispatching Most around the local guitar shops to seek out a replacement (Beck's regular spare, a Telecaster, was having tuning problems), he wound up with a stripped 1954 maple-neck Stratocaster, and made that his trademark as well.

The tour moved on, through Philadelphia, Toronto, Detroit, Dallas, Cleveland, Oklahoma City, Miami, Seattle... Learning from the lessons that were so painfully taught to other British bands of the age (most notably Cream, whose American workload played its own part in curdling the group), Beck's itinerary was relaxed, even enjoyable.

There was time for sightseeing, time to take in other performances, even the opportunity to play the occasional unscheduled show – back in New York City on Hallowe'en, the Jeff Beck Group were among a handful of stars who turned out for a benefit for the beleaguered African nation of Biafra that stands as the direct precursor of all the charitable concerts that would follow during the decades to come, from the Concert for Bangladesh to Live Aid and beyond. Indeed, the event was one of several similar benefits that Scene proprietor Steve Paul put together – six weeks earlier, on 12 August, the first Operation Airlift Biafra Benefit featured Joan Baez and Jimi Hendrix; tonight, the highlight of the show was a dramatic closing jam between Beck and Rick Derringer of the Scene's house band, the McCoys.

Another visit to the Scene in early November allowed Beck to join Most at Terry Reid's first ever American performance, the opening night of a 16-day residency; another saw the entire band troupe into Mirasound Studios to record two deliciously laconic versions of BB King's "Sweet Little Angel". And one more saw Beck hook up with Peter Grant and Jimmy Page as they dropped off the masters for the first Led Zeppelin album to Atlantic Records.

The album had been recorded quickly; as fast, in fact, as the New Yardbirds changed their name. Lead Zeppelin was the name that had been bandied around for Beck and Page's two-year-old venture with Keith Moon and John Entwistle, and Page had always had a fondness for it. The only adjustment he felt was necessary was in the spelling; he remembered, as did so many others, the cautionary tale of the aspiring young guitarists who, anxious to discover the secret of Hank Marvin's magical sound, ascribed it to the fact that he played lead guitar – that's lead, the metal.

Led Zeppelin might have defused Keith Moon's original pun a little, but it also avoided a lot of confusion later on – beginning just days after the band returned from Scandinavia, and moved into Olympic Studios, to bang down the live set they'd just tweaked to perfection. "I Can't Quit You Baby", "How Many More Times", "Dazed And Confused", the newly-composed "Communication Breakdown", the acoustic instrumental "Black Mountain Side"... within no more than 36 hours (and, according to Page, as few as 15), Led Zeppelin I was complete.

They were proud of it, too, as Page told Beck when they settled to listen to a white label test pressing of the album. And Beck agreed that they ought to be, at least until the needle hit the third track on side one and "You Shook Me" shook out of the speakers. "I looked at him and said 'Jim... what?' and the tears were coming out with anger. I thought 'This is a piss-take, it's got to be.' I mean, there was Truth still spinning on everybody's turntable... Then I realised it was serious."

Page desperately defended himself, at the time and, as Led Zeppelin's renown grew, into the future. "It was a total freak accident", he insisted. "I remember hearing the Muddy Waters EP it was on, (and) it was our sort of material." Besides, he pointed out, the two performances were approached from very different angles – so different, in fact, that when Page was reminded that John Paul Jones had played organ on Beck's recording, he shrugged, "he probably didn't know it was the same number, because the two versions were so different." He certainly "didn't say anything about it – 'oi, I've just done this with Jeff.' Because they were so different."

Peter Grant, too, sided with Page – and that despite his frequent insistence that it was he, rather than Ken Scott or even Mickie Most, who produced Truth. From the outset, there was no question that Grant would assume the management of this new band; and, again from the outset, his devotion to his new charges overpowered every other consideration. Grant told journalist Chris Welch that there was no question of Led Zeppelin 'ripping off' Beck and/or Truth; insisted that, though he did give a white label advance copy of Truth to Page, "because I assumed he'd want to hear what Jeff had done", Page never actually listened to the record. "Some time later, Jimmy asked me why I hadn't told him that Jeff had done 'You Shook Me'. I told him about the white label... and he hadn't even heard it."

Neither, if one accept Grant's tale, had he noticed the song at any of the Beck concerts he attended over the years (and, according to Rod Stewart, there was a lot); neither had its presence in the live set arisen in any of Page's many conversations with one of his oldest, closest, friends. In fact, he would have yet another opportunity to hear the song that very day, as Page joined the Jeff Beck Group en route to their next gig in Miami, to thrill the first-night audience by jumping up on stage with Beck for a quick jam... the first time the pair had shared a stage since October 1966. Journalist Dave DiMartino was among the hundreds crammed into Thee Image that evening and, aged 15, he declared the show "the best concert of my life."

The tour reached California at the end of November, for a pair of shows at the Shrine, and twice that many at the Fillmore West. Both cities feted the band as returning heroes, and were rewarded with gigs that merited that approval. The Jeff Beck Group's time in LA, however, is best remembered not for the concerts, but for their encounter with the GTOs, the singing, dancing groupie aggregation who were currently recording their own album with producer Frank Zappa.

As his appearance on TV's *Man Alive* earlier in the year made clear,

Beck had little time to spare for groupies. Zappa, however, was another matter entirely – the pair first met on one of the American's visits to London the previous summer, and quickly hit it off. One night at the Speakeasy, the two spent the entire evening locked in conversation, sitting at the bar drinking Scotch together; a few nights later, Beck and Wood joined Zappa and Jimi Hendrix on a social call to the flat where Tomorrow were then living, and where Zappa cohort Suzy Creamcheese rechristened Woody "a darling little munchkin."

The moment Zappa heard Beck was in town, he sent a message to the hotel – "Meet us at the studio, and bring the band if you want." Then, to spice the invitation up a little, he mentioned the artists he was working with.

Over the last few years, Zappa had become something of an *eminence gris* to the American groupie scene, less through his patronage of them than for his fascination with the scene itself. Cynthia Plaster Caster certainly recalls him as "my patron", recalling how Zappa flew her to Hollywood and presented her with an address-book full of musicians' names and numbers, "so I could build up a collection. His record company gave me an advance because Frank had this dream of financing an exhibition of my casts in a gallery or museum."

The museum exhibit never occurred, but Zappa's fascination only gathered momentum until 1969, when he hit on the delightfully inverted idea of forming a bunch of groupies into a group of their own. He settled upon the GTOs – Girls Together Only (or Occasionally or Often, depending upon the mood), an already coalesced aggregation of Laurel Canyon ladies whose specialty was dancing together at various Hollywood clubs clad only in skimpy white T-shirts and diapers, and revelling in the evocative identities singer Tiny Tim had already conferred upon them: Miss Sandra, Miss Sparky, Miss Pamela (Miller – later to marry singer Michael DesBarres), Miss Cinderella, Miss Mercy and Miss Christine, Zappa's own housekeeper.

"We called ourselves the Laurel Canyon Ballet Company", recalled Miss Pamela and, one night at a Mothers show at the Shrine Auditorium, while Zappa was "wandering around after the show... I made a point of slamming into him on the dance floor." Soon, Miss Christine was inviting the others up to Zappa's home, actor Tom Mix's old mansion in Laurel Canyon, to entertain the other guests by singing and dancing to his Mothers of Invention records.

It was a great act – at least, Zappa thought it was, and he was soon laying plans to incorporate their routine into in three of his own shows at the LA Shrine. There, *Rolling Stone* described their performance as "beautifully choreographed, and so what if one of the Mothers thinks they're astonishingly flat and can't carry a tune in a bucket?" Another band member, Bunk Gardner, recalled them as "vampirish, black lipstick, black mascara, black everything", and though he found them "a little bit too unattractive for my tastes", Zappa's enthusiasm knew no bounds, especially now that he had his own record label, Straight, up and running.

Permanent Damage remains a landmark in groupie history, a not-altogether listenable but certainly ear-catching period piece that peaks, perhaps, with Miss Christine's discussion of Cynthia Plaster-Caster's diary, but also includes odes to Captain Beefheart's shoes ("The Captain's Fat Theresa Shoes") and LA scenester Rodney Bingenheimer ("Rodney") – the first boy Miss Pamela ever kissed in Hollywood!

The Mothers of Invention were responsible for most of the musical accompaniment on the record; however, the Jeff Beck Group's arrival in town quickly inspired Zappa, as producer, to rope some fresh talent into the proceedings. Beck, Hopkins and Stewart were all invited down to the studio, where the GTOs quickly christened Stewart "Rodney Rooster" and spent the entire afternoon glancing over as he sat in one corner, giggling and making coy comments.

In musical terms, however, they seemed distinctly unimpressed by his presence. While Beck and Hopkins worked around the backing tracks to the three songs Zappa had pulled out for their approval, Stewart simply paced around the studio grumbling to himself, then finally announced his departure: "There's nothing for me to do, so I'm off."

It took a frantic deputation of GTOs to bring him back to the studio – they waited until Beck had finished his latest solo, of course, then fanned out across the neighbourhood in search of the pouting performer. They finally located him sitting on the steps outside a nearby school, still sulking. But he allowed himself to be drawn back to the studio and, once he'd been reassured that he wasn't just there under sufferance, he happily turned in backing vocals to the last of the session's three songs, "Shock Treatment." History then draws a politic veil over the events of the rest of the evening...

The party returned to London the day after the final Fillmore show, 9 December – just in time for Hopkins to drift down to Stonebridge Park Studios in Wembley to take part in the Rolling Stones' *Rock'n'roll Circus* TV spectacular. Four days later, on 13 December, Beck motored down to Canterbury to catch his first glimpse of the burgeoning juggernaut that was Led Zeppelin.

With Led Zeppelin I scheduled for release the following month, Zeppelin would begin gnawing away at the US concert circuit by opening for Vanilla Fudge in Denver on Boxing Day, before launching into a string of solo dates, almost every one handpicked by Grant from his experiences with the Beck Group. That band's tours had introduced him to the cities that were interested in the kind of music both bands played; now he was out to consolidate that interest and transform it into devotion. In Britain, on the other hand, the band was still fulfilling the kind of engagements that Grant had been landing for the Yardbirds – the Marquee, various universities, the Bristol Boxing Club, the Bath Pavilion, and tonight, the Bridge Country Club in Canterbury.

It was not a representative show, or so Page told his distinguished visitor later. "Things went slightly wrong", Beck laughed, recounting the unscheduled explosion of Page's amplifier. Beck recalled "I went 'What's up with that, Jim?' and then I realised it was my amp, because my roadie had moonlighted and rented Jimmy my equipment. And he'd changed the impedance on the back, so it sounded like a pile of shit." Nevertheless, after weeks of hearing the grapevine (or, at least, Peter Grant) extolling the virtues of Led Zeppelin, Beck finally understood what the fuss was all about.

"I could see the potential. It was just amazing, blew the house down, blew everybody away." Everything the group was tailored for success, at least when he compared them with his ragtag little band. "(They) had a better-looking lead singer... he had golden curly locks and a bare chest, and the girls fell in love with him. They also had Bonzo on drums, creating all sorts of pandemonium." It was "a much better package than I had", and Beck freely admitted, "I was blind jealous, (although) maybe jealousy is the wrong word, because it's a negative emotion. But envy and frustration all rolled into one, because... I couldn't (even) find a drummer or a singer who wanted to experiment and do outrageous stuff. I wanted to break barriers and you need people around you to help you do that. And money! I couldn't even spring for a session, let alone keep them all on retainer.

"So obviously they did better."

CHAPTER
TWENTY-ONE

The Jeff Beck Group was to spend much of the festive season of 1968 lying dormant. They stirred for a Christmas show at the Middle Earth, staged tonight at the Roundhouse, but other gigs around the UK were cancelled, together with a short run of American shows that Peter Grant set up in the hope of keeping the group's momentum bubbling. Beck, however, refused to travel. He was exhausted, he said; plus, he and Celia (plus 18 cats and two dogs) were moving into their own new home, a 500-year-old cottage in Egerton, Kent. Grant didn't argue with him. He simply replaced the group with those other clients of his – Led Zeppelin.

While he waited, Stewart finally made a start on that long gestating solo record, flitting between Lansdowne and Morgan Studios with both Wood and Waller in tow, as he pieced together what would emerge a surprisingly mature, and extraordinarily courageous blending of folk, blues and straight ahead rock'n'roll. Stewart himself later dismissed An Old Raincoat Won't Ever Let You Down as "naïve", even claiming that the five self-composed songs on the record were achieved as much by luck as judgement – "I told people what sort of sound I wanted, then I'd bring home the tape without the vocals on it, and write words to fit the sounds. It was a strange way of going about things, but it worked."

Indeed it did. Every facet of Stewart's past career was highlighted, from the down at heel folkie who used to busk a raw version of Ewan MacColl's "Dirty Old Town", through a reunion with the Mike D'Abo songbook across a soon-to-be-classic reading of "Handbags And Gladrags" and onto the late-1960s rocker who kicked the Stones' "Street Fighting Man" into touch – and that despite the band having originally set out to record Little Richard's "The Girl Can't Help It." "During the session, for no apparent reason, I started singing 'Street Fighting Man,' adding much confusion to an already bewildered band." Even more confusing were the elements of another Stones number, "We Love You", that pianist Ian McLagan slung into the mix as the song faded out.

On the face of it, Little, on the new album, gelled with the music he'd been making with the Jeff Beck Group, at least in terms of volume and attack. But if you strip away the more overt aggression (and overlook Beck's insistence that his band could never have played the folk songs that Stewart was then writing), the old principle of taking the blues and fucking them up remains in perfect focus. And what wouldn't one give to have heard Beck's lead guitar, rather than Wood's, behind Stewart on the album's centrepiece, "Blind Prayer"?

The sessions would be slow going, woven in and around the musicians' (and the studio's) availability, and also around Stewart's reluctance to let Beck know too much about what was going on. Beck, however, already knew as much as he needed to. "We all knew Rod was recording", Nicky Hopkins later said, "but I don't think anybody took it too seriously – we knew what he was like when he got together with Wood and Waller, and the rest of his band was basically just friends that he'd called up and ask if they fancied a blow. Plus, Rod was never great at spending money, so he was booking the studios at the most ridiculous times to get the cheapest rates."

The full Jeff Beck Group finally reconvened on 14 January 1969 for a gig at the London Marquee; and it was immediately apparent that the recent rest had done them good. Their performance, *Melody Maker's* Chris Welch determined, "proved why they have been so successful in America", and even a smattering of equipment problems as the set got under way could not dent the band's confidence. Welch continued, "Jeff himself was in good form... (he) blew some nice blues and shone on his flag-waving piece 'Beck's (sic) Boogie.' Nicky Hopkins' piano came through loud and clear and gave the band a highly distinctive sound. Rod Stewart, a most under-rated singer, leapt and sang with his usual enthusiasm... The band as a unit are often a little rough, but are happily different and unpretentious, and once they get up a head of steam can blow many a group offstage."

In fact, Beck himself was less than happy with the performance – "We're all lazy bastards, I'll admit. The band has been rusty because we haven't been playing much recently." Neither would they be. Beck would drop by the Speakeasy to jam with Noel Redding one night, and the full band played a one-off show at the Toby Jug pub in Tolworth, just up the road from where Beck grew up. (His father attended the show. "He doesn't play round here so often", Beck Senior told a local journalist. "But I've got all his records!") Any intentions Peter Grant might have had of stringing together a longer sequence of shows, however, was stymied when American band Moby Grape arrived in town to launch their first British tour. Beck promptly loaned them the bulk of his own band's equipment.

The Toby Jug show also served another purpose, warming the band up for their first meaningful trip back to the recording studio since they completed Truth. Epic, the Jeff Beck Group's American label, had been agitating for a single for a few months now – although "Ol' Man River" had been on the schedule for a while, nothing from Truth ever hit them as being appropriate, while Most's suggestion that Beck simply cut the long-delayed follow-up to "Love Is Blue" fell on deaf ears as well. The label wanted something by the Jeff Beck Group itself, Rod Stewart vocal and all.

The problem was, of course, they had nothing to record. "Mother's Old Rice Pudding" remained the only new composition in the band's repertoire – and though they'd introduced a handful more covers, Beck couldn't help thinking that the group had already worked most of them to death on their last American tour. One idea did keep coming to mind, though. Elvis Presley's NBC TV comeback special *Elvis* was still fresh in a lot of people's minds – screened just six weeks earlier, Beck and the band themselves watched it in their LA hotel room and, afterward, all were smitten with an almost evangelical fervour: the King was back. What better way could there be to welcome him, then, that to deliver up a cover of one of his own greatest oldies, "All Shook Up"?

The song made sense in other ways as well. There was something of a rock'n'roll revival underway at the time – the Who had unearthed sundry old Eddie Cochran numbers for their live show; John Lennon was pondering a Plastic Ono Band whose live set would revolve around "Blue Suede Shoes" and "Hound Dog"; the Stones had reinstated Chuck Berry in their set to devastating effect. Bill Haley's "Rock Around The Clock" would soon be back on the British chart.

Mickie Most agreed. He was an Elvis nut as well – indeed, a few years down the road, he would have a full-time Elvis clone on his own RAK label as Mud arose from the early 1970s Glam-Rock movement, to spearhead their own rock'n'roll resurgence. "All Shook Up" it was, and on the B-side, a look back at another of Beck's formative influences, with a song written by the Shadows' Hank Marvin, "Throw Down A Line".

The problem was, as the session got underway, Beck couldn't help feeling that Most wasn't actually there; that he didn't, to put it bluntly, give "two fucks" about the Jeff Beck Group. "I think he just wanted to maintain his factory production-line hit thing, and we were just floundering about, trying to find a groove. The talent was there, but Mickie didn't have a fucking clue about what heavy rock was." The Jeff Beck Group, he insisted, was "pioneering big time"; all they needed was a sympathetic ear in the studio, to help them get their bearings. Instead, Most just let them get on with it.

The performance itself "wasn't too bad", Beck mused 35 years later. "If it doesn't sound toe-curlingly bad now, then it could've been pretty good." But far from standing as a finished master, the two songs the band recorded that afternoon were little more than a demo – and, as the session wore on, Beck was shocked to discover that he didn't care if they ever completed it. "All Shook Up" remained close to his heart. But "if you told me that I was going to have to play "Throw Down A Line" in front of a million people, I'd have run away." Neither was Hank Marvin himself especially disappointed by the non-appearance of Beck's version; he recorded the song in his own right that summer, pulled Cliff Richard in to handle lead vocals and wound up with a Number 7 hit – Cliff's last-but-one UK Top 10 hit for five long years.

There was another reason why the Jeff Beck Group never returned to the studio to complete that (or any other) single. According to Nicky Hopkins, they really couldn't stand to be that closely confined with one another. "There was so much unhappiness in the group. Woody was always moaning about something, and Mickey Waller was always demanding more money. Rod was – he was just Rod, and we could deal with that.

"But Ron and Mick were constantly going on about something, and it really was causing problems in the group. So Jeff called me one day and said 'Look, I'm thinking about getting rid of Wood, but I'm not sure how Mick will respond,' so I said, 'Maybe Mick could go as well, and we can start again with a whole new rhythm section.' It couldn't hurt, could it? So that's what happened." According to Woody, Peter Grant dropped the axe by telephone on 11 February – he remembered the date because it was his girlfriend Krissie's 21st birthday.

Stewart himself was aghast when he heard what was being planned. The Jeff Beck Group's next American tour was now just a week away, and he knew from experience how hard it was to break in just one new band member, let alone two. Besides, the Wood-Waller pairing was "the tightest rhythm section I ever heard" – that was why he'd retained it for his own album sessions. "I said it was a big mistake. But (Beck) wanted to get rid of them, and he wouldn't change his mind."

America, Beck responded, was no problem. They'd just cancel the first two weeks worth of shows – at the Fillmore East on Valentine's Day, the New York State University, the Kinetic Playground in Chicago, the Kiel Auditorium in St Louis and the Memorial Auditorium in Worcester. And, as for new musicians, he already had that in hand as well.

Headlining the Marquee back in April, Beck couldn't help noticing the bass player with the support group, New Nadir – Doug Jerebine was a New Zealander who, Beck determined, had all the power and presence that the Beck Group demanded. He now went under the name Doug Blake, but Beck tracked him down and lured him in regardless. (According to Beck biographer Annette Carson, he was then playing with Junior Walker and the All-Stars.)

The drum spot, meanwhile, was to be plugged by a player of somewhat wider renown. Tony Newman was drummer with Sounds Incorporated, an instrumental band that had been kicking around since the early 1960s, most notably as the backing band for any number of visiting American rockers (Beck's beloved Gene Vincent included), but also as an attraction in their own right – they scored a couple of minor UK hits in 1964 after Brian Epstein began taking an interest in their career; they contributed the horn section to the Beatles' "Good Morning Good Morning", and were the opening act at the Fab Four's New York Shea Stadium show. The group itself had slowed down after that as session work began subsumed their own activities and, when Beck called Newman, Sounds Incorporated had already called it a day. The drummer accepted the job on the spot.

As with Viv Prince and Jet Harris, back at the birth of the band, Beck was following his idealistic instincts, as much as his musical tastes, when he recruited Newman. "I'd seen (him) playing with Little Richard and Gene Vincent, and I thought 'this guy's a total thug, but he's got the chops. He could stand up and play, which I thought was cool, and still keep two bass drums going. I knew he was my guy... a total lunatic, and he fed the excitement back into the band that Mickey Waller had lost."

The only difficulty was, "Rod didn't like him because he was too uncouth, too loud." As with so much about the Jeff Beck Group, the very qualities that most enamoured Beck were those that least pleased Stewart. But that wasn't Beck's problem. Rod would just have to deal with it.

There was another change in the air, as the American dates drew closer. Beck was also having second thoughts about Nicky Hopkins. "(He) wasn't putting any muscle into the stage shows. Because of his status as a session man, he couldn't fit into the wildness of stage, so he was completely the wrong person." One night on stage, Beck laughed, Wood wandered over and flicked a cigarette ash onto Hopkins' shoulder. "It was still there at the end of the gig." Hopkins would survive the proposed purge, however. "He was a luxury that we thought might help out to do more poppy, Motowny rock stuff, (because) that was where I was headed, customising Motown into heavy rock. We had to make a wider line between guys and the Hendrix and Cream kind of stuff, and having a piano removed all of that."

Unaware of his narrow escape, Hopkins recalled the new line-up rehearsing hard, even taking a trip into the studio to cut the jam "Blues Title". According to Stewart, however, Blake himself "rehearsed with us just once, the night before we went onstage." Either way, the new look group departed for the US on 27 February 1969.

The tour itself would now launch at the Alexandria Roller Rink in Alexandria, Virginia, and immediately it was obvious that things simply weren't going to work out. Though Blake never put a foot wrong in rehearsal, onstage he proved totally unsuitable – to the band, to the performance, to the needs of a large-scale show. "We died the all-time death", Stewart shuddered. A heated meeting backstage following the show saw the hapless New Zealander sacked on the spot – and a hasty phone call made to Ron Wood to ask whether he would overlook the sacking that had wrecked his girlfriend's birthday and fly out to the States on the first flight he could find.

Woody refused. Though less than a month had elapsed since their firing, he and Waller had already struck up a new partnership with Leigh Stephens, the former frontman with Blue Cheer, who was now based in London following that band's implosion. Things were still in the earliest phase, but Wood was determined. It would take a hell of a lot more money than he had ever previously been offered to persuade him to drop everything for a band that had already sacked him once.

To his amazement, Beck was equally determined to have him back. A lot was hanging on this tour, financially and otherwise, but they were already earning enough to make it worth Woody's while. Although the actual amount that he received remains in question – Wood once claimed it was £2,000 per show, although Nicky Hopkins said it was considerably less ("That was more than we earned from some gigs") an agreement was finally thrashed out. At least one more show, at the Boston Symphony Hall was cancelled while they awaited Wood's arrival; finally, on 7 March, the tour could resume, with two shows crammed into one day – a replacement date for the cancelled State University concert in the afternoon, then the Island Garden Arena in nearby West Hempstead that evening.

Disaster was still waiting in the wings, however. Just three gigs later, at Chicago's Kinetic Playground, a passing stranger took it upon himself to spike Stewart, Wood and Hopkins's joint. "Luckily, I had only one tiny little smoke of it", Beck recalled, "but it knocked them sparko and I don't think they ever recovered from it. They were acting like a bunch of schoolkids." Topping a bill that already threatened their supremacy, via the inclusion of the newly solo (and fast-rising) Van Morrison, the Jeff Beck Group's performance was so erratic that at least one group of fans was standing at the box office demanding their money back before the show was even four songs old.

"Nobody knew what they were doing", fan Marty Lake still seethes, almost 40 years on. "Beck would play one song, Wood would start another and Stewart was just giggling to himself. We sat through this for three songs... which was actually more like a dozen, because everyone was playing something different... and that was it. We were out of there."

But such external disruptions only masked the nature of the Jeff Beck Group's real problem. "After the night of the sackings", Stewart swore, "the band was never the same again." The gigs went ahead as planned, and there were no major knockdown battles to speak of. But the magic that marked the Jeff Beck Group's last American visit was sorely lacking. Wood was clearly playing the part of a mercenary sessionman, making it clear at every opportunity that he would be just as happy to fly home as drag around on a bad-tempered bus. And there was also a sense of staleness, the knowledge that the vast majority of the band's live set had now been in place for close to two years without any sign of new material pushing into view. "Mother's Old Rice Pudding" continued to evolve, but it remained little more than a masturbatory gesture at a time when the release of the first Led Zeppelin album had raised the musical bar higher than the Jeff Beck Group now seemed capable of leaping.

Led Zeppelin I was issued on schedule, in January 1969, and immediately listeners were drawn in one of two directions – either it was, as *Rolling Stone's* John Mendelsohn pointed out, no more than an inferior twin of Truth, offering "little that... the Jeff Beck Group didn't say as well or better three months ago"; or, as *Oz* enthused, one of those rare LPs that so defy "immediate classification or description, simply because (they are) so obviously a turning point in rock."

Both opinions are valid. The patent lifting of "You Shook Me", after all, was only the first of the debts that Led Zeppelin I owed to Truth; elsewhere, "Black Mountain Side" echoed the acoustic interlude offered by "Greensleeves", while the very sound of the two albums posited heavy blues extremes towards which no other act of the time dared to journey. Zeppelin even borrowed Beck's typographer – Royal College of Art student George Hardie worked with photographer Stephen Goldblatt on the Truth sleeve, and was rewarded with an introduction to Peter Grant. He went on to design the sleeve to Led Zeppelin I.

For all these similarities, coincidences and borrowings, however, Beck is honest in his assessment of the two records. "The thing with Truth was, it was never really developed. We had a sound, and it turned out to be a colossally influential one, but we weren't interested in just making the same record again and again. Which means I've had to sit back here for the past 30 years, watching people perfect it and, when Led Zeppelin started doing huge concerts, I was sitting in my garage listening to the radio, and going 'what's going on? I started this shit, and look at me!'"

Ultimately, what Led Zeppelin had and the Jeff Beck Group didn't, is vision. Even before he ever put his finger on a life beyond the Yardbirds, Jimmy Page knew he would be in control of his destiny. "The one thing I was sure of was that I was going to produce the band myself, because I knew about the studio," he told journalist Nick Kent. "I'd been an apprentice for years, and I'd discovered things that someone like Mickie (Most) didn't have a clue even existed." The Jeff Beck Group, on the other hand, was beholden to Mickie Most for permission to even think about going into the studio.

Without even appearing to question the right, Led Zeppelin took absolute control of everything they did. Everything. Although Peter Grant still operated out of the RAK Music Management offices on Oxford Street, and RAK financed the physical recording of Led Zeppelin I, it was clear from the outset that there was no room for Mickie Most in the new set-up. And why, Most himself asked, should there be? Displaying every last ounce of the arrogance and self-confidence which both friends and enemies admired in him, and a shameless ability to revise history, he threw his own opinion on Led Zeppelin into the same camp as the band's detractors.

Yes they were a great band, yes they had some good ideas. But whatever Led Zeppelin might have achieved so far, he'd already been there, done that, and bought the souvenir T-shirt. "Truth was a forerunner to Led Zeppelin", he declared. "A great album – which I made."

Now he was wondering whether it might be time to make another, a question that Beck himself had already answered. Led Zeppelin I not only infuriated him, it alarmed him as well – muscling into a musical constituency that he already considered his own, and doing so with such assurance that, even as Zeppelin's first American tour opened to a storm of enthusiasm, the musicians themselves were already looking towards their next album. If the Jeff Beck Group had any hope of keeping up with these newly enriched Joneses, they needed to get themselves into the studio.

"The sales of Truth had tailed off", Beck explained, "we hadn't anything to tell the radio stations about why we were touring again without a record, and attendances were dropping off, which was a drag. We were in that dark area between 3,000 seaters and the big stuff, which wasn't really that widespread at the time", but the lack of any new point of interest saw the Group as likely to play "ice rinks to six people" as they were to pack "three thousand in a two-thousand seater, with people busting down the doors to get in."

It was clear what they needed to do – but just in case anyone had missed the point, a mid-tour missive from Mickie Most spelled it out in back and white. "Mickie was telling us that the attendances weren't good enough for us to make money, that we were undoing the good work we'd done last year with Truth. Other bands were coming in and steamrollering us..." And, of course, Led Zeppelin were steamrollering them.

In Miami, teenage fan DiMartino caught them at Thee Image and immediately revised his opinion about the best gig he'd ever attended... "Zeppelin were stunning." He acknowledged that they were "like Jeff Beck." But they were "noisier, looser, more extreme."

A few nights later at the Fillmore East, Zeppelin's performance was so intense, and the audience reaction so hysterical, that the headlining Iron Butterfly delayed their onstage arrival by 45 minutes in the hope that the crowd would calm down. They hoped in vain, and Led Zeppelin never went out as a support group again.

Beck watched all of this unfold, and he knew that the stakes had been upped so high that nothing short of perfection could top them. Led Zeppelin's next American tour was scheduled to begin in April – less than two months away. If the Jeff Beck Group was ever going to grab back their crown, they needed to do it now.

Today, Beck's admirers can look back on the turmoil of these times, and with hindsight washing over their judgement, comprehend the guitarist in the light of his subsequent activities. Bernie Tormé, for example, speaks for many when he says, "I don't think Beck ever got the credit for the way he changed the world: there was literally no-one else around. And when other people poked their heads up, they were basically imitation white blues players. I loved Clapton in the Bluesbreakers and Cream – but, knowing what I know now, Clapton was really just recycling Freddie King, louder, for white Europeans... In his own unbeatable way, granted. But not like Beck, who single-handedly created an entire genre, psychedelic heavy guitar. At the time he was the touchstone, the one every guitarist listened to."

More than money, more than touring, more than anything, the band now had to get home and give them something new to listen to. And that meant getting off the road and getting down to some serious songwriting. Two dishevelled weeks into a six-week tour of the United States, Beck announced he'd had enough – and did so as publicly as he could, live on air with Detroit DJ Russ Gibb, following two nights (21/22 February) at the local Grande Ballroom. "The next thing we're gonna do? We're going home on Monday." The group played one final show in Minneapolis the following evening, then fled. In fact, as Hopkins recalled. "We'd wake up one morning in the States and (Jeff) had left the night before and was in England. It was ridiculous."

The cost of cancellation was high, of course. Industry sources estimated the band had turned their back on a quarter of a million dollars in tour revenues alone, and many times more damage to Beck's own reputation. Among the cancelled dates was a run at the Fillmore

West, and Bill Graham spoke for many of his colleagues when he asked whether any promoter in his right mind would even contemplate booking a Beck tour, knowing that he might just as easily blow it out on a whim?

Graham himself took to demanding a deposit from Beck before he would even consider booking him into one of his venues; other promoters, Beck admitted, were content with hanging "a big neon sign over my head, saying 'Unreliable Motherfucker.' For a while, people wanted my grandmother as a hostage before they'd let me do anything."

Even the loosely floated notion that Beck's health was suffering – the faithful old standby that had served him through the Yardbirds – was no longer holding water. If he was that ill, maybe he shouldn't have been touring in the first place. "There has been a genuine health problem", a RAK spokesman tried to assure cynics. "We know this is the usual excuse but, in Jeff's case, this is true. He will be resting for a while, and then he hopes to get an album and possibly a single together in the next few weeks." And therein lay the true nature of the health problems.

"(A new) album was needed desperately in order to finish the tour", Beck reflected. "Back then, the rule of thumb was, an album per tour. You didn't try to tour twice on the same album. We were doing the same small circuit, Detroit-Cleveland-Boston, playing small ballrooms, and we'd have been going back trying to do the same act again – it wouldn't have worked."

CHAPTER
TWENTY-TWO

Work towards the Jeff Beck Group's second album got underway at De Lane Lea Studios in London on 3 April, with a fresh stab at the Elvis song they'd already demoed back in February, "All Shook Up". It went well, as well – so much so that seven days later, they would assault a second Presley number, "Jailhouse Rock". It was only later that Nicky Hopkins admitted, "of course they kept doing Elvis songs. They didn't have anything else, and if Mickie hadn't put his foot down and started talking about the publishing the whole album would have been old rock'n'roll covers."

If Most did convince the band otherwise, then that was one of the few concrete contributions he made to the entire record. Mindful of the mess they'd made of their last studio sojourn, Beck opened the sessions by asking whether Most might step aside once again and let the band bring in an outside producer – someone who maybe understood their music a little better. He tried to be diplomatic about it as well, but Most was furious. "I could hear them shouting at one another", Hopkins reported. "Jeff was saying he wanted a different producer, so Mickie said maybe they should bring in another guitar player as well, because that was the only way they were going to get anything done."

Neither did matters improve once they got down to recording. Most had already resigned himself to the album being a rush job, but even he wasn't prepared for how little preparation the band had actually done.

Beck had already decided that the new album needed to move in a different direction to its predecessor. The problem was, he didn't know what that direction was. He couldn't simply remake Truth "because we'd already done it once", and Zeppelin had done it again. He decided to wing it. "I didn't know what I was gonna do in the morning at breakfast... that whole album was pretty well dreamt up on the spot." Indeed, if Truth had been blighted by a paucity of new material, this new set was to be devastated by it.

Reiterating the lament he first sang around Truth, Beck reiterated, "what we needed was, we should have got a good writer in. And that really was all we needed, a great songwriter, someone like Elton John or Steve Harley. We needed a great writer, we needed a lyricist." Instead, they had Rod Stewart.

"Rod had started writing by this time", Beck continued, "but his lyrics were pretty awful (Stewart himself calls them "silly"). The pair did manage to hatch the rudiments of three songs – "Spanish Boots", "The Hangman's Knee" and the hard-riffing "Plynth (Water Down The Drain)", all conceived according to the same regimen Stewart had devised for his own solo songwriting sessions. Beck would come up with a clutch of guitar lines, then Stewart would take them home and "come up with some ridiculous lyrics which we pinned on some of my riffs."

Wood, too, threw himself into the process – "(he) came up with some pretty cool licks", Beck mused. "'Water Down The Drain' was his bass line." Other ideas, Stewart said, would be hatched at Wood's mum's council house. "We used to sit around with two bars of the heating on, with Mrs Wood coming in and saying 'don't waste the electricity, turn that other bar off'."

Nicky Hopkins' much vaunted songwriting abilities, however, were confined to a clutch of co-writes, and just one original song – "Girl From Mill Valley," a paean to his girlfriend of the time. "I suppose it does look strange", Hopkins admitted, "Jeff talking about how I was brought in to help with the songwriting… But I never claimed to be a songwriter as such; what I brought to the group was the shading that took, say, a very ordinary song and gave it something more interesting. I was a catalyst rather than a composer." Except they were not allowing him to catalyse – Beck later claimed that "Girl From Mill Valley" was only recorded "(as) a way of keeping (Hopkins) quiet, because he wasn't really doing much in terms of a feature," then revealed that the composer wasn't even responsible for all the keyboards. John Paul Jones dropped by to add the Hammond organ.

Mickie Most was no help whatsoever. He just wanted the job done as quickly as possible, overlooking even the most glaring errors (a two-bar drop-out during "Spanish Boots" the most obvious) in his haste to wrap up one session and get the next one underway. "We didn't get time to redo anything", Beck mourned. "Mickie was 'I got Lulu or Herman coming in at four'."

At the time, he tried to put a brave face on Most's treatment of the band. "All (Mickie) wants to do is make hit records", Beck told *Zig Zag* magazine that summer, "and all I want to do is play my music. When 'Love Is Blue' was recorded, he was terribly difficult to work with. He really let me know who was boss. But when he went to the States and saw us play, and realised just how huge the market was, he did a big swallow and said 'What have I been doing all this time?' And now he's a lot more lenient as to what material we recorded; in fact, he's enjoying what we're doing now."

No he wasn't. He was simply putting up with it, in the hope that the breakthrough enjoyed by Truth might be amplified by this latest project. Indeed, if any one song summed up the sessions, it was "Mother's Old Rice Pudding", the only "new" number in the band's existing live set, and purportedly the model around which the entire funky ethos of the set was built. Unfortunately, it was also indulgent, untogether and went on way too long – faults, said Beck, that still stand as "a snapshot of the situation at the time. With the bad feeling in the band, it's obvious what was going on."

Into the midst of this unfolding nightmare, there wandered a Swedish camera crew, led by director Lasse Hallstrom, visiting London to film a 30-minute TV documentary about the local music scene. Mickie Most was just one of the programme's several focal points – Paul Jones, Amen Corner, busker Don Partridge and Eurovision hopeful Clodagh Rodgers were also profiled, while Most's empire would reappear via a short sequence with Terry Reid.

Kram (Hug in English) was broadcast in Sweden on 28 April 1969, and included excerpts of the band recording "Water Down The Drain" and some footage of Beck overdubbing guitar on "Mother's Old Rice Pudding." But more memorable were the confrontations that the cameras caught, like Stewart approaching Most to request some guidance with his vocal, only to be told "sing it however you want", and later, as an out-of-sorts Beck complained about the haste with which they were expected to record, an exasperated Most moaned back about Beck's own unreliability.

"We're trying to bundle everything into one day", Beck complains. "Well, not really", Most snaps back. "We have been... you didn't show up last Saturday, we're supposed to be doing this over two Saturdays and you didn't show up last Saturday. You went home early Friday, because you didn't feel well, didn't show up Saturday, so that's a day and a half lost."

"That's what I mean, we're trying to cram it all into one session", Beck reasons. "It's very difficult, looking at a blank wall trying to get inspiration for this sort of stuff." He could probably knock off everything in the next two hours, he said, but he'd prefer to be given four, "just to be on the safe side",

"Yes", replies Most. "But the rest of the world can't sit around waiting for Jeff Beck." No less than during the recording of "Hi Ho Silver Lining", Mickie Most had his sessions mapped out with almost military precision – two hours for the backing track, from 11 till 1. Break for lunch for an hour, and then work on the vocals till 5. Mix and overdub until 7, and then home for dinner. Repeat as necessary, over however many days. Record complete.

Beck was throwing that entire plan into the garbage, but finally Most gave way. "We are behind, and I'd like to have finished today, but we're (also) behind with the cover, and if it's going to be rubbish for a couple of hours then forget it. I haven't gone through a week of this..."

The album was to be titled Cosa Nostra Beck Ola, a name derived in part from Grant's affectionate nickname for Beck (after the old Rockola jukeboxes), and in part from a pun hatched by Mickie Most, playing on a double-meaning that, sadly, went right past the record company. Cosa Nostra is, of course, an alternate name for the Sicilian Mafia, and that, said Most, "suits the band's music. It's evil." But it translates as "our thing", and that is exactly what the album was intended to represent – the Jeff Beck Group's own personal "thing."

Beck himself regarded the completed Cosa Nostra Beck-Ola with an almost bitter weariness. Penning the liner notes, he mused, "With all the hard competition in the music business, it's almost impossible to come up with something totally original. So we haven't." He was selling himself short, although it was only in hindsight that the album's greatest strengths became evident.

Cosa Nostra Beck-Ola was marketed as the guitarist's latest rock album, and was left sprawling in the mud in comparison with Truth. What Epic and Columbia should have done was call it what it was – rock's first funk record, the consequence of all those nights the Jeff Beck Group spent speeding across America with James Brown, Motown and Stax pounding out of the radios; of those concerts where any number of local support bands spliced their own formative influences with psychedelic fashion; and, most of all, the music that Stewart, Beck and Wood, at least, had each spent the last near-decade listening to.

Recalling those evenings sitting around the two bar electric fire, Wood described his and Stewart's songwriting procedure – "Take the bit where the Temptations do this, and Booker T does that... the Meters, Gladys Knight, James Brown... Rod always idolised Sam Cooke..." Add to that the Sly sensations that draped "Mother's Old Rice Pudding" months before it arrived in the studio and, when they threw it all in together, the only thing that stopped anyone from noticing what they'd accomplished was, the actual timing of the accomplishment's release.

A month before Sly and the Family Stone became superstars at Woodstock, six months before Jimi Hendrix took a similarly blindfold plunge with his own Band Of Gypsies funk experiment (then reiterated his own affection for Beck by borrowing a riff from "Rice Pudding", for his own "In From The Storm"); and a full year before Beck himself went to Detroit to record at the Motown Studios, Cosa Nostra Beck Ola laid the foundations for an entire new musical hybrid.

If only there had been more of it. An amusing exchange in Kram, presumably shot after the band had listened to a playback of the album-so-far, sees Beck asking what the eighth song is. Most turns around and tells him, "there isn't one."

And so it proved. Although a couple of out-takes have surfaced, both on the 2004 CD remaster and in the researches of sundry scholars and collectors, the seven tracks which made up the final album were all that they completed. The album sessions were not the Group's sole concern, after all. Although the cancelled American dates had been lost, a clutch of fresh shows had been scheduled for early May – two in New York (originally the final shows of the last tour), four nights at the ever-faithful Boston Tea Party and a final blast at Yale University's Woolsey Hall on 9 May.

A new act needed to be rehearsed in time for that, and the new songs had to be broken in even sooner – on 25 April, less than 24 hours after they'd finished mixing the album tapes, the Jeff Beck Group played their first live show since returning from America (and their last before returning there) at the latest in the London Lyceum's series of Friday night 'Midnight Court' concerts.

Al Stewart had been originally scheduled to headline, while Caravan, Ron Geesin and the newly-emergent Edgar Broughton Band completed the menu. Ticket sales, however, were sluggish and when Beck was leapfrogged to the top of the bill less than a week before showtime the night sold out straight away. It was a great gig. No less than five of the new album songs were featured in the set – both Presley covers, plus "Plynth", "Spanish Boots" and the restructured "Rice Pudding". Truth supplied the rest of the set – there was no room for the hit singles now.

Small Faces keyboardist Ian McLagan was in the audience that evening, with bandmates Kenny Jones and Ronnie Lane. Their own band had just been shattered by the departure of vocalist Steve Marriott, off to form his Humble Pie supergroup. Mac was well-accustomed to Rod Stewart by now – they'd gigged together in the past, and were recording together on the Stewart solo sessions, which were still dribbling along. But it was only when he saw him up on the Lyceum stage, cocksure and camp, such a natural showman, that the three Faces suddenly realised that they were looking towards their own future. "I could hardly take my eyes off (Rod)", Mac later remarked. "He was so flash!"

There again, the entire Jeff Beck Group was on form that evening. "Nicky really blew my mind", Mac continued. "Hunched over the piano at one side of the stage, not even looking at his hands, his fingers were all over the place. He made it look so easy, but he had no ego." The band as a whole, Mac enthused, "was great"; the entire night was "fantastic." He was not to know that the next time Rod Stewart and Ron Wood stepped onto a British stage, it would be in the company of McLagan, Jones and Lane themselves.

The Jeff Beck Group's fourth American tour kicked off at the Fillmore East on 2 May. Joe Cocker shared the bill with them, and Stewart later admitted, "following him onstage scared the living daylights out of me." Cocker was still a comparative unknown in America – his earth-shattering performance at Woodstock was still a masterpiece waiting to happen, and his UK chart-topping rendition of the Beatles' "With A Little Help From My Friends" had climbed no higher than Number 68 in the States. But Stewart knew who he was, and knew precisely how tightly Cocker would wind the Fillmore audience around his finger. He needed to be on great form to have even a hope of following Cocker... and even greater form the night Cocker joined the Group themselves on stage to trade vocals on a song or two.

Stewart's nervousness was not helped by having strained his vocal chords, a malady that at least some of the audience was quick to notice. "The excitement was slightly dampened", *Cashbox's* review mused, "but the rest of the group, especially pianist Nicky Hopkins, took up the slack nicely." Nevertheless, the majority of the review was devoted to Cocker's performance, while reviews elsewhere on the tour suggested that Stewart was not the only star who needed to look to his laurels.

"Jeff Beck is dead", announced Boston's *The Tech*. "(He) could be fantastic if he wanted to. Listen to "Jeff's Boogie", "Happenings Ten Years Time Ago" and other early Yardbirds material. Presently, however, he's on a big ego trip, and it's too bad..." Too bad, because Led Zeppelin were now muscling so formidably into Jeff Beck Group territory that even the most devoted acolyte was drawing parallels between the two bands, and finding Beck wanting.

Neither was the new material at all likely to resurrect the Beck Group's reputation. Having blown out a string of gigs in order to hustle an album into life, the band now discovered that it was all in vain. Delays at the record company, problems with the sleeve design (mysteriously, a reproduction of René Magritte's La Chambre d'Ecouté had been chosen for the front cover), and a log-jam of similarly high-profile releases all jousting for daylight all saw Cosa Nostra Beck Ola's release pushed back to mid-June, ensuring that the band would spend the next six weeks touring a record that nobody even had a chance of hearing – and which they might not want to hear again.

Without exception, live performances of the latest songs were, at best, meandering, at worst unfocussed. While Led Zeppelin were tearing up the concert circuit with some of the most incendiary performances of the age, the Jeff Beck Group was foundering badly, as though they already knew the game was up. "We're going home to cut the third album", Beck insisted during an interview in New York, but even he didn't sound convinced.

In fact, the band followed Mickie Most into Advision in mid-May, to cut half a dozen songs with Donovan. Although the singer's public profile remained high, there was a growing feeling within the RAK hierarchy that he was, as Beck puts it, "getting (into) a rut, strumming his acoustic guitar" and spending less time writing the kind of structured songs that Most most admired in favour of looser watercolours that would then be moistened in the studio and allowed to run where they would.

Certainly the material that Donovan was stockpiling for his next album was pointing him in a considerably less disciplined direction than the run of hits that preceded it – gone was the razor-sharp pop vision of "Hurdy Gurdy Man", "Sunshine Superman" and "Jennifer Juniper"; in their place came silly singalongs like "I Love My Shirt" and "Happiness Runs", pseudo-mystic mumblings like "Atlantis", and so on.

He was spreading himself thin. The constant touring and TV work demanded by his American success necessarily consumed a lot of his time, but there was also a sense that Donovan was turning into some kind of rent-a-hippy TV personality and losing great swathes of his audience in the process. Released as a British single in late 1968, "Atlantis" sank almost as thoroughly as the legendary civilisation it deified; in the US, it was his first big hit in a year.

Mickie Most seized upon one last, inspired gambit. Instinctively, he knew that Donovan's traditional audience had little time for the growing sensitivity and politics that now fired the Scotsman's muse, just as he was aware (or had finally accepted) that Jeff Beck's hard-rock constituency really didn't appreciate his dips into Top 20 fodder. But what if one was to combine the two – place Donovan in a setting the 'heavies' might appreciate, at the same time as pushing Beck towards the teenies he had hitherto regarded as beneath him? It was definitely worth a try, particularly when Beck, for once, greeted the idea with the utmost enthusiasm.

It was a dynamic collaboration. According to Beck, Donovan "walked into the studio, picked up a guitar and strummed the song, while we joined in and wailed behind him. Sometimes these things work and sometimes they don't, (but) this session just burst into flames."

What most impressed him was the sheer spontaneity of it all. Although they'd really only planned to record a couple of songs, they would wind up with half-a-dozen, several of which were more-or-less written on the spot. Indeed, as a laughing Beck pointed out, "a song with a title like ("Goo Goo Barabajagal") isn't something you sit at home planning for six months." That wouldn't hold it back, however. "Goo Goo Barabajagal" reached Number 12 in the UK that summer, Beck's biggest hit since the Yardbirds days – and Donovan's last hit single ever.

"It was a pretty damned good idea, and a great record", Beck continued. "It was a nonsense lyric, which was perfect because I can't stand love songs or any of that wistful sentimental shit; and it was a funky groove Tony Newman came up with this funky groove which you'd die for, a really hip groove, and the notion of that, plus my guitar with Donovan, seemed to work on that particular track. I love quirky surprises, and that really fit the bill."

Surprising, too, is the pervasive legend that, among the backing vocalists on the single, was the young Suzi Quatro, a tale that is even relayed in the booklet accompanying Donovan's 2005 box set. Unfortunately, it isn't true, as Quatro herself explains. "The Donovan album I sang on was Cosmic Wheels, and the track was 'Music Maker'."

Indeed it did. "Everything else this week fades into insignificance against this gem of a record", trumpeted the *New Musical Express'* review. "This totally compelling, marvellous little single is the kind of song from which pop standards are made. (And) though it's Donovan's song, the importance of the Beck Group's contribution cannot be understated."

The remainder of the session was equally radiant. "Bed With Me" (as in "won't you go to...") was an infectious, breathy romp that was immediately selected as the B-side of the single (and, just as immediately, retitled "Trudi" so as not to offend the Powers That Be), while "Stromberg Twins" was a half-skewed Beach Boys pastiche that was "written in California about two girls and a carburettor." "From Here On In, Your Guess Is As Good As Mine", and "Suffer Little Children" are at least remembered fondly by both Donovan and Beck.

But though Donovan's own next album was titled for the hit single, the Jeff Beck Group were otherwise conspicuous by their absence – and have remained so. Donovan would finally allow "Homesickness" to shine amid his HMS Donovan album, and "Stromberg Twins" was eventually released aboard the CD remaster of the Barabajagal album. But the collaboration that Beck is convinced could have formed the basis for a full Donovan/Jeff Beck Group album was otherwise abandoned. "We should have done that", Beck admitted. "But then Donovan had to go off on tour, and then we broke up, so that was the end of it."

CHAPTER
TWENTY-THREE

That break-up was to be a slow, almost interminable affair. It commenced just days after the Donovan sessions, as Beck and Nicky Hopkins fell into an argument over the Jeff Beck Group's future that ended with Hopkins walking out of the band forever. "4 June 1969", Hopkins reflected. "I don't know why I remember it."

Throughout his time with the Jeff Beck Group, Hopkins' biggest bone of contention was the band's sheer unreliability. "We could have made it so big", he said in 1973. "Every opportunity was there, and we blew it by constantly cancelling tours." What made things especially galling for Hopkins was the knowledge that he could have been making a tidy, not to mention satisfying, living as a sessionman alone.

He toured because he enjoyed it, because it got him out of the studio where he'd spent most of his career. But, if he wasn't touring, he still wanted to be working, and he worked hard to schedule his future commitments so that everything fell into place alongside one another. The loss of the third American tour infuriated him, but his efforts to push Beck into promising that it would not happen again were doomed to failure. Finally he snapped. Management was a problem, the roadies were a problem, and Jeff Beck was "totally unsuited to be leading a successful band." "I told him, 'if you can't guarantee work, then I'll go somewhere else that can,'" Hopkins recalled, and it was only pride, he laughed, that prevented him from calling Jimmy Page right then, and asking if the job was still available. "Well, pride and the fact that I knew he'd say no."

Woody was the next to make his dissatisfaction known. The same week that Hopkins quit the band, the *New Musical Express* reported that Wood, too, was leaving, to join forces with the former Small Faces as lead guitarist. He was already rehearsing with the trio at the Rolling Stones' studios in Bermondsey, south London, and though "no definite date has been set" for the band's relaunch, the union was set to enjoy a low-key launch-of-sorts, opening for PP Arnold at a Cambridge University May Ball a few days later.

Art Wood, Ronnie's brother, was in charge of putting the band together, an ad hoc affair that would be loose enough to give the students their money's worth, and entertaining enough to maybe have some kind of a future. Though Wood's own band, the Artwoods (and, as they faded, the Saint Valentine's Day Massacre) were both long gone, but his record label, Fontana, retained sufficient faith in the bandleader to offer him unlimited studio time in which to carve out a future. Quiet Melon, as Wood had already christened his new project, was the vehicle with which he'd achieve that.

Brother Ronnie was an inevitable inclusion; so, at his suggestion, were the rest of the Small Faces, Ronnie Lane, Ian McLagan and Kenny Jones. Bassist Kim Gardner was happy to give it a go, and when Woody mentioned the outing to Stewart, he was begging to be included as well.

Stewart had finally wrapped up An Old Raincoat Won't Ever Let You Down, and was justifiably thrilled with what he'd accomplished. But he was also at a loose end. The album would not see the light of day for at least another six months, the Jeff Beck Group was at another of its standstills, and the only piece of even putatively paid work Stewart had all summer was a favour for John Peel. The DJ had just signed an Australian band, Python Lee Jackson, to his Dandelion label, but was having trouble getting a decent vocal out of singer David Bentley. Would Stewart come down and lay down a few guide vocals, just to show Bentley how it was done?

Stewart agreed, and took his fee in carpeting for his car. Three years later, the best of the three songs he recorded with the band, "In A Broken Dream," was riding high up both the British and American charts, buoyant on the brilliance of the most recognisable voice in contemporary rock – and Stewart wasn't owed a penny in royalties. He didn't even still have the carpeting, either. "I was conned."

That unpleasantness was far off in the future, though. For now, the May Ball offered Stewart an irresistible opportunity to celebrate his own record's completion – the pay was pretty good as well. The band was set to collect a £200 fee, plus all the champagne and strawberries they could devour.

There was little time in which to plan for the show, although the nature of May Balls themselves scarcely demanded the utmost professionalism. Rather, the concerts were staged to mark the end of the undergraduates' University year, with all the drinking, carousing and generally bad behaviour that that entailed. Any musicians fortunate enough to be engaged for such an occasion was required to do little more than make a lot of noise, play some songs that the students might recognise through their haze, and keep the party spirits up as high as they possibly could. Which was one thing that the Small Faces contingent, at least, would have no trouble pulling off.

A set list was worked out, one that revolved almost exclusively around the kind of classic rock and blues numbers that everyone in the band was familiar with. With 45 minutes to fill, Art Wood remembers simply working up a list of "mainly standards… a lot of blues numbers". "Got My Mojo Working", "What'd I Say" and "Hoochie Coochie Man" are among the few that anyone involved can actually remember. "It was a general piss-up", Ian McLagan confirmed, "and we went on without any rehearsal."

The show went well – high-spirited, chaotic and wild. "We came off the stage, ready to have a beer and go home", Art Wood continued. "So everyone started having a few drinks and throwing strawberry pies at each other. When the promoter came up to us and said PP Arnold wasn't going to play, and would we go back on for another £250? We were back up there as soon as he said it."

The evening was an absolute triumph; the very next day, in fact, Art Wood was on the phone with a Cambridge-based promoter, Rufus Manning, lining up a few more shows – a second May Ball at Oxford University, and another University show somewhere in Surrey, where they ran into Long John Baldry and keyboard-player Jimmy Horowitz and promptly added them to the line-up for the night.

According to Baldry, at least one more show followed – he recalls playing "two or three (gigs), but there might have been more." It was not, to his mind, a serious project: "I just went along and we did what we did. I remember showing up and doing silly things." In fact, he later admitted to not even being sure what the group was called – "Quiet Melon... Deaf Melon...."

Kim Gardner agreed. Talking in 1996, he admitted, "I never thought of Quiet Melon as anything more than a chance to mess around with some friends, and I don't think anybody else did... it was fun, but to be honest, I'd completely forgotten about it until a couple of years ago when suddenly people began asking me about it and I had to sit back and think about it."

The reason for that sudden revival was Art Wood's rediscovery of the tapes that Quiet Melon recorded for Fontana, around the same time as the live shows: as he told *Record Collector* magazine, "I swept up the leaderless fragments of the Small Faces – Ronnie Lane, Ian McLagan and Kenney Jones – plus Ron (Wood) and Rod Stewart, and dragged them all down to the studios."

Retaining the Quiet Melon name – "I wanted (one) that wouldn't immediately be associated with the Artwoods". The team quickly recorded four songs, Wood originals with the working titles "Diamond Joe", "Engine 4444", "Right Around The Thumb" and "Two Steps To Mother". But that was as far as the matter went. Though the performances clearly presaged much of what the Faces would aspire towards on their own first recordings, with Stewart's share of the vocals a simultaneous link to the Jeff Beck Group, Philips, Fontana's parent label, was not impressed. "We delivered the tapes (and they) said they weren't good enough, and called a halt to my free studio time. I told them I'd done my bit and it was up to them if they didn't want the stuff."

Agent Manning took over now, offering the tapes to various other labels. The Beatles' Apple and Kit Lambert/Chris Stamp's Track Records were both interested for a time, but eventually moved away – apparently, Stewart's still-complicated management situation turned them off. Warner Brothers were keen, too, but would take so long to make their decision that, by the time they did get back to Wood, he'd lost interest, and the band had lost patience. Kim Gardner was now rehearsing alongside Tony Ashton and Roy Dyke in the brilliant Ashton, Gardner & Dyke; Lane, McLagan and Jones were back in Bermondsey; and Wood and Stewart, though their hearts, too, lay in south London, had rejoined the Jeff Beck Group for its final, painful weeks of life.

Jeff Beck shared their lack of enthusiasm. Another live show had just bitten the dust – the Jeff Beck Group was meant to have played the Marquee on 6 June, but Hopkins' precipitous departure knocked that one on the head. They were meant to be getting some serious practice time as well but, with Stewart and Wood running around with their friends, it was easier just to quietly cancel the rehearsals and stay at home with Celia.

Only Tony Newman's continued enthusiasm prevented Beck from calling it a day then and there; without him, Beck admitted, the group might not even have hung together long enough to make their last ever UK appearance, accompanying Donovan through "Goo Goo Barabajagal" on *Top Of The Pops* on 26 June. It might have already been buried by the time their second album, Cosa Nostra Beck-Ola, was actually released.

Once again, the album appeared in the US first at the end of June, with the British launch held back until September when the group was scheduled to launch its next UK outing. The band itself was back in the US on 1 July, to catch the first reviews of the record – and, for a moment, the mood in the party could not help but brighten.

"This is a brilliant album", declared *Rolling Stone*, "dense in texture, full of physical and nervous energy, equally appealing to mind and body." It possessed, raved writer Ben Gerson, "a guiding intelligence which allows these five excellent, assertive musicians to work with, and not against, each other."

How wry were the looks that shot between the quartet as they read those words – and how quickly were their egos deflated by the events unfolding around them. The Jeff Beck Group had a month's worth of gigs ahead of them, yet they had barely settled into their New York hotel rooms, than they learned that the Powers That Be had decided to regard the tour as a simple promotional outing – a billing which did not decrease the group's workload, but which would certainly impact upon their earnings. Negatively, of course.

Tempers were fraying. Stewart picked up the phone and asked the desk to put him through to Beck's room. Beck wasn't registered at the hotel. "It was getting too ridiculous for words near the end", Stewart sighed. "We were trying to hide from each other all the time. One would stay at the Hilton, and the others would stay at Hotel Third On The Bill around the corner." No prizes for guessing who was staying at the Hilton.

The tour opened in Schenectady, in the backwoods of New York State; moved on to the Fillmore East, where Jethro Tull and Soft White Underbelly – the future Blue Öyster Cult – awaited them; and then hit a pair of festivals, the 16th annual Newport Jazz Festival in Rhode Island, on Independence Day, and the New York Pop Festival on Randalls Island the following day.

Both offered up some ferocious competition: Blood Sweat and Tears, Ten Years After and Jethro Tull joined the Jeff Beck Group at Newport, where they played beneath the somewhat deceptive banner of "an evening of jazz rock." A festival-best audience of 24,000-plus, however, was not disappointed – indeed, demand for tickets for the weekend was so vast that, two days after the Jeff Beck Group's appearance, a scheduled performance by Led Zeppelin came close to being cancelled as the city fathers rose in protest at the invasion.

In the end, Peter Grant – ferociously dividing his time between Beck's gigs and Zeppelin's – was able to calm their ruffled feathers, but the lesson had been learned. The following weekend was intended to treat Newport to the American debut of Blind Faith, Eric Clapton and Ginger Baker's first post-Cream endeavour. With less than a week to go, the show was scrapped.

The New York Pop Festival passed off more calmly, but still eardrums were ringing as Steppenwolf and Grand Funk Railroad threw their amps into overdrive alongside Beck, Tull and – strangely in such company – John Sebastian.

And the itinerary yawned on through the late July and August heat: the first Spectrum Music Festival in Philadelphia, alongside Sly & the Family Stone, the Mothers of Invention, Savoy Brown and Ten Years After; the Laurel Festival in Maryland, where the same line-up (plus the Guess Who) would ignite a miniature riot; the Schaefer Music Festival Series in Central Park, the Mountain Rock Festival in Ellenville and, finally, an ambitiously arranged, but somewhat tentatively organised weekend bash in the upstate New York community of Woodstock.

Beck loathed the schedule; the band loathed the money they were receiving for each performance. According to Wood, it was Newman who finally made them see the error of their ways and convinced them that you couldn't just roll over and take whatever was offered to you because you'd never be offered anything more. He was, Wood smiled, "a real businessman. 'You mean you're being paid what? Mickie Most is doing what? You need somebody to get organised.' And on and on." Finally, his words got through.

Just hours before taking the Central Park stage, Wood, Stewart and Newman announced that they not only wanted a pay rise, they wanted to see the cash up front before they would ever take the stage again. They would receive their money – somehow, on a Saturday, Peter Grant was able to produce the cash. But even with dollars in their pockets, the band played like condemned criminals.

"Beck was just a mess", one onlooker growls 35 years later. "None of them seemed to care, they were just up there going through the motions. I'll tell you how bad it was. You know how everyone goes on about Hendrix doing 'The Star Spangled Banner' at Woodstock? And how magical it was?

"Beck played it at Central Park... this was before Woodstock, remember, so it was before Hendrix did it... and people just booed. There were all these kids in the crowd who'd come down from an anti-war protest somewhere in the city, and the National Anthem was like dog-shit to them because it glorified the establishment, everything that people should have been fighting against. So when Beck started playing it... what the fuck did he think he was doing?"

CHAPTER
TWENTY-FOUR

Not every moment of the tour was a gruelling, grinding horror, of course. Soon after arriving in New York, Beck ran into Bruce Wayne, one of the Yardbirds' former roadies. He was now working with the Vanilla Fudge, who themselves were in the studio recording a jingle for Coca-Cola. Guitarist Vinnie Martell had fallen ill... would Beck be interested in filling in for him?

He was. He'd been a fan of the band since their earliest days, quaaluding up the chart with their signature massacre of the Supremes' "You Keep Me Hangin' On"; he could still remember the thrill he felt, sitting around with John Bonham and Jimmy Page one night, listening to the Fudge's Near The Beginning live album. "When it came to the "Shotgun" track, it was a revelation, particularly Carmine (Appice)'s drumming. I just knew that I had to work with that rhythm section."

Now he was, albeit for no more than four or five minutes – but from the moment he plugged in, he knew that wouldn't be sufficient. "I always fancied myself as a bit of a lunatic, but even I couldn't stand the pace around these two, charging around all day, looning everywhere!"

He would be granted another opportunity to experience the sheer euphoria of playing alongside the Americans at the Singer Bowl Music Festival, on 13 July. Vanilla Fudge and the Jeff Beck Group were co-headlining a bill that also featured Ten Years After and the Edwin Hawkins Singers. "It was one of those riotous sorts of days," Beck recalled. "Everyone's energy level was 100% and we were throwing things at one another on stage. I threw a mug of orange juice at Alvin Lee and it stuck all over his guitar. It was just one of those animal things..."

Better was to come, however. Although they weren't on the bill, members of Led Zeppelin were at the festival as well, and Zeppelin roadie Richard Cole recalled a drunken John Bonham ambling onto the stage during the protracted rendition of "Rice Pudding", having a few words with Newman (misidentified as Waller in Cole's Stairway To Heaven memoir), and then "(grabbing) the drum sticks and immediately (begin) pounding out a stripper's rhythm." Which only halted when he did indeed start to strip.

"The gig ended up in what they call a nine-man jam", Stewart remembered. "The stage was full of people – John Bonham, Jimmy Page, Beck, me, Robert Plant, the guy who used to play bass for Jethro Tull (Glenn Cornick), we were doing 'Jailhouse Rock' and it was fucking incredible."

There were four drummers – Bonham and Newman were joined by Ten Years After's Ric Lee and the headliners' Carmine Appice; and

Bonham himself ended the evening by stripping off all his clothes and being arrested. "And the Vanilla Fudge couldn't follow it", Stewart recalled. "They just couldn't. They packed up later that night."

In fact the group would stumble on for a few months more, fulfilling the last handful of engagements they'd scheduled. But the rhythm section, Carmine Appice and Tim Bogert, had seen their future and they had no intention of letting it out of sight. Backstage after the Singer Bowl show, they cornered Beck and Stewart and offered them a place in a new band, a new "shit-hot" band, where "every night could be like the Fillmore."

Beck was stunned. Painfully conscious that his own group was unlikely to survive for much longer, he had already mapped out a vague game plan for the future – with 'vague' being the operative word. "I planned to have three months off work", Beck told *Melody Maker* later. "I'd been working hard for nearly two years, and I'd come to the end of what I felt was the first chapter of my career." As for what he would do after that, though, he didn't have a clue. "I had to decide. The others wanted to do their own thing. They weren't happy, and we'd come to the end of a phase of music that we were involved in. I didn't know musically what I wanted to do." Then he met the Fudge. "We spent an evening together talking and I was so proud that they were soon to be my bass player and drummer!"

Beck was sold on the idea from the outset and so, for a while, was Stewart. Gradually, however, his enthusiasm began to fade, even as Beck's continued to skyrocket. Fresh tensions began to tear into the Jeff Beck Group, fresh ruptures that left Stewart sometimes staring at his bandmate, and wondering whether he'd even be able to get through the night without killing him, let alone put together a whole new band, and continue the charade for who knew how many years to come?

Beck was different. Although he insisted "I need friends rather than business colleagues", somehow, he was able to switch himself on and off, to regard the people he played with as musicians alone, and not even worry about such things as friendship and relationships. Maybe it was the years he'd spent in the Yardbirds, where he was the new boy and the butt of the jokes, but Beck no more looked for comradeship among his bandmates than a bus driver expects to be friends with his passengers.

Stewart wasn't like that. The last few years had taught him a lot about music, and he knew that his future was bound up in it – the pride he felt in his still-unreleased solo album told him that. But making music was like making love. You can do it with someone you don't like, but how much more fun to be with a friend? Jeff Beck was not a friend. Neither were Bogart and Appice, and the more he thought about the new group the less entranced by the prospect he became.

"Carmine and Timmy were two incredibly nice guys", Stewart reflected a couple of years later. "(But) I wasn't really knocked out by the things the Fudge were doing at the time." Left to their own devices, the Jeff Beck Group "could've played together for years, and still come up with nice stuff." But the twist in the dynamic that the two Americans would necessarily induce was one manoeuvre too many.

On 25 July, the Jeff Beck Group arrived in Detroit to play the first of three nights at the Grande ballroom. Even before they touched down, however, it was clear that nobody was in any mood to go on stage. A row before their last gig, in Lowell, Massachusetts, was still festering, and when it refused to clear up Beck cancelled the first show. (Procol Harum stepped in to replace them.)

The following day dawned brighter. Nobody mentioned the cancelled show, but when Beck went off for a local radio interview nobody contradicted him when he told the band "see you at soundcheck." The interview, too, went well. He chatted about the Donovan single, and discussed plans to cut another one with Terry Reid. He explained away Nicky Hopkins' departure, then talked some more about the Jeff Beck Group's projected third album.

The union with Appice and Bogert was on his mind, of course, but the actual identities of his new bandmates remained a closely-guarded secret – nothing could be uttered publicly until the Vanilla Fudge completed their final string of engagements, a short European jaunt during September. Neither did he suggest that they were anything more than a journeyman rhythm section. There would be two new faces in the band, that was all, to replace Wood and Newman.

Then he returned to the hotel, and Stewart dropped his bombshell. Appice and Bogert had themselves arrived in Detroit, intending to sit down and make concrete plans for their future. Before they'd even opened their mouths, however, Stewart delivered his decision. He wanted no part of the new group. Either the Jeff Beck Group would continue on with Wood and Newman, or it didn't continue at all.

Yet Wood and Newman were themselves uncertain whether they wanted to continue on. Wood's own enthusiasms were almost exclusively aimed towards the rehearsals he'd been having with the Small Faces back in London, and in the fast-dawning realisation that Stewart would be the ideal frontman for any new line-up they conceived. Newman, on the other hand, had all but declared a one man war against Peter Grant and his lawyer, Steve Weiss, bucking furiously against their tight-fisted handling of the band purse strings, even as he hit out at the band's own lack of professionalism. "Jeff's group has always been unstable, ever since I joined it. There were always undercurrents going on, and disputes happening all the time. In the eight months I was with the group, we rehearsed about twice, which is ridiculous."

Money was a constant thorn in everybody's side. "We never got paid", Stewart complained. "Woody and I were in the band, and we never used to get paid. Jeff used to go off in the limo, and have Woody and me call for a taxi." On one occasion, Wood revealed, he and Stewart were so broke and hungry that they were reduced to shoplifting eggs from the Horn & Hardart automat. On another occasion, in Boston, Beck's seemingly impulse purchase of a £1,000 hot rod, while his band mates were bartering for beer money, raised tensions even higher.

But Beck himself later admitted that even he didn't have a clue how the band's finances were arranged. As late as a 1973 interview with *Crawdaddy* magazine, he acknowledged, "I'm still waiting to see the accounts from 1968 through 1970. (Management) were saying 'Hey look, we're selling out, we're doing 6,000 people at the gate, getting $8,000 or $9,000 a gig.' That was the most we ever earned. (But) none of the guys were getting paid, and they just wanted to know where the hell this money was going. Of course I got the rap for it. (But) we were getting ripped off... fleeced."

Stewart's refusal to even think about trying to put the group back on an even keel was the final straw. The Jeff Beck Group played their Saturday night show in Detroit, and then Beck went home. The final night in Detroit was cancelled, and the rest of the tour as well. It was over.

Stewart is convinced that, had the Jeff Beck Group just been able to hold on for another two weeks to fulfil the final show on their summer 1969 American tour schedule, history might have been completely rewritten. Even before the three day Woodstock Festival got underway, everybody involved knew that it was going to be a big deal... maybe the biggest deal any of them had ever been involved in. It would be filmed for a sure-fire blockbuster movie; it would be recorded for a sprawling, multi-disc live album; it would afford its participants more exposure than a lifetime spent on the road. With hindsight in overdrive, Stewart was convinced, "if we'd done it, I think we would have stayed together."

Beck, however, had other ideas. Like Stewart, he knew exactly what the Woodstock festival portended... and he didn't like it. So far as the singer was concerned, the festival was already over, the movie was already in the cinemas and Rod had risen triumphantly out of it, to become the greatest superstar the world had ever seen. Now he was making certain that everyone else was aware of that as well. Finally, Beck cracked. "Rod was so cocksure that I wouldn't blow the gig that he got a power trip going, and started really becoming an asshole. And I just thought 'right, what do I do?'

"We were booked to play, we were in all the advertising, but it just wouldn't have worked. Things in the band had deteriorated to the point of almost disappearing up their own bum. There was such a bad vibe, and I knew that if we played Woodstock and it failed, then I'd never be able to live with myself. But if we didn't do it, we could always just guess. Plus, I did not want to be preserved on film. If that thing hadn't been filmed, I'd probably have said 'okay let's do it.' But I knew it was going to be a big-time film, and if we fucked up and we were on film, forget it. I wasn't strong enough to do it at that time."

Those other open-air shows that season had already convinced Beck that "we weren't used to doing big outdoor gigs – and while a lot of other people on the bill probably weren't used to them either, they went into Woodstock with a positive attitude. I just didn't have that at the time. I didn't have the confidence in myself to do it. Up against Sly & the Family Stone? You're crazy! You need a camaraderie thing for that, and we didn't have it."

Back in London, Beck tried to play down the collapse of the Jeff Beck Group – or, at least, the ugliness of that collapse. "We're disbanding very shortly", he told the *New Musical Express*. "Ronnie... is leaving because he wants to play lead instead of bass, and I wish him the best of luck." There were, however, "no bad vibes or anything like with most other groups"; in fact, he now claimed, the decision to split had, in fact, been made "after our second-to-last tour of the States. We were all exhausted, the group had seen America and they've seen enough of it."

Stewart read those words and shrugged. "Do you know, in the two-and-a-half years I was with Beck, I never once looked him in the eye? I always looked at his shirt or something like that."

"The end of the band was messy", Beck admits. "I suppose what we did in an 18 month period was more than a lot of people do in an entire career. But with that volatile kind of vibe going, it was inevitable that it wouldn't last. It couldn't."

The Jeff Beck Group's name would continue to appear in the advertising for a few more shows – just as he had at the end of the Yardbirds, Peter Grant continued booking them shows, just in case there was a change of heart, or a sudden influx of enthusiasm. But the Bilzen Festival in Belgium on 23 August and the Isle Of Wight festival the following weekend both passed off without the band's appearance, and Beck, still glorying in the need for understatement, explained simply, "I knew we wouldn't be ready." Bob Dylan was headlining the Isle Of Wight event, and "(he) can control all that, there's magic coming out of him." Beck couldn't.

The musicians splintered to the winds. Newman joined a new band, May Blitz, as they launched into one of the hardest-rocking careers of the early 1970s – quite coincidentally, they wound up on the newly-formed Vertigo label, where Rod Stewart would briefly rank among their labelmates: An Old Raincoat Won't Ever Let You Down was released by the same company in February 1970. Wood, of course, was still teamed up with the Small Faces and Stewart was joining him as well, convinced that he'd be able to make a go of both life in a band and his own solo career. Paramount among the new union's immediate plans was a debut album that would include a reworking of Beck-Ola's "Plynth".

Beck was sorry to see him go. Right up until the bitter end, he'd been hoping that Stewart might have a change of heart, and give the Jeff Beck Group another try. What did it matter that the two men couldn't stand one another? On stage and on record, they were an unbeatable combination, and surely that was where it mattered the most?

Appice and Bogert told him to stop worrying – they already had a new singer lined up, Rusty Day, from the Amboy Dukes. They had just three more shows to play, and then rehearsals could begin.

Beck baulked a little. It sounded "okay on paper", he mused, but he did wonder how it might balance out, "three Americans and me the only English person." He agreed, however, to at least see how things worked out, even if it meant having to swallow another bitter pill and relocate to the United States. Just a few weeks earlier, he'd told the *NME*, "I don't mind working there, but it's such a long way. It's bad enough just visiting for a few weeks, let alone buying a house and living in the middle of all that rubbish." Now, however, he was agreeing to at least a protracted stay, joining his new bandmates on Long Island while they got the band off the ground. Grant and Beck made arrangements to fly back to New York on 3 November.

They would not make the flight. Early in the morning of 2 November, Beck decided to give his 1923 A-Ford a final late-night drive before being garaged for the duration. Suddenly a tyre blew and the car went into a skid, piling into a passing Morris. "It wasn't the speed", Beck was at pains to explain, later. "The front tyre completely blew out. With a transverse front string, I didn't stand an earthly. And with cross-ply tyres, it was like I was on ice. I just went straight across the road."

The driver of the other car received a broken knee. Beck, however, was flung onto the road. When the ambulance arrived, it was to find him concussed, with breaks to his nose and possibly his pelvis. He had broken a tooth and cut up his face. As he was rushed into intensive care at the Royal West Kent Hospital in Maidstone, there were even fears that he might be paralysed, possibly permanently.

Either way, there was no way he would be moving to the US, no way he would be hooking up with Appice, Bogert and Day. No way, in fact, that he'd be doing anything for the next six months. And when he did return to action, it was to find that Bogert and Appice had already wandered off to form the grisly bombast of Cactus, and Rod Stewart was telling all who would listen just what an absolute horror life with Jeff Beck had been.

"I've said so many nasty things about Beck", he told *ZigZag*. "And they're all true."

CHAPTER
TWENTY-FIVE

It would be more than two years before Beck finally linked up with Tim Bogert and Carmine Appice, years during which he both launched and lost an altogether wholly redirected Jeff Beck Group, built around jazz pianist Max Middleton. It also featured drummer Cozy Powell and vocalist Bob Tench, former frontman with the British funk band Gass (he was replaced in that outfit, incidentally, by Carl Douglas – later to top the UK chart with the anthem "Kung Fu Fighting").

Around the same time as another beat-boom survivor, Eric Burdon, was getting funky with the American band War, but certainly following the blueprint laid down by Beck-Ola, this new-born Jeff Beck Group debuted in Detroit, recording at the Motown studios, which is where Suzi Quatro became a witness to the proceedings. "My brother heard Mickie (Most) was in town to record Jeff Beck at Motown, so he arranged for Mickie to come and see (my band Cradle) play. Jeff, Cozy and Mickie came together. Mickie didn't like the band, but loved me; apparently, Jeff says he told Mickie 'forget the others and sign the bass player.' After the show, I accompanied them to Motown studios and did a little jam with Jeff and Cozy playing (the James Gang's) "Funk 49"."

The Motown sessions were eventually scrapped as Beck acknowledged trying, but failing, to crystallise the strivings that marked out so much of Beck-Ola. Two subsequent albums continued the search, though, as 1971's Rough And Ready was followed by the next year's Jeff Beck Group, and right at the end, Beck finally found what he'd been looking for. In the studio with Steve Cropper, the Memphis-born guitarist with Booker T & the MGs, Beck conceived an album which slammed soulful instrumentals into passionate vocal numbers, made a masterpiece of Mar-Kays bassist Don Nix's "Going Down", and a swampy blues shaker out of "Sugar Cane", a song that Beck and Cropper wrote themselves and which still stands among the guitarist's finest moments.

This restyled Jeff Beck Group shattered in 1972 when Beck finally linked with Bogert and Appice. But, perhaps inevitably after all this time, the long-awaited union never lived up to the promise the founding musicians perceived when they first discussed joining forces. Too bombastic, too pompous, too run-of-the-mill, their live show was little more than deafening flash, their first album was deservedly crucified and attempts to cut a second disc foundered on the awful realisation that Rod Stewart, of all people, had got it right way back when. "All that noise!" he shuddered.

By the end of April 1974, Beck, Bogert & Appice was no more, and Beck was pondering his next move – a possible solo album backed up by members of Zzebra, a hook-up (caught on BBC TV's *Music On Two*) with jazzrockers Upp... and a party being thrown by socialite Sally Payne, at her home on the Portobello Road, towards the end of May.

The guest list was stellar; by the time Beck arrived, Mick Jagger, Rod Stewart and Ron Wood were already there, and, when a pile of musical instruments somehow appeared before them, of course they had to jam.

Wood recalled the moment for *ZigZag*. "I was playing drums, Mick was playing piano, Rod was singing and Beck on guitar. That was the first time that Rod and Jeff had really had a confrontation since (the band broke up)", and there was a little "animosity", as Wood put it, sparking between the pair, little jabs aimed at upstaging the other, false musical cues and surprises. But the jam went on into the early hours regardless, and might even have continued had Payne's neighbours not started to kick up a fuss.

The law arrived to break up the party and the quartet went their separate ways, at least for a few days. But when Wood made his solo debut at the Gaumont State in Kilburn on 14 July, Beck and Stewart were both in the audience and, the following February, when Jagger found his own band in need of a guitarist, to replace the errant Mick Taylor, Beck was one of the first names he turned to.

Taylor's departure was a bolt from the blue. One day the Rolling Stones were packing their suitcases, ready to return to the studio; the next, Jagger was at an after-gig party for Eric Clapton, listening to Taylor explain why he wouldn't be joining them.

"He just said he'd played with us for five years, and he felt he wanted to play some different kind of music. So I said, 'that's okay, that's fine,' and that was that. We were due to return to Munich about two or three days later to start recording, so I really didn't have much time to talk to him. I'm sorry to see him go, but I think people should be free to do what they want to do. I mean, it's not the army, it's just a sort of rock'n'roll band."

"A sort of rock'n'roll band." Of all the epithets which have been thrown at the Rolling Stones over the last 35 years, Jagger's is probably the most understated. Without the Stones to provide competition, the Beatles would never have achieved half the marvels they did. Without the Stones to give the evidence, rock'n'roll might never have been the demon beast it became. And without the Stones to write them, we would never have had a lifetime of songs which aren't simply part of our culture, they are what shaped that culture.

And here they were, without a lead guitarist. A lesser band in a similar position, with a new album on the shelves and a world tour in the offing, might have been pole-axed by a shock like that. But Jagger was adamant that the Stones were in no hurry to replace him.

"Mick was in on only half the sessions for (the recently released) It's Only Rock'n'roll because he was in hospital. We had two sessions and he didn't come to the first one. So it's not really any great difficulty." Taylor's departure "just means we're missing one guitar player, which we'll no doubt find. At the moment, though, we're not really looking for anyone because we're recording, you know?"

Besides, the band was often at its best when it was on its improvisatory uppers. It's Only Rock'n'roll was a critical and commercial smash, but it also rates among the patchiest albums in the Stones' canon, a half-formed mass of slick arrangements and rent-a-riff rocking, the sound of a band switching on the auto-pilot because there wasn't a cloud in the sky.

Taylor's departure changed that, and the sessions the Stones were now contemplating would reap all the wild winds there were. Hosting auditions even as they held down sessions, the band would rediscover a looseness they had not enjoyed since the halcyon days of Let It Bleed; more importantly, they would rediscover roots which the Stones' absorption into the body politick of Modern Rock had all but cast adrift.

Black And Blue, the album which would finally emerge from five months of recording and rehearsing, has been described as the Stones' most divisive album ever, a headlong dive into disco and dance which betrayed every scything riff Richard ever unleashed. But look again at that title, and forget the bruised-bints-in-bondage ads which drummed up so much controversy upon the album's original release. Black, as in the music which the Stones always loved the most, Blues as in the music they made at the start. Put the two together and Black And Blue was more than a new Rolling Stones record. It was also an affirmation of everything they had done since they first stumbled out of suburbia.

Checking into the Munich Hilton and, booking into Munich Musicland, the four-piece Stones (plus a passing Nicky Hopkins) eased gently into their latest album sessions with a loose limbed take on Eric Donaldson's "Cherry Oh Baby." Keith Richard's fascination with reggae, most evident (if evidently unfulfilled) in the Stones' occupation of Dynamic Studios in Kingston, Jamaica, for Goat's Head Soup two years before, was well-known, but "Cherry Oh Baby" was their first serious assault on the genre.

It was also, even at this early stage, one of the best they would ever achieve. Lacking the weighty reverb with which mainstream reggae was already becoming fascinated; hamstrung by the Wyman-Watts rhythm section's apparent uncertainty, "Cherry Oh Baby" was still at least as successful a stab at white boy reggae as anything Eric Clapton (the only other practitioner of note) had achieved. More than that, it would remain so until Keith Richard himself eclipsed it, with his solo rendition of "The Harder They Come" a couple of years later.

Certainly the Stones themselves were unable to improve on this prototype. First tackled on 15 December, the final day of the band's eight-day stint in the studio, this pioneering backing track would eventually form the basis for the released version of the song.

Indeed, these initial sessions not only proved more productive than subsequent histories let on, they also illustrate just how far from the band's minds any final album concept was. "Fool To Cry", a gorgeous ballad spiralling straight out of the laid-back vibe of It's Only Rock'n'roll, was taped on 12 December; an instrumental backing track for "Wind Call", an equally evocative slow roller, followed. If the Stones really were, as Black And Blue would subsequently insist, about to go disco, right now they were among the last to know.

The sessions broke up for Christmas, to reconvene in Rotterdam on 22 January 1975. By now, the band had drawn up their own list of possible replacements for the errant Taylor, a shopping list which the Anglo-American music press was swift to augment with some suggestions of its own.

Rory Gallagher was an early candidate on this media wish list; so was Mick Ronson, David Bowie's former lieutenant, at an apparent loose end since the demise of Mott The Hoople. Neither, of course, was actually approached by the Stones, though as Ronson reflected a decade later, "the Stones announced they were looking for a blonde guitarist who could do his own make-up, and I suppose I fit the bill."

In fact, the band were looking for nothing of the sort; all the guitarists on their shortlist were decidedly dark-haired, and a little too craggy to paint up as well. Americans Harvey Mandel and Muscle Shoals sessioneer Wayne Perkins were both in contention; so was Ron Wood, as he ran down the last months of the Faces; and so was Jeff Beck.

"I went over there and I found they wanted me to join", Beck recalled. "I couldn't believe that. I mean, the money was tempting, I could have made a fortune and never had to work again. But I would have been half-dead, and my reputation would have been shot."

Over the next 18 days, the Stones' mobile studio was working 24 hours a day as the band, now augmented by keyboardist Billy Preston, jammed with a steady stream of guests, then played back the tapes to see who fit in best. "We... had to play with a lot of people, basically", Jagger acknowledged. "It was just gonna take a long while before we knew what we were gonna do... I knew it was gonna be a bit of a problem 'cause those things really do take time. It's not like employing a cook or something. You've gotta have the guy, you've gotta like him, as well as like the way he plays. And how can you know if you like him or not? It's even difficult to know how he really plays. It's really hard. It's tough going. Ask the Average White Band. They rehearsed a thousand fucking drummers, right?"

More than a dozen basic tracks were recorded during this period of searching, including several seemingly endless instrumental jams and a handful of still unfulfilled songs in the making: "English Rose", "I Got A Letter" and "Man Eating Woman". There were also some typically energetic covers: the blues standard "Rock Me Baby", Jimmy Reed's "Shame Shame Shame", Martha and the Vandellas' "Heat Wave", the Stones' own "Monkey Man" and finally, a clutch of tracks which, remixed and substantially overdubbed, would be resuscitated for 1981's Tattoo You: the driving "Slave" (familiar from bootlegs as "Black And Blue Jam") and "Worried About You". Two years on from that, on, another Rotterdam out-take, the funky instrumental "Cellophane Trousers", would metamorphose into "Too Tough", from the Undercover album.

Unfortunately, details of who played on what remain sketchy, with the

Stones' own subsequent rerecordings, not to mention various period bootlegs, only adding to the uncertainty. The otherwise marvellous Reggae'n'Roll, for example, insists that all seven tracks within were recorded with Jeff Beck, despite Beck having fallen from contention very early on. The guitarist later said he simply slipped a note under Jagger's door, saying "sorry lads, I've got to go home." But a legend which is too good to be completely apocryphal insists he dropped by to work through just one song, a version of his own "Freeway Jam", before exiting with the words, "call me when you've got a rhythm section." Jagger and Richard were apparently happy with the one they already had, because Beck was never invited back.

Harvey Mandel and Wayne Perkins were luckier; as late as 22 March 1975, when the sessions relocated to Munich Musicland, they were still in contention, impressing the Stones sufficiently that both would take the spotlight on the completed Black And Blue. Mandel plays lead on the opening "Hot Stuff" and another mighty ballad, the painfully evocative "Memory Motel"; Perkins joins him on the latter, playing acoustic guitar, then shines in his own right on "Hand Of Fate". He would also overdub some lead onto the December take of "Fool To Cry", a chain of events which prompted Marshall Chess, the Stones' manager, to unofficially announce Perkins' permanent recruitment into the group.

Immediately, *Rolling Stone* leaped into action, tracing Perkins to Keith Richards' London home and requesting an interview. Chess demurred. "I think you better wait awhile. There's somebody else over there right now, auditioning for the job."

That, of course, was Ron Wood.

"I wanted someone that was easy to get on with", Jagger told Rolling Stone, "someone that wasn't too difficult, that was a good player and was used to playing on stage." Tacitly, he thus acknowledged why Perkins, at least, had not got the job; a brilliant guitarist, he was also primarily a studio musician, "and it's quite a lot to ask of someone to come and do a big American tour with a band like the Stones. I wanted someone that wasn't going to be phased out."

The first sign of Woody being in serious contention for the gig can be gauged from one of the Rotterdam out-takes, where he joins the Stones for a version of "Act Together", a Jagger-Richard composition which Wood himself recorded for his own I've Got My Own Album To Do solo set the previous year. Digging deeper into his relationship with the band, Wood had also enjoyed both Mick and Keith's personal presence on that album; had appeared, as one of several uncredited co-conspirators, on the "It's Only Rock'n'roll" backing track, and had in fact been close friends with Keith since the early 1960s.

However, his recruitment was by no means an open and shut case. Wood was still a member of the Faces at this time; and, while that band was clearly spiralling to its death, torn apart by Rod Stewart's superior solo success, still the group's internal politics refused to admit that the combo was at an end. Studio time had been booked in Los Angeles, an

American tour was scheduled for the spring of 1975, and there was a string of summer festivals to look forward to in Britain.

Wood admitted the Stones job was "a very tempting little carrot", but was adamant, "I suppose that I would join the Stones in another time. A lot of my roots and influences are in that band. But it could never happen when I'm with the Faces. The Stones know that because they dig the Faces, too."

At the same time, though, Wood knew that only a fool would walk away from such an offer. The Faces were a great band, but the Stones were an institution. In late March, he rejoined the Stones in Munich, and quickly made his presence felt on the still germinating album. He was included in the photo shoot which produced Black And Blue's memorable gatefold jacket; his backing vocals were overdubbed onto five of the eight tracks which were now in contention, while his actual audition appears to have been the pounding 12-minute jam (recorded on 2 April) which would, at less than half its original length, appear on vinyl as "Hey Negrita."

The Munich sessions concluded on 4 April 1975. A week later, with Rod Stewart having announced that he would not be available for the Faces' British dates (he blamed tax reasons), Wood agreed to become a temporary Stone. He would complete their new album, tour the US through the summer, then rejoin the Faces for their own American and Far Eastern tours beginning in August. He would be back with the Stones for a Christmas tour of Europe, but remained convinced that his entire tenure with the group was "just an arrangement if I've got time."

Of course, it was time alone which could determine what happened after that, but Marshall Chess, at least, was overjoyed by the combination. "Woody and Keith are both primarily known as brilliant rhythm guitarists. That allows a certain cross-trading of riffs that they've never had before."

From Munich, the band headed – with Woody still aboard – straight to a rented mansion in Montauk, NY, to begin rehearsals for the American tour, a 58-date outing which included debut shows in Brazil, Mexico and Venezuela. The new boy made his first appearance with the band in mid-May, two weeks before his 28th birthday, rolling down Fifth Avenue in New York on the back of a flatbed truck. He is still there today.

CHAPTER
TWENTY-SIX

Wood's enrolment as a Rolling Stone brought an end to another of the most enthralling musical soap operas of the mid-1970s – the Faces.

The band's first album, the sensibly titled First Step, arrived less than a year after the collapse of the Jeff Beck Group, and showed the old Stewart-Wood partnership to be flourishing under this new regime. But supporters of the band, as opposed to any individual member, would argue that, from the outset, the singer's partnership – with Wood, and with the band itself – was doomed.

Aide from touring and recording with the Faces, Stewart was also to maintain his own separate, solo career, following An Old Raincoat Won't Ever Let You Down with four further albums, all recorded while he remained a member of the band. It was his third set, autumn 1971's Every Picture Tells A Story (and the attendant single "Maggie May") that finally skewed the balance between the two sides of his public life. But the Faces, too, managed five albums during this period, and in musical terms, there was little to choose between either career. The Faces frequently backed Stewart on his solo work and, if their work as a band had more of a musically dilapidated feel to it, their contributions to Stewart's albums could scarcely be faulted.

But the strain of their singer's double life was lethal all the same. Every time the group stepped out, their own self was eroded a little further, whether it was by promoters who insisted on renaming the group "Rod Stewart and…"; by journalists whose interviews wound up fixating on the frontman's activities; or by the public, who bought Stewart's solo records in droves but proved harder to convince when it came to the band. Between 1971 and 1975, Rod Stewart alone scored three British Number 1 singles. The Faces only just scraped together three Top 10 hits though they scored three Top 3 albums.

But still the end of the Faces was slow in coming, and, no less than the death of the Jeff Beck Group, painful in arrival. What became their final studio album, 1973's Ooh La La, was recorded in much the same mood as blighted Cosa Nostra Beck-Ola: drummer Kenny Jones recalled "nobody went into the studio with a song" and, the delicious "Cindy, Incidentally" notwithstanding, it shows. Stewart, who was already under suspicion of keeping his best songs for his own albums, didn't even turn up at the studio for the first two weeks, and bassist Ronnie Lane, who wound up writing half the finished record, was approaching the end of his patience. The album was barely on the shelves when Lane quit to form his own band, Slim Chance (a name he originally offered to the Faces).

Lane was replaced by Tetsu Yamauchi, who had taken over from Andy Fraser in Free; ironically, the Faces turned to him only after Fraser himself had already turned the job down. But the Faces were clearly on their last legs. Despite its undeniable strengths, "Pool Hall Richard" – the new boy's debut with the band – wasn't even given an American release; instead, the Faces' biggest market was introduced to Yamauchi via Coast To Coast: Overture And Beginners, a distinctly substandard live album that sounded exactly like what it was – a contract-filler.

The album was unanimously trashed in the media, where every journalist apparently had his own vision of what a Faces live record should sound like (none of which were met by the actual thing), but still the band went out with a bang. "You Can Make Me Dance, Sing Or Anything" may not have become the biggest hit single they ever enjoyed, but it was the epitome of everything the band had ever represented. As epitaphs go, it was unsurpassable, which was just as well. With the band members now ripping one another apart in the press, it was the only one they got.

Seven months before the Faces finally collapsed, Stewart headed over to Muscle Shoals Studios to begin work on his next solo album. It was the first time he'd ever recorded outside of Britain, the first time in a decade that Wood was not by his side. Instead, producer Tom Dowd recruited the old Stax Records house band of Duck Dunn, Al Jackson Jr, Booker T and Steve Cropper, Jeff Beck's sparring partner on the Jeff Beck Group album.

But the change did Stewart good. His most powerful album yet, Atlantic Crossing entered the UK chart at Number 1 and spawned two chart-topping singles, "I Don't Want To Talk About It" and a reworking of the Sutherland Brothers' "Sailing", which remained at the top for eight weeks.

The Faces' final tour took place shortly after Atlantic Crossing was released. It was a completely different band to any that had operated in the past: Jesse Ed Davis joined Wood on guitar, and a 15-piece string section, brought in against the wishes of the rest of the group, was on hand to translate Stewart's latest ballads to the live arena. But the portents were unmistakable and, on 19 December 1975, Stewart quit the band. Tours of Australia, Japan and Europe were promptly canned, while the singer himself hightailed it over to Hollywood to set up as a tax exile.

His romance with actress Britt Ekland, meanwhile, catapulted him any number of rungs above the Cockatoo-Haired Plonker status he'd hitherto enjoyed. Beautiful, elegant, sophisticated and Swedish, Ekland might be better-remembered today for who she is, as opposed to what she did (pub quiz question – name three movies in which she starred), but glamour was a powerful drug and she dispensed it like candy. Stewart's social status had just soared from broken-down Volkswagen to showroom Lamborghini; now it was time to make music to match.

Stewart began work on A Night On The Town, his eighth solo album, in November 1975, the moment he got off the road with the Faces and some weeks before the group's demise was officially announced. And there were a few songs there that proved he could still make slobbering, three-chord rock when he wanted to – a romp through "The Wild Side Of Life" quickly became the blueprint for Status Quo's hit reinvention of the same song; a lazy lament utterly transformed the Manfreds' "Pretty Flamingo"; and then there was the horn-honking Stonesy groove of "The Balltrap", a Stewart original that could easily have been written in the same burst of boozy creativity that served up "Stay With Me" and "Cindy Incidentally" – "you didn't know my name", he lamented, "not even when I came." What a lad.

Flip the disc, however, from the "fast half" to the "slow half", and the new Rod flashed for all to see... not only that, he flashed his lady as well, as Ekland half-gasped, half-purred, across the fade of "Tonight's The Night" and a nation's DJs glanced nervously towards the lyric sheet, in the hope that her flawless French did not conceal something rude. Then, when they couldn't answer that question, they assumed it did, and started fading the record early, even after it topped the US chart. But the joke, as Stewart himself pointed out, was on them. People were so busy listening for a hint of smutty French that they didn't even pay attention to the English portion of the lyrics. "Spread your wings and let me come inside" indeed.

More opprobrious attention was directed towards "The Killing Of Georgie (Part One and Two)", the six-plus minute epic which closed the "slow half" and which detailed, with almost chilling precision, the last hours on earth of a gay friend of Stewart's, mugged and murdered by a New York street gang – although not, queerly enough, because he was gay. "He just pushed his luck a little too far that night." At a time when more and more rock stars felt duty-bound to climb aboard one issue-drenched bandwagon or another, it was refreshing to come across a protest song that simply protested. Still, the anti-gay lobby frowned disapprovingly upon the song, so it seems odd to recall that, of all the controversies that littered A Night On The Town, the most contentious was still to come.

Three singles were pulled from Tonight's The Night: the title track, "Georgie" and, more than a year after the album's release, a lovely cover of Cat Stevens' "The First Cut Is The Deepest" – released in the UK in April 1977, double A-sided with Atlantic Crossing's "I Don't Want To Talk About It." It was a well-chosen single, too – both its predecessors were Top 5 hits, but this new offering went all the way, topping the chart at the end of May and remaining there for a month.

Just two weeks into its run, however, retailers across the country noticed something had gone terribly awry. Although the charts insisted Stewart was still Number 1, it was the Sex Pistols' "God Save The Queen" that was actually selling the most... as many as two or three times more than Stewart, by some estimates. 1977 was Queen Elizabeth's Silver Jubilee year, June was the month in which the celebrations reached their peak. It was unthinkable that a bunch of foul-mouthed, anti-monarchist punk rockers should be allowed to spoil the party by topping the charts in the very week that the nation was united in its love for Her Majesty. With the Pistols at Number 2, Stewart remained King until the crisis was past.

Tonight's The Night was also significant as the first release on Stewart's own, newly-inaugurated Riva label. Named for a speedboat he once spotted in the south of France (where else?) and instantly recognisable with its roaring lion and tartan logo, Riva was modelled on his close friend Elton John's Rocket label, itself a prodigious little concern that would ultimately establish itself among the most quietly successful of all artist-owned record labels.

Riva would not prove so noteworthy – eight of the label's first ten 45 featured Stewart, whether they were fresh solo releases, reissues of old Faces numbers or even a pseudonymous slide into traditional Scottish balladry via the Atlantic Crossing Pipe & Drum Band's impassioned rendering of "The Skye Boat Song." Not until the arrival of John Cougar Mellencamp in 1979 would Riva boast another artist whose profile even threatened to approach Stewart's own. For a long time, however, it didn't even need one.

Bouyed by the success of the album, Stewart set about forming a new band – one in which, he laughed, he was finally the boss. "We can cut out a song whenever we want. With the Faces, you couldn't do that. You'd have to go through a bloody board meeting or something. It'd take six months to get anything done."

The nucleus of the group was built around former Family and Cockney Rebel guitarist Jim Cregan and – stunning everyone who remembered the demise of the Jeff Beck Group – former Vanilla Fudge drummer Carmine Appice. But Stewart was adamant that this new line-up should catch the eye from every direction. Ever since he first saw Fleetwood Mac back in the late 1960s, he admitted, he'd nursed the dream of leading a band that had three guitarists. With Cregan joined by Strider's Gary Grainger and Billy Peek from the Chuck Berry band, that dream came to fruition, and it sounded amazing; the version of "Get Back" which Stewart contributed to the movie soundtrack All This And World War Two positively leaks guitars over everything and, in concert, the wall of noise grew even louder.

Stewart toured through late 1976, and then moved straight into the studio to begin work on a new album, confidently expected at this stage to emerge a double. It would not, in the end, turn out that way; the glut of new material that Stewart envisioned having ready for the set turned out somewhat thinner than he had hoped, while the slowly-crumbling state of his relationship with Ekland was also a distraction.

Ironically, the rumours that had percolated all year finally hit the headlines towards the end of 1977, just as Stewart's latest single, "You're In My Heart", immortalised their love with some of his clumsiest (but, oddly, most affecting) lyrics yet: "You're Celtic, you're United", he crooned, "but baby I've decided, you're the best team I've ever seen."

Elsewhere, he rhymes "yarns that were so lyrical" with "the attraction was purely physical", while his attempt at disguising the object of his affections ("the big-bosomed lady with the Dutch accent") is itself so poetic that any laddie falling in love for the first time and hearing "You're In My Heart" come over the radio would have it seared into his soul forever.

Recorded in LA, where Steve Cropper and British blues legend John Mayall were among the old pals who dropped by the studio to play a note or two, Foot Loose And Fancy-Free, the suddenly apt title of Stewart's new album, appeared in November 1977. An immediate hit, of course, its impact was only strengthened in the UK by a chart-topping reissue of Atlantic Crossing early in the New Year. Ultimately climbing to Number 3, Foot Loose remained on the British charts for half a year; in the US, it reached Number 2 and was still on the listing 12 months later.

Its success – and its unimpeachable highlights – could not disguise a few weaknesses, however. Stewart had always had his old faithful fall-backs in the studio, the song styles that he could turn out with his eyes closed, but Foot Loose seemed to be dominated by them – a demonstration, sniped the critics, of why it's called showbusiness, rather than show-art. There were the bleeding heart ballads; there were the trousers-round-your-knees rock'n'rollers; there was the classic soul retread ("If Loving You Is Wrong"); there was the audacious epic – nodding towards drummer Appice's past, Stewart grasped "You Keep Me Hangin' On" with distinctly Fudge-stained fingers. Unfortunately, while one could (and still does) admire the sheer audacity of the performance, one did have to ask – why did he bother? Beyond allowing the boys in the band a chance to shine, that is.

Not until the end of the album did Foot Loose again hit the heights with which it was ushered in, as Stewart reflected again on the death of a romance and wondered who was really to blame. "Ever since I was a kid in school", announced "I Was Only Joking", "I've messed around with all the rules" – and then it proceeded to document them, with an honesty that could have been cloying if it wasn't so crippling. According to guitarist Cregan, by the way, no-one in the band even heard the song's lyrics until Stewart actually came in to record them; and, when he did, he was constantly glancing up at everyone in the room, "to see if they thought the song was too corny."

Guilt and recriminations notwithstanding, foot loose and fancy free in his own right, Stewart spent the last half of 1977 being linked with every eligible young female on the Hollywood radar, from English actress Susan George to *Playboy* centrefold Marcy Hanson, from Bebe Buell to Bianca Jagger, from Miss Universe runner-up Siv Aberg to Texan thespian Alana Hamilton – and anybody who guessed that she might turn out to be 'the one' was swiftly proved correct. In March 1978, Ekland moved the last of her possessions out of the house she and Stewart once shared in the LA suburb of Carolwood. Within an hour, the gossips reported, Hamilton was moving hers in.

Stewart's other great love, the Scottish national football team, were also on the move that summer, as they qualified for the World Cup competition (held that year in Argentina), and Stewart was in the studio with the entire squad of players, recording a new single to celebrate their achievement, "Ole Ola". It was not the greatest record he ever made (it's not even the best the Scottish team ever made), but it was one of the most heartfelt – and, with Scotland the only British side to have made it through to the finals, the entire island got behind the record. It soared to Number 4, outperforming both "I Was Only Joking" and "Tonight's The Night" and doing a lot better than the footballers as well.

Equally surprising was the news that Stewart had a new album ready to go – and one that, if the pre-release word was anything to go by, proved that he was as aware of Foot Loose And Fancy Free's failings as any of its critics. It was called Blondes Have More Fun and, more than any other album in his catalogue so far, it was set to divide Stewart's audience almost irreparably.

Ten songs, all but one of them self-composed, offered more bang for the buck than either of its predecessors, and most of his albums before that. More importantly, however, the album dangled Stewart's very reputation over such a precipice that even he admitted, "I knew when I went into it that I was putting myself out on a limb. I thought 'this is a bit of a dare – let's see what happens to it'."

"It" in this instance was the album's opening track, and first single, the five minute slab of unadulterated disco that dared to ask "Da Ya Think I'm Sexy". And it is hard to say, today, precisely what it was about the record that was to set so many spines a-bristling. The Rolling Stones had already proven that rockers could disco with "Miss You", while the song's lyric (and that key question) was so clearly related in the form of a story – a humorous story at that – that the fools who rushed to condemn Stewart for his vanity must have been deaf as well as stupid.

"The song's not about me", Stewart confirmed. "Although I'm certainly sexy to a point, I am but a narrator, telling a story." But he certainly set tongues wagging when he proclaimed "Sexy" to be as great a song as "Maggie May", while Carmine Appice only threw a few more cats into the pigeonloft when he described Stewart's aims as "Hollywood rock'n'roll. Glamour, crazy press stuff. If you're in the music business (that phrase again!) and live in Los Angeles, you should go along with everything involved. It's like the movie stars lived."

Ah, but which movie stars? Rolling Stone's Paul Nelson was unerringly accurate when he noted that Stewart had suddenly acquired "this kind of Jayne Mansfield image; a really trashy, not even movie-star image, but movie starlet, a sort of male tart. And he apparently likes it."

Of course he liked it. "They say 'fucking Rod's gone Hollywood, right?' What the fuck am I (expected) to do?" His penchant for blondes, teasingly parodied in the new album's title, sleeve design and even his own newly-dyed hair... but taken desperately seriously by an awful lot of awful people; his love of glamour; his "tartiness" indeed, all were seized upon by those who would clatter him to the floor. But, again, "What the fuck am I going to do? Wouldn't your first choice be some gorgeous 21-year-old blonde before it would be that sweet secretary down the hall with the thick arse?"

Later, he conceded, his opponents did hit the occasional right mark – the latest tour, across the US through late 1978, was a vaudeville spectacular, with Stewart flaunting himself like the cheapest hooker in town. And he confessed, "I really didn't concentrate on my singing. I was definitely more concerned with showing off the anatomy than trying to prove my vocal prowess." But still, "I (do) like all that. It might look silly, but it makes me feel sensuous. I'm very comfortable being a star. I rather enjoy it, in fact. I look in the mirror ever so much."

Further fuel was added to the fiery controversy after Stewart acknowledged accusations that the song's melody had been lifted from Brazilian singer Jorge Ben Jor's "Taj Mahal". "I was in Brazil and that song stuck in my head. I didn't copy it on purpose. I was with Elton John and we drank too much. I remember almost nothing from that trip." The ensuing legal dispute ended with Stewart agreeing to pass all royalties from the song on to UNICEF, but the knockers weren't satisfied. It was bad enough, the moaners moaned, that Stewart had sold out so comprehensively. The fact that he hadn't really even written the sell-out just cheapened him even further.

Yet, chop your way through the undergrowth of ugliness that surrounded (and still surrounds) Blondes Have More Fun, and the album remains one of Stewart's most gallant, and absolutely defiant records ever, with "Da Ya Think I'm Sexy" only the first departure from formula, cliché and Another Rodders Record.

As if to deliberately ensure that the critics' wrath would not wear thin, "Da Ya Think I'm Sexy" was just the first of a pepper-mill full of infuriating song titles – "Dirty Weekend", "Attractive Female Wanted", "Scarred And Scared", "Ain't Love A Bitch." He sneaked a smidgen of smut into the album's one cover, an otherwise reasonable facsimile of the Four Tops' "Standing In The Shadows Of Love." "Didn't I treat you right now baby, didn't I??" he whispers. "Didn't I do the best for you, now didn't I? Didn't I screw you right?" And, if you propped the gatefold sleeve up alongside the stereo while the record played, the 12-inch Rod in its tight spotted jumpsuit really did look an utter pillock.

But this was certainly one book you could not judge by its cover, as one song ("Attractive Female Wanted") emerged a deliciously lascivious rock-reggae lurch, the title track slammed straight out of the old-school Faces factory; "Scarred And Scared" rode a harmonica line straight out of some long-forgotten Eagles number; and "Ain't Love A Bitch" revealed itself to be another of those heart-stopping ballads Stewart had been fabricating forever, and as beautiful as any of them.

Stewart himself does the record a gross disservice today, as he falls so meekly in line with the critics of the day and writes the album off altogether. "I don't know what I was doing", he sighed. "It sold six and a half million copies, and not a decent track on it." But remarks like that simply make you want to pull his hair and tweak his nose. The reviews were rotten, but the public knew precisely what it was doing. Blondes

Have More Fun was, and is, a great album, one of Stewart's all-time finest; and, while "Sexy" topped the chart across most of the world – it became his third American Number 1, his fifth British chart-topper, his first Swedish and so on – Blondes itself emerged his most successful LP ever.

Yet it also marked something of a watershed in Stewart's career. In April 1979, even as "Ain't Love A Bitch" marched out to become his 19th American Top 100 hit, Stewart and Alana Hamilton married, five days before the groom's next US tour kicked off and, Hamilton later acknowledged, just weeks before the couple's first child would begin to 'show.'

Stewart himself has since admitted, "after 'Da Ya Think I'm Sexy', for a couple of years I almost lost interest in music altogether. In fact, between the summer-long concerts, the thrill of marriage and the joys (and everything else) of fatherhood, it is hardly surprising that 18 months would elapse before Rod Stewart was back on the new release sheets – 18 months during which his enemies sharpened a few more barbs, his supporters dreamed up a few new responses, and "Da Ya Think I'm Sexy" found its way into another few million homes – three million in America alone, courtesy of its inclusion within Stewart's third compilation album in six years, Rod Stewart's Greatest Hits.

And the album that did eventually break this silence, 1980's Foolish Behaviour, simply picked up where Blondes left off, leading in with the passionate, sultry funk of "Passion", marching on with the nostalgia-soaked "Oh God, I Wish I Was Home Tonight" and filling in around those two peaks with another clutch of righteous rockers, bellicose ballads and a handful of moments of unfettered fun (a great cover of Smokey Robinson's "My Girl").

It didn't do as well as Blondes, of course; in fact, its Number 12 placing marked Stewart's lowest US chart peak since Smiler, back in 1974. But the hard work was already done. Chart positions be damned; Stewart was already established as part of the musical furniture: a superstar whose lust could not be dimmed by either flop singles or low sales; an icon for whom the changing fashions of the quarter-century since then have scarcely been worth noticing.

The past, however, contained sufficient demons that Stewart was constantly battling to resolve them – whether in song, where past love affairs undoubtedly fired many of his most accomplished lyrics, or in person, when, in late 1982, he allowed Carmine Appice to set up a meeting with a mutual associate he'd not seen in more than eight years: Jeff Beck. It was a short meeting, but a friendly one, as though both men had grown enough to put their sometimes rancorous past behind them. When Stewart made the tentative suggestion that they keep in touch, Beck wholeheartedly agreed.

CHAPTER
TWENTY-SEVEN

Beck's own career had taken a number of shocking twists and turns in the years since Beck, Bogert & Appice laid down their instruments, as the guitarist plunged headlong into jazz-rock pastures that may have satisfied his own urges to keep moving forward and never play the same thing twice ("which, of course, is a lot easier if you're not actually playing tunes to begin with", sniped one disgruntled British critic), but did little to thrill the core audience that was still nursing fond memories of the Yardbirds and Truth.

It was some six months after that late-night Portobello party, in October 1974, that Beck finally got to work on the album which his supporters had been demanding all along, an instrumental set which would showcase his abilities, and his alone. Produced by George Martin, Blow By Blow itself came as an immense shock to Beck.

"I had no idea I was going to be a solo guitarist", he confesses. "I always thought I had to have a singer, a frontman, and many people over the years have asked me where was the new Rod Stewart – after Rod left – 'why didn't you?' Well, it was simply because there ain't another Rod Stewart, and to be seen to be looking for one by choosing somebody similar was just silly. Had there been someone else with their own thing going, in the way that Rod had, that would have been different.

"But once I got on the stage, and started to play lots of instrumental stuff, I found I really enjoyed it. To have people clapping me – in the past, well, were they clapping Rod or Bob (Tench) or Timmy (Bogert)? Or were they clapping me? When you have a lead singer, you don't know that. Unless you get a roar of approval during a guitar solo, you really don't know who they're clapping for."

There was much to applaud on Blow By Blow, beginning with a startling revision of the Beatles' "She's A Woman" and peaking with the latest manifestation of one of Beck's most valued personal friendships, with Stevie Wonder. Back in 1972, the Jeff Beck Group album featured a devastating instrumental version of "I Can't Give Back The Love I Feel For You", a cut from Mrs Wonder, Syreeta Wright's recently released Syreeta debut album; Beck's next, with Beck Bogert & Appice, included a near-definitive take on Wonder's own "Superstition"; Blow By Blow now served up two new Wonder compositions, "Cause We've Ended As Lovers" and "Thelonius". "He's such a ball of energy", Beck told the British music paper *Sounds*. "He could give you 50 hours of unrecorded material!"

Blow By Blow was the album which saw Beck's funkiest instincts come to the fore, transporting him further than ever from his roots as one of Britain's prime guitar gods and pinpointing a direction he had never seriously considered – one in which the instrumentation was the idol and the instrumentalists were simply the vehicles which carried it to the stage. His plaintive request to Mickie Most back in 1966, "I want to be a pop star", had finally come to pass, in the most unexpected, and most un-pop, way imaginable.

Verbally extravagant critic John L Walters (not to be confused with the late BBC producer John Walters, or movie director John Walters) once described Beck as "a serious artist in an idiom that is increasingly difficult to take seriously, though there are moments when his guitar playing transcends the stereotype." Blow By Blow, and the two or three years that followed, were among those moments.

He guested on a stream of albums by jazz-funk great Stanley Clarke and, once he was joined by Czech keyboard genius Jan Hammer, early into the Wired sessions, suddenly the sky was the limit. Credited to Jeff Beck with the Jan Hammer Group, a 1977 live album (the adventurously titled Live) remains one of those albums which one either loves with scientific passion... or loathes with the hatred normally reserved for watching a couple of computer geeks discussing the best way to upgrade their operating system. Technically it's brilliant. But it ain't rock'n'roll.

Beck acknowledges this, but only gently. "The 1970s were the perfectionist times, where everybody did spend months and months of time doing ridiculous amounts of tweaking and preening the record, and it didn't really appeal to me, that stuff." Both in the studio and in concert, he was growing restless once again.

"Really, I can't imagine anything worse than sitting in the back row of some huge auditorium, hearing this big noise coming out of the speakers, which is totally out of scale with the size of the guy on stage. It must get very boring after a while."

It must. It does. Even as he completed his first album of the 1980s, There And Back, he found himself looking further back, to the last years of the 1960s.

"We made Truth in two weeks, Beck-Ola in four days, and I do miss that kind of schedule. I loved it, because the hysterical pressure is what's lacking nowadays. Everybody's in slippers and pipes and they can take five years over one guitar solo and that's not my cup of tea at all. If Little Richard had done that with "Lucille", "Lucille" wouldn't have existed. Or "Hound Dog". I know Elvis used to do 25 takes, but it was 25 takes all in one day, not spread out over six months. I like the danger and excitement elements, and that's very hard to get."

More recently, however, there were signs that Beck was interested in reclaiming his rock crown, moving away from his solo career to concentrate instead on a succession of high-profile one-offs and guest appearances, all of which dallied closer to the mainstream than he'd ventured in a decade.

Alongside Eric Clapton, he was a highlight of the 1981 Amnesty International benefit, *The Secret Policeman's Other Ball* – the pair sashayed through the old Robert Johnson staple "Crossroads", Beck's "Cause We've Ended As Lovers" and Bobby Bland's "Farther Up The Road." The following year, a reissue of "Hi Ho Silver Lining" nibbled the lower reaches of the chart; and, in March 1983, Beck jammed alongside Les Paul for the benefit of American television's *Rock'n'roll Tonight* and, again at Clapton's behest, threw himself enthusiastically into a charity project that lay close to the heart of almost every musician of his generation.

Ronnie Lane, ten years out of the Faces, had been stricken by Multiple Sclerosis, and ARMS (Action Research into Multiple Sclerosis) was a fund that Lane himself set up, to try and raise funds for, and research into, the devastating condition that would eventually kill him. (Lane passed away in May 1997.) On 20 September 1983, Beck, Clapton and Jimmy Page all appeared at an ARMS benefit concert at the Royal Albert Hall and, within days, had agreed to take the event further afield, with a nine-date tour of America.

Rod Stewart was waiting for Beck when the outing reached California. He was working on his next album, and was wondering whether Beck might be interested in doing something with him... for the album, for a single, or simply for the hell of it. Beck nodded – why not? A few nights later, he joined Stewart and his band for dinner at a local Indian restaurant, to learn that the singer had already booked the studio for their reunion... for the following morning. And, as if to emphasise the sheer spontaneity of the entire affair, Stewart left Beck to decide what song they would do.

Beck decided on Curtis Mayfield's "People Get Ready", an old Impressions number that he and Stewart had been united in adoring throughout the Jeff Beck Group years, and which Beck then revisited onstage with Beck, Bogert & Appice – although, according to Beck, the decision was actually made by the only guitar he had to hand that evening, a battered old relic with one string missing, and an inability to portray any chord apart from 'D'. And "People Get Ready" was the only song Beck could think of that itself was in 'D.'

He worked out a rough arrangement, then headed up to Stewart's house. The singer was on the phone at that time, "not interested at all". But Beck went upstairs and began playing, and as soon as Stewart heard what he'd come up with, "he ran up the stairs and the next day we cut it in about two hours."

The performance was peerless. But Stewart's vagueness over the recording's eventual fate was no act. Two years would pass before "People Get Ready" was finally released (on Beck's 1985 Flash album); in the meantime, Stewart wanted to know whether Beck might be care to contribute to a clutch of his own new songs; songs that this time were scheduled for his then-gestating Camouflage album, and of which the highlight was the rip-roaring "Infatuation".

Trading unashamedly upon the reputation that "Da Ya Think I'm Sexy" kickstarted, "Infatuation" completed (with "Passion") a triumvirate of 45s that was as stunning as the "Maggie May"/"You Wear

It Well"/"Angel" triptych that first confirmed Stewart's solo success. Certainly Beck was impressed; even though he later complained that Stewart was never even present at the sessions when he taped his guitar parts, the success of the single prompted Stewart's label, Warner Brothers, to demand more of the same... a fully-fledged reunion across Stewart's next American tour.

Stewart was up for it; Beck, who hadn't toured for three years at that point, no less so. "What was spoken about was a very attractive offer financially, and also I wouldn't have to bear the brunt of headlining a tour", he reasoned. "So I thought 'People are going to love this; if it turns out anything like we've been discussing, it's going to be great."

What the pair discussed was essentially a Rod Stewart show, but with plenty of room within the set list and the arrangements for Beck to stamp his own mark on the performance. "I'll have a spot in the middle of the show. Then I'll finish up with the new tracks from his album, bugger off to get a drink or two, and come back at the end." A massive itinerary was drawn up, 70 cities in four months ("Can you believe that? Four weeks is long enough for me"); the media went into publicity overload – sales of Truth and Beck-Ola even started to climb.

And then the tour started, and Beck came crashing back to earth. "As each day passed, and I was out on the road with him, it was painfully obvious that we weren't going to come remotely close to what I had in mind." Stewart's set was more than halfway through by the time Beck was finally ushered on stage, to run through the instrumental "The Pump" before the star of the show appeared for a medley of "Rock My Plimsoul" and "I Ain't Superstitious". He remained onstage for four more songs – "Infatuation", "Young Turks", "Bad To Me" and "People Get Ready", and that was it. That was the extent of the great reunion.

"I was a sideshow", Beck mourned. "I thought, when I came on (the tour), we were going to go places, blow up a few buildings. But he had no plans for that at all. I was sent packing after about ten or 15 minutes."

What was even worse was that, Beck had more or less been warned of precisely this kind of disappointment, shortly after the reunion was first announced. Keith Altham, the veteran British PR man whom Beck had known since the Yardbirds days, had made no secret of his scepticism, going so far as to offer Beck a seemingly irresistible wager – that he would not last 12 nights on the tour. Beck laughed, shook hands and sauntered off into the sun. Now he was regretting that precipitous wager, a regret that grew even stronger when he learned that Altham himself was joining the tour to handle press for Stewart.

He flew over to the US, joined up with the tour in Philadelphia and, before the gig began, decided to take a walk around the evening's venue. Stewart's dressing room "was about the size of a suite in the Waldorf Hotel. It was wall-to-wall with flowers, there were buckets of champagne everywhere and food piled up on the table."

Next door, he found the band's dressing room, about half the size of Stewart's, with half as many flowers, and one bottle of champagne. Then came the road crew's quarters: "no flowers", said Altham, "and just a bottle of Southern Comfort. (And) right at the end of the corridor was a door with Jeff Beck's name on it." Altham knocked, then walked in.

Beck looked up; then, without saying a word, he took out his cheque book. A decade later, invited to host Rod Stewart's induction into the Rock 'n' Roll Hall Of Fame, Beck uttered words that summed up his feelings that night in Philly, and on so many other nights at the end of the 1960s. "We have a love-hate relationship. He loves me and I hate him."

But he also acknowledges that, if he hadn't met Rod Stewart that night in the Cromwellian and suggested they form a new band together, the course of his entire career might well have been very different indeed.

Almost a quarter of a century after the Jeff Beck Group broke up, and ten years after "People Get Ready", *Vox* magazine asked Beck why, in all that time, he'd never settled down with another singer; had given over most of his catalogue to instrumental recordings.

Eyes wide as though he couldn't believe he was being asked something so imbecilic, Beck simply answered from the heart. "Because I've had the best singer in the world. I had Rod. It's hard to come to terms with any other singer who doesn't have that incredible grit. I was completely spoiled. You don't realise how good it was until you try someone else, and they're all trying to sound like Rod."

To that recommendation, of course, one can add the world of guitarists who all try to play like Jeff Beck, the planetful of rhythm sections who can only dream of sounding like Wood and Waller (or Dunbar, or Newman), and the entire universe full of records that have since walked in the footsteps of the Jeff Beck Group. Their time together may have been brief, and their relationship scarred by more warring and worry than any single group should ever have to bear. But they achieved more than most other groups as well, and blueprinted a musical genre that is still as vivid and vital as it ever was in its prime.

"I get a bit uncomfortable when I see interviews where Jeff seems embarrassed about his legacy in heavy metal", concludes Bernie Tormé. "Hell we all are. 99.9% of everything to do with 'heavy metal' should have been slaughtered at birth. But that doesn't change the fact that what he did was total genius and he should be really proud of it. It was emotional rough and visceral, incredible guitar. Personally I'm not so sure about his later stuff, it seems to me to be a bit lacking in the glands department. But God knows he deserves every bit of success he gets because he was the instigator."

In September 1967, *Melody Maker* indulged its passion for compiling rock lists by publishing short profiles of the seven greatest guitarists of the day ('The Magnificent Seven', of course) – Eric Clapton, Jimi Hendrix, Pete Townshend, Jimmy Page, Peter Green, Steve Winwood (surprisingly) and, "the enigma of the seven", Jeff Beck. You could add a handful more to the innings – Davy O'List, Syd Barrett, Mick Taylor – but still it was a prescient list. Forty years on, those same names remain high in the pantheon of rock guitar godhood, men who created the world as they wanted to see it, and then let their audience in to admire what they'd done.

The years that followed, however, were not always kind to the members of that elite; they would see most of them fall by one wayside or another. Of course, some would return from their own personal abysses, others would at least recover their poise and only a handful truly slipped too far. Beck, however, never slipped, never let go, never once took his eyes off the vision that set him on his path in the first place.

Beginning with 1985's Flash, three new albums over the next 10 years saw Beck finally able to indulge his fascination with spontaneity, with his tribute to Gene Vincent and Cliff Gallup, 1989's ferocious Crazy Legs, at least giving the impression of a succession of manic moments, strung fortuitously together into one of the greatest albums of his entire career.

It was Beck's final album of the 20th century, however, that finally returned him to basics. "There's more of me on Who Else! than on any other album I've ever made", he insisted. "There was more decision-making, more packing and slicing, more saying yes and no than I've ever done before. In the past, you see, I was playing with great players, and..." with the spectre of the Jan Hammer era again looming over his shoulder... "I was letting them have the run of the show. There's a certain code within me – I can't just turn around and tell them to shut up and do what I want them to. But now I can. This time around, it's my turn to run things, and I'm making the most of it."

It was Beck who thought of adding a vacuum-cleaner to the intro of "Psycho Sam"; Beck who came up with the 7/8 time signature which powers "Blast From The East"; and Beck who would finally decide whether or not bandmate Jennifer Batten's dream of completely, and dramatically, rearranging his 1960s signature theme, "Beck's Bolero", would finally escape from the rehearsal room.

He readily acknowledged that the incentives behind this astonishing rebirth were not wholly musical; openly admitted that money was not as plentiful as it might be; acknowledged that the succession of dodgy contracts that he signed during his youth have ensured he sees very little from the succession of hits (and subsequently, hit compilations) he enjoyed with the Yardbirds and the first flush of solo success.

Peter Frampton, one of Beck's 1960s/70s superstar contemporaries, once explained, "When you're young, someone wants to give you money to make music – of course you're going to say yes. You're not thinking of this as a career, you're not thinking 'Ooh, will I get paid for these records when I'm old and grey?' and neither were the people you were signing with. It was something which was happening at the time, in the moment; nobody knew that in 30, 40, years time, people would be reissuing all those records on CD, and if you'd told them they wouldn't have believed you. Now, of course, it's happening, and people are making money of those records, and it can be galling. But you have to put it behind you and get on with what you're doing now, making money in the present, rather than trying to live off your past."

Wise words, and – peering out from behind a mountain of Yardbirds compilations, repackaging and recycling three years' worth of devastating creativity, with very little reward for its builders – Beck not only agrees with them, he's living them. "A lot of people think of me as being something from the 1960s, but I haven't played with the Yardbirds for decades, and I doubt I'd even remember how to, any more. I've moved on so many times since then..."

Where Who Else! went, its successors travelled even further, astonishingly contemporary records which, had they come spinning out from the godheads of modern techno – the Prodigy, Underworld, Orbital, whoever – would be held up as one of THE sonic achievements of the first decade of the 21st century. Beck's willingness, meanwhile, to couple these advances with some breathtaking glances back at his past – linking with Chicago *wunderkinds* White Stripes, to recreate a mid-1960s Yardbirds set at the Royal Albert Hall in September 2002, for example – ensured that even at his most fearlessly contemporary, he continues to lead by example. And how does he do that?

Because he's Jeff Beck, that's how. And that's the Truth.

JEFF BECK GROUP DISCOGRAPHY

This discography is designed to reflect the contents of this book only –
that is, the careers of Jeff Beck, Rod Stewart and Ron Wood between
their respective recorded debuts, and the demise of the Jeff Beck Group
in mid-1969. It is arranged in chronological order to allow readers and
collectors to trace the development of those careers.

JB – recording features Jeff Beck; RS – Rod Stewart; RW – Ron Wood
*NOTE: radio sessions are noted by recording date. Broadcast dates were
frequently several days, and occasionally weeks, later.*

1963

Late: THE TRIDENTS (JB)
Session: Keep Your Hands Off My Baby/Trouble In Mind
(Trouble In Mind included on Beckology box set 1991)

1964

EARLY: THE TRIDENTS (JB)
Session: Wandering Man Blues/That Noise
(Wandering Man Blues included on Beckology box set 1991)
EARLY: THE TRIDENTS (JB)
BBC radio (live session – uncertain broadcast): Nursery Rhyme
(included on Beckology box set 1991)
2 February: LONG JOHN BALDRY &
THE HOOCHIE COOCHIE MEN (RS)
Live, Birmingham Town Hall: Bright Lights Big City
(featured on box set Rod Stewart 1964-1969, 1999)
JUNE: LONG JOHN BALDRY & THE HOOCHIE COOCHIE MEN (RS)
Single (United Artists UP 1056): Up Above My Head
JUNE: JOHNNY HOWARD BAND (JB)
Single (Decca F11925) Rinky Dink/Java
mid: ROD STEWART
Demo session: Bright Lights Big City/Ain't That Loving You Baby/Don't
You Tell Nobody/Just Like I Treat You/Moppers Blues/Keep Your
Hands Off Her
(featured on box set Rod Stewart 1964-1969, 1999)
late: THE BIRDS (RW)
Session: You're On My Mind (demo)/You Don't Love Me (demo)
(featured on The Collectors Guide To Rare British Birds, 1999)
OCTOBER: THE BIRDS (RW)
Single (Decca F12031): You're On My Mind/You Don't Love Me
OCTOBER: ROD STEWART
Single (Decca F11996): Good Morning Little Schoolgirl/I'm Gonna
Move To The Outskirts Of Town

November: PHIL RYAN & THE CRESCENTS (JB)
Single (Columbia DB 7406) Mary Don't Weep/Yes I Will
Estimated: JEFF BECK & JIMMY PAGE
Jam session: Steelin'/Chuckles
(featured on Blues Anytime Volume Three compilation, 1968)

1965

January: FITZ & STARTZ (JB)
Single (Parlophone R5216): I'm Not Running Away/So Sweet
8 March: THE YARDBIRDS (JB)
Radio Luxembourg – The Friday Spectacular: For Your Love
16 March: THE YARDBIRDS (JB)
BBC radio – Saturday Club: I'm Not Talking/Guitar Boogie/My Girl
Sloopy/For Your Love/Just Like I Treat You
18 March: THE YARDBIRDS (JB)
BBC TV – Top Of The Pops: For Your Love
Granada TV – Scene At 6.30: For Your Love
19 March: THE YARDBIRDS (JB)
Rediffusion TV – Ready Steady Go!: For Your Love
22 March: THE YARDBIRDS (JB)
BBC radio – Top Gear: Someone To Love Me/I Ain't Got You/For Your
Love/I'm Not Talking/Steeled Blues
24 March: THE YARDBIRDS (JB)
TWW TV – Discs A Go Go: For Your Love
25 March: THE YARDBIRDS (JB)
BBC TV – Top Of The Pops: For Your Love
April 1965: THE BIRDS (RW)
Single (Decca F12140): Leaving Here/Next In Line
April 1965: THE YARDBIRDS (JB)
Session: Heart Full Of Soul (sitar version)
(featured on Shapes Of Things box, 1984)
1 April: THE YARDBIRDS (JB)
BBC TV – Top Of The Pops: For Your Love
2 April: THE YARDBIRDS (JB)
Rediffusion TV – Ready Steady Goes Live: For Your Love
9 April: THE YARDBIRDS (JB)
BBC radio – Saturday Swings: Too Much Monkey Business/Hush A
Bye/I'm A Man/Runaround/For Your Love/Spoonful
30 April: THE YARDBIRDS (JB)
BBC radio – Joe Loss Pop Show: For Your Love/I Ain't Done
Wrong/I'm Not Talking
1 June: THE YARDBIRDS (JB)
BBC radio – Saturday Club: I Wish You Would/Steeled Blues/Heart
Full Of Soul/Respectable
4 June: THE YARDBIRDS (JB)
BBC radio – Saturday Swings: Pretty Girl/Steeled Blues/Heart Full Of
Soul/I'm Not Talking/I Ain't Done Wrong/Louise

4 June: THE YARDBIRDS (JB)
Rediffusion TV – Ready Steady Go!: Heart Full Of Soul
9 June: THE YARDBIRDS (JB)
BBC radio – The Ken Dodd Show: Heart Full Of Soul
BBC radio – Top Gear: I Ain't Done Wrong/I've Been Trying/Heart Full
Of Soul/Guitar Boogie
13 June: THE YARDBIRDS (JB)
ABC TV – Thank Your Lucky Stars: Heart Full Of Soul
30 June: THE YARDBIRDS (JB)
TWW TV – Discs A Go Go: Heart Full Of Soul
JULY: THE YARDBIRDS (JB)
Single (Columbia DB 7706): Evil Hearted You/Still I'm Sad
2 July: THE YARDBIRDS (JB)
BBC radio – Joe Loss Pop Show: Heart Full Of Soul/I Ain't Got
You/For Your Love
3 July: THE YARDBIRDS (JB)
BBC radio – Easy Beat: I Ain't Done Wrong/Heart Full Of Soul
6 July: THE YARDBIRDS (JB)
Rediffusion TV – Ready Steady Go: Heart Full Of Soul
8 July: THE YARDBIRDS (JB)
BBC TV – Top Of The Pops: Heart Full Of Soul
30 July: THE YARDBIRDS (JB)
Rediffusion TV – Ready Steady Go: My Girl Sloopy
AUGUST: THE YARDBIRDS (JB)
Five Yardbirds EP (Columbia SEG 8421): My Girl Sloopy/I'm Not
Talking/I Ain't Done Wrong
5 August: THE YARDBIRDS (JB)
BBC radio – Saturday Swings: I Ain't Done Wrong/Hush A Bye/San Ho
Zay/Heart Full Of Soul/I've Been Trying/Love Me Like I Love You
6 August: THE YARDBIRDS (JB)
BBC radio – You Really Got…: I Wish You Would/For Your Love/Love
Me Like I Love You/I'm A Man/Too Much Monkey Business/Heart Full
Of Soul
9 August: THE YARDBIRDS (JB)
BBC radio – The Beat Show: Heart Full Of Soul/Love Me Like I Love
You/I Ain't Done Wrong
10 August: THE YARDBIRDS (JB)
National Jazz & Blues Festival/US TV – Shindig: Heart Full Of
Soul/For Your Love/My Girl Sloopy/I'm A Man/I Wish You Would
SEPTEMBER: CHRIS ANDREWS (JB)
Single (Decca F12236) Yesterday Man/Too Bad You Don't Want Me
23 September: THE YARDBIRDS (JB)
NBC TV, USA – Hullabaloo: I'm A Man
26 September: THE YARDBIRDS (JB)
ABC TV – Thank Your Lucky Stars: Evil Hearted You
27 September: THE YARDBIRDS (JB)
BBC radio – Saturday Club: My Girl Sloopy/Evil Hearted You/The
Stumble/Still I'm Sad/The Train Kept A Rolling

28 September: THE YARDBIRDS (JB)
Granada TV – Scene At 6.30: Evil Hearted You
29 September: THE YARDBIRDS (JB)
TWW TV – Discs A Go Go: Evil Hearted You
OCTOBER: THE BIRDS (RW)
Single (Decca F12257): No Good Without You/How Can It Be
OCTOBER: THE YARDBIRDS (JB)
Single (Columbia DB 7706): Evil Hearted You/Still I'm Sad
1 October: THE YARDBIRDS (JB)
Rediffusion TV – Ready Steady Go: Evil Hearted You
4 October: THE YARDBIRDS (JB):
BBC radio – The Beat Show: Still I'm Sad/Heart Full Of Soul/Evil
Hearted You
8 October: THE YARDBIRDS (JB)
BBC radio – This Must Be The Place: For Your Love/Heart Full Of
Soul/Still I'm Sad/Evil Hearted You
9 October: THE YARDBIRDS (JB)
BBC radio – Easy Beat: Evil Hearted You/Still I'm Sad
21 October: THE YARDBIRDS (JB)
BBC TV – Top Of The Pops: Evil Hearted You
29 October: THE YARDBIRDS (JB)
Rediffusion TV – Ready Steady Go: Evil Hearted You/Still I'm Sad
NOVEMBER: ROD STEWART
Single (Columbia DB 7766): The Day Will Come/Why Does It Go On
13 November: THE YARDBIRDS (JB)
RTB TV, Belgium – Adamo Show: Still I'm Sad/For Your Love
16 November: THE YARDBIRDS (JB)
BBC radio – The Sound Of Boxing Day: The Train Kept A
Rolling/You're A Better Man Than I/Smokestack Lightning/Still I'm Sad
DECEMBER: STEAMPACKET (RS)
Rehearsal: Can I Get A Witness/Baby Take Me/Oh Baby, Don't You Do
It/Lord Remember Me
(featured on box set Rod Stewart 1964-1969, 1999)
---: THE NIGHTSHIFT (JB – alleged)
Single (Piccadilly 7N 35264) Stormy Monday/That's My Story

1966
3 January: THE YARDBIRDS (JB)
US TV – Shivaree: I'm A Man/Heart Full Of Soul
4 January: THE YARDBIRDS (JB)
US TV – 9th Street West: I'm A Man
10 January: THE YARDBIRDS (JB)
US TV – The Lloyd Thaxton Show: Shapes Of Things/For Your Love
28 January: THE YARDBIRDS (JB)
San Remo Festival/Italian TV: Questa Volta/Pafff... Bum
FEBRUARY: THE YARDBIRDS (JB)
Single (Columbia DB 7848): Shapes Of Things/You're A Better Man
Than I

February: THE YARDBIRDS (JB)
Single (Ricordi SIR 20-010, Italy): Questa Volta/Pafff... Bum
3 February: THE YARDBIRDS (JB)
French TV: Shapes Of Things
18 February: THE YARDBIRDS (JB)
Rediffusion TV – Ready Steady Go: Shapes Of Things/You're A Better
Man Than I
20 February: THE YARDBIRDS (JB)
ABC TV – Thank Your Lucky Stars: Shapes Of Things
28 February: THE YARDBIRDS (JB)
BBC radio – Saturday Club: You're A Better Man Than I/Shapes Of
Things/I've Been Trying/Dust My Blues
MARCH: THE YARDBIRDS (JB)
Yardbirds' Eye View sessions: Jeff's Blues/What Do You Want/Pounds
And Stomps/Someone To Love Me Part Two/Chris' Number/Crimson
Curtain/Like Jimmy Reed Again/Here Tis
(all featured on Shapes Of Things box set, 1984)
1 March: THE YARDBIRDS (JB)
Rediffusion TV – Five O'Clock Club: Shapes Of Things
2 March: THE YARDBIRDS (JB)
TWW TV – Now: Shapes Of Things
4 March: THE YARDBIRDS (JB)
Rediffusion TV – Ready Steady Go: Shapes Of Things
10 March: THE YARDBIRDS (JB)
BBC TV – Top Of The Pops: Shapes Of Things
12 March: THE YARDBIRDS (JB)
BBC radio – Easy Beat: You're A Better Man Than I/Shapes Of Things
16 March: THE YARDBIRDS (JB)
Granada TV – Scene At 6.30: Shapes Of Things
17 March: THE YARDBIRDS (JB)
ABC TV – Where The Action Is: Shapes Of Things/Train Kept A
Rolling/I Wish You Would/You're A Better Man Than I
31 March: THE YARDBIRDS (JB)
BBC TV – Top Of The Pops: Shapes Of Things
APRIL: ROD STEWART
Single (Columbia DB 7892): Shake/I Just Got Some
1 April: THE YARDBIRDS (JB)
Rediffusion TV – Ready Steady Allez: Shapes Of Things
29 April: THE YARDBIRDS (JB)
Rediffusion TV – Ready Steady Go: Jeff's Boogie
MAY: THE YARDBIRDS (JB)
Single (Columbia DB 7928): Over Under Sideways Down/Jeff's Boogie
1 May: THE YARDBIRDS (JB)
NME Poll Winners Concert/ABC TV: The Train Kept A Rolling/Shapes
Of Things
4 May: THE YARDBIRDS (JB)
BBC radio – Parade Of The Pops: Shapes Of Things/You're A Better
Man Than I

6 May: THE YARDBIRDS (JB)
BBC radio – Saturday Swings: Jeff's Boogie/You're A Better Man Than I/The Sun Is Shining/Over Under Sideways Down/Baby Scratch My Back/Shapes Of Things
27 May: THE YARDBIRDS (JB)
Rediffusion TV – Ready Steady Go: Over Under Sideways Down
8 June: THE YARDBIRDS (JB)
BBC TV – A Whole Scene Going: Over Under Sideways Down
JUNE: THE BIRDS (RW)
Sessions: Run Run Run/Run Run Run (alternate version)/Good Times/Say Those Magic Words (alternate version)/Daddy Daddy (alternate version)/La Poupee Qui Fait Non
(featured on The Collectors Guide To Rare British Birds, 1999)
JUNE: THE BIRDS (RW)
The Deadly Bees soundtrack session: That's All I Need
9 June: THE YARDBIRDS (JB)
BBC TV – Top Of The Pops: Over Under Sideways Down
9 June: THE YARDBIRDS (JB)
BBC radio – Joe Loss Pop Show: Over Under Sideways Down/Shapes Of Things/Jeff's Boogie
11 June: THE YARDBIRDS (JB)
BBC radio – Easy Beat: Rack My Mind/Over Under Sideways Down
15 June: THE YARDBIRDS (JB)
US TV – It's A Mod Mod World: Turn Into Earth/Over Under Sideways Down
JULY: THE YARDBIRDS (JB)
LP The Yardbirds (aka Roger The Engineer) (Columbia SX 6063): Lost Women/Over Under Sideways Down/The Nazz Are Blue/I Can't Make Your Way/Rack My Mind/Farewell/Hot House Of Omagarashid/Jeff's Boogie/He's Always There/Turn Into Earth/What Do You Want/Ever Since The World Began
22 July: THE YARDBIRDS (JB)
Rediffusion TV – Ready Steady Go: Farewell/Lost Woman
27 July: THE YARDBIRDS (JB)
BBC TV – Hey Presto! It's Rolf: Rack My Mind
SEPTEMBER: BIRD'S BIRDS (RW)
Single (Reaction 591 005): Say Those Magic Words/Daddy Daddy
OCTOBER: SHOTGUN EXPRESS (RS)
Single (Columbia DB 8025): I Could Feel The Whole World Turn Around/Curtains
OCTOBER: THE YARDBIRDS (JB)
Single (Columbia DB 8024): Happenings Ten Years Time Ago/Psycho Daisies
OCTOBER: THE YARDBIRDS (JB)
Blow Up soundtrack recording: Stroll On
19 October: THE YARDBIRDS (JB)
BBC TV – Top Of The Pops: Happening Ten Years Time Ago

24 October: THE YARDBIRDS (JB)
US TV – Milton Berle Show: Happenings Ten Years Time Ago
--- PAUL YOUNG (JB)
Single (Philips PF 350316 – Sweden) I'm Not Running Away
(B-side only)

1967
FEBRUARY: JOHN'S CHILDREN (JB)
Single (Columbia DB 8124) But She's Mine (B-side only)
MARCH: JEFF BECK
Single (Columbia DB 8151): Hi Ho Silver Lining/Beck's Bolero
MARCH: THE BIRDS (RW)
Session: Granny Rides Again
(featured on The Collectors Guide To Rare British Birds, 1999)
7 March: JEFF BECK GROUP
BBC radio – Saturday Club: Let Me Love You/Stone Crazy/I Ain't
Superstitious/Hi Ho Silver Lining/I'm Losing You
27 April: JEFF BECK
BBC TV – Top Of The Pops: Hi Ho Silver Lining
15 May: JEFF BECK GROUP
BBC radio – Monday Monday: Let Me Love You/Rock My Plimsoul/
Hi Ho Silver Lining
17 May: JEFF BECK
Dutch TV – Moef Ga Ga: Hi Ho Silver Lining
18 May: JEFF BECK
BBC TV – Top Of The Pops: Hi Ho Silver Lining
JULY: JEFF BECK
Single (Columbia DB 8227): Tallyman/Rock My Plimsoul
JULY: CRAZY BLUE (RS)
Session: Stone Crazy (two versions)/Fly Right Baby (one version of
Stone Crazy featured on box set Rod Stewart 1964-1969, 1999)
4 July: JEFF BECK GROUP
BBC radio – Saturday Club: Rock My Plimsoul/This Morning/Tallyman
Summer: ROD STEWART
Sessions: Little Miss Understood (demo)/Come Home Baby (with
PP Arnold) (featured on box set Rod Stewart 1964-1969, 1999)
14 September: JEFF BECK
Dutch TV – Moef Ga Ga: Tallyman
OCTOBER: JOHN WALKER (JB)
Single (Philips BF 1612) I See Love In You (B-side only)
9 October: JEFF BECK GROUP
BBC radio – David Symonds Show: Rock My Plimsoul/Let Me Love
You/Walking By The Railings
NOVEMBER: ROD STEWART
single (Immediate IM 060): Little Miss Understood/So Much To Say
1 November: JEFF BECK GROUP
BBC radio – Top Gear: I Ain't Superstitious/Beck's Bolero/Loving You
Is Sweeter Than Ever/You Shook Me/You'll Never Get To Heaven

December: SANTA BARBARA MACHINE HEAD (RW)
Sessions: Albert/Porcupine Juice/Rubber Monkey

1968
February: 1968: JEFF BECK
Single (Columbia DB 8359): Love Is Blue/I've Been Drinking
March: PAUL JONES (JB)
Single (Columbia DB 8379) The Dog Presides (B-side only)
14 April: JEFF BECK
Swiss TV – Hits A Go Go: Love Is Blue
May: THE CREATION (RW)
Single (Polydor 56246): Midway Down/The Girls Are Naked
Summer: THE CREATION (RW)
Singles (Hit-Ton, Germany): Mercy Mercy Mercy/For All That I
Am/Uncle Bert
July 1968: JEFF BECK GROUP
LP Truth (Columbia SCX 6293): Shapes Of Things/Let Me Love
You/Morning Dew/You Shook Me/Ol' Man River/Greensleeves/Rock My
Plimsoul/Beck's Bolero/Blues DeLuxe/I Ain't Superstitious
17 September: JEFF BECK GROUP
BBC radio – Top Gear: You Shook Me/Shapes Of Things/Sweet Little
Angel/Mother's Old Rice Pudding/Rock My Plimsoul
November (released December 1969): GTOs (JB/RS)
LP Permanent Damage (Straight Records STS 1059)
Eureka Springs Garbage Lady/Fat Theresa Shoes/Shock Treatment

1969
February: JEFF BECK GROUP
LP sessions: All Shook Up/Throw Down A Line/Sweet Little
Angel/Jailhouse Rock
(all featured on CD remaster Beck-Ola 2004)
April: JEFF BECK GROUP
Swedish TV – Mickie Most documentary: Plynth/Rice Pudding
June: JEFF BECK GROUP & DONOVAN
Session: Goo Goo Barabajagal/Trudy (Bed With Me) – single (Pye 7N
17778)
Homesickness – LP HMS Donovan (Dawn DNLD 4001,
1970)/Stromberg Twins (featured on CD remaster Barabajagal
2005)/Suffer Little Children/From Here On Your Guess Is As Good As
Mine (both unreleased)
June (released February 1970): ROD STEWART (RS/RW)
LP An Old Raincoat Won't Ever Let You Down (Vertigo VO 4): Street
Fighting Man/Man Of Constant Sorrow/Blind Prayer/Handbags And
Gladrags/An Old Raincoat/I Wouldn't Ever Change A Thing/Cindy's
Lament/Dirty Old Town
June: QUIET MELON (RS/RW)
Session: Diamond Joe/Engine 4444 (both featured on box set Rod
Stewart 1964-1969, 1999) + untitled instrumentals

26 June: JEFF BECK GROUP & DONOVAN
BBC TV – Top Of The Pops: Goo Goo Barabajagal
Summer: PYTHON LEE JACKSON (RS)
Single (Youngblood 017 – 1970) A Broken Dream/Doing Fine
Single (Youngblood YB 1077 – 1976) The Blues/Cloud Nine
JULY: JEFF BECK GROUP
LP Cosa Nostra Beck-Ola (Columbia SCX 6351): All Shook Up/Spanish
Boots/Girl From Mill Valley/Jailhouse Rock/Plynth/Hangman's
Knee/Rice Pudding
SEPTEMBER 1969: JEFF BECK GROUP
Withdrawn single (Columbia DB 8590): Plynth/Hangman's Knee

FURTHER READING/BIBLIOGRAPHY

The most valuable biographies in my own research library were: *Jeff's Book* by Christopher Hjort and Doug Hinman (Rock'n'roll Research Press, 2000), *Crazy Fingers* by Annette Carson (Backbeat Books), *Rod Stewart: The New Biography* by Tim Ewbank and Stafford Hildred (Portrait Books, 2003); *Rock On Wood – The Origin Of A Rock'n'roll Face* by Terry Rawlings (revised edition: Helter Skelter 2005); and, for their detail on Mickie Most and Peter Grant's early careers, *The Record Producers* by John Tobler and Stuart Grundy (BBC Books, 1982) and *Peter Grant: The Man Who Led Zeppelin* by Chris Welch (Omnibus Press, 2002).

Other worthy additions to the bookshelf include: *Yardbirds* by John Platt, Chris Dreja and Jim McCarty (Sidgwick & Jackson 1983) and *Our Music Is Red With Purple Flashes: The Story of the Creation* by Sean Egan (Cherry Red Books, 2004).

Numerous other volumes detail different aspects of the Jeff Beck Group's career. Those referred to most frequently while writing this book include: *Rock Family Trees* by Pete Frame (Omnibus Books, various editions); *The Great Rock Discography* by Martin Strong (Canongate Books, various editions); *Guinness Book Of British Hit Singles... Albums* (Guiness World Records, various editions); *Top Pop Singles... Albums* by Joel Whitburn (Record Research, various editions); and *In Session Tonight* by Ken Garner (BBC Books, 1992).

Back issues of the following magazines and periodicals were similarly invaluable: *Circus, Classic Rock, Creem, Disc, Live! Music Review, Goldmine, Melody Maker, Metal Hammer, Mojo, New Musical Express, Record Collector, Rolling Stone, Sounds, Uncut, ZigZag.*

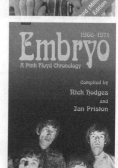

CHERRY RED BOOKS

We are always looking for interesting books to publish.
They can be either new manuscripts or re-issues of deleted books.
If you have any good ideas then please
get in touch with us.

CHERRY RED BOOKS
A division of Cherry Red Records Ltd.
Unit 3a,
Long Island House,
Warple Way,
London W3 0RG.

E-mail: iain@cherryred.co.uk
Web: www.cherryred.co.uk